MODERN EDUCATIONAL THEORY AND PRACTICE

MODERN EDUCATIONAL THEORY AND PRACTICE

[Strictly According to the UGC Syllabus for B.Ed. Course]

BHARAT SINGH

ANMOL PUBLICATIONS PVT. LTD.
NEW DELHI - 110 002 (INDIA)

ANMOL PUBLICATIONS PVT. LTD.
H.O.: 4374/4B, Ansari Road, Darya Ganj,
New Delhi-110 002 (India)
Ph.: 23261597, 23278000
B.O.: No. 1015, Ist Main Road, BSK IIIrd Stage
IIIrd Phase, IIIrd Block,
Bangalore - 560 085 (India)
Visit us at: www.anmolpublications.com

Modern Educational Theory and Practice

First Published, 2004

Reprint, 2006

Reprint, 2008

PRINTED IN INDIA

Printed at Mehra Offset Press, Delhi.

Contents

PART TWO : STAGES OF EDUCATION

Preface

Education is a vast discipline and Teachers' Training is a vital part of it. The responsibilities of the educationists and educators are focused on the task of providing better training to the future teachers for their better learning and proper development. Needless to say that this responsibility can only be exercised, if the trainers are equipped with the required knowledge of the subject concerned. That's why it becomes essential for making adequate provisions for each course to the student-teachers or teacher trainees. The present series is designed for providing a solid workable base for all course-papers. It has been prepared strictly according to the syllabus of the B.Ed class, prescribed by the UGC for different universities.

No doubt, there are so many other books on the subject, available in the market, written by worthy authors. However, every writer has his or her own style and way of presentation. The present work also has its own features and characteristics.

In preparation of this series of texts, the editor had to refer to the works of other authors and information sources. The editor feels a deep sense of gratitude for incorporating their ideas in the text. Hopefully, this series would serve as a 'ready to refer' tool for all teachers, teacher-students and others.

—**Editor**

1

Introduction

The history of educational administration in India has its formal beginning in 1775. The East India Company administration had set up three schools, for the running of which a sum of Rs.1 lakh had been approved. This sum was not utilised for twenty years. In 1853, Lord Macaulay formulated an educational policy, and a year later, in 1854, Sir Charles Wood introduced the system of aid for educational institutions. At the same time, the Directorate of Public Instruction was established. In 1882, the Hunter Commission came forth with a number of suggestions for the improvement of administration in education. In 1921, because of the dual administration set up in the country, state legislative assemblies and the ministry of education came into existence. At this stage,. the Indian ministers had great and burdensome responsibilities, but of rights and authority they had almost none. In 1929, the Hertog Committee recommended the setting up of an Educational Advisory Council, and this was done in 1935. In 1944, the Sargent Commission, defined national development as the goal of education, and also recommended that greater liberality should be introduced into administrative matters. In 1948, the University Education Commission, too, recommended a number of improvements in the administration of higher education in the country. In 1952-53, the Secondary Education Commission laid even more emphasis upon the improvement of the administrative structure concerned with education, because, according to the Commission, in any attempt at educational reconstruction, under any kind of scheme, the administrative sphere is of particular significance because it is the administrative machinery which is responsible for the growth and improvement of various educational institutions. Hence, it was felt that the goal of education could not be achieved without the necessary improvements in educational administration.

The Central government formulates the general educational policy and is also responsible for the growth of education in the Union Territories and the areas governed by it. At the central level, the following is the structure of educational administration:-

1. Education Minister
2. Minister of State of Education
3. Deputy Minister of Education
4. Education Secretary
5. Advisor, Deputy-advisor, Programme Department.
6. Director,
   (i) Project
   (ii) Adult Education
   (iii) Statistics and Information
7. Joint Secretary
   (i) Programme Controller
   (ii) Education Advisor
   (iii) Deputy Secretary (school division)
   (iv) Deputy Secretary (UNESCO division)
   (v) Assistant Educational Advisor (Publication unit)
8. Director (Internal Finance)
9. Joint Secretary.
   (i) Director (Administration)
   (ii) Deputy Secretary (Book improvement)
   (iii) Deputy Secretary (Hindi section)
   (iv) Special Officer (Sanskrit)
   (v) Sub-education Advisor, Deputy Secretary (Youth Services)

10. Joint Educational Advisor

    (i) Sub-advisor (higher education)

    (ii) Deputy Secretary (foreign scholarships)

    (iii) Sub-advisor (union territories)

11. Educational Advisor (Technical)

    (i) Sub-advisor (technical education division)

At the central level, the direction of the educational policy is in the hands of the Central Education Advisory Board, which is headed by a famous educationist and educational administrator. The central government has also set up some specialist institutions for encouraging education in the country. They are

University Grants Commission. Its function is to maintain harmony and balance in the sphere of higher education, and to nourish it by giving the necessary grants. It came into existence in 1953.

National Council of Educational Research and Training. This body was founded in 1955. The institution has many other bodies under its control. Article 48 of our Constitution speaks of providing free education to all children upto the age of 14, and the task of achieving this objective has been entrusted to this institution. In the sphere of primary education, this institution performs the functions of educational planning, administration, preparation of literature, collection of statistical data and making arrangements for directing the development of education.

Thus, we can see that the central government has accepted a part of the burden of education. For this reason, mutual and cordial relations between administrative institutions is essential, though the greater responsibility of administration lies with the States, since education is, constitutionally, a state subject. The departments of education of the states are the main agencies for preparing educational plans and implementing them. It is very unfortunate that proper attention has, so far, not been given to their development. During the British period, these departments were set up for the implementation of a very limited number of projects. Even today, the structure which was then created has not be modified. Their methods of working and programmes are generally similar.

We must also keep in mind that administration implies confidence, direction, courage, enthusiastic leadership and ability to maintain human relations successfully. For this purpose, sufficient stress can hardly ever be laid upon the fact that suitable employees must be recruited. Most of the major shortcomings of the education departments of our states are directly related to their employees. Some of these shortcomings are: dearth of officers at the highest levels, untrained employees, unsatisfactory scales of pay and conditions of service, unsatisfactory modes of recruitment, inadequate arrangements for in-service education, and an inadequate number of workers.

At the state level, educational administration is structured thus:

1. Education Minister (2) Deputy Minister of Education, (3) Educational Secretary, (4) Joint Secretary, Education, (a) Additional Secretary, (b) Deputy Secretary, (c) Assistant Secretary (5) Educational Director, (6) Additional Director of Education, (7) Deputy Director of Education, (8) Assistant Director of Education, (9) Regional Director of Education, (10) District Inspector of Schools, (11) Deputy Inspector of Schools. (12) Sub-deputy Inspectors.

There are Regional Inspectoresses for the education of girls. The accompanying chart will clarify the nature of educational organisation suggested by the Secondary Education Commission. These days separate directorates are being establishment at almost every level. The necessary steps in this direction have been taken in Uttar Pradesh.

The function of the Education Secretariat and Directorate is to ensure that the government's educational policies and schemes are implemented. They offer recognition and affiliation, maintain the strength of the educational administration, give grants and aid, formulate the curriculum, recommend text-books and inspect schools. The following table will clarify the local administrative structure in the educational sphere:-

	Local Level
District Board	Municipal Board
	Education Supdt.
Dy. Inspector	
Sub deputy Inspector	Sub-deputy Inspectors
Panchayat Samiti	
Education Expansion Officer	
ADO (Education)	
Basic Education Officer	
Adult Education Officer	

The basis of local administration is decentralisation, and what is needed is that the local administration strengthened and made effective.

Mechanism Suggested By The Kothari Commission

	Ministry of Education	
State Board of Vocational Education	Education organisation	State Board of Education
		Higher Secondary Board
		Examination Board
	District Education Office	District Education Board (District Level)
	Block Education Office	Block Education Committee
		Block Level

The faulty administration of education in India is responsible for the failure of education in achieving its goals. The administrators have formed a class of their own, a caste which has become a symbol of the growing alienation between education, the educator and the process of education. According to the Kothari Commission educational administration in India lacks many things which it ought to possess. This administration is burdened with administrative and financial work, in the main, and it limits itself to collecting statistical data about finances and education, and preparing reports about them.

The following are the problems of educational administration in India-

1. Various ministries implement different educational programmes falling within their jurisdiction, for instance, medicine, engineering,, social planning, etc. Because of this many difficulties arise in achieving harmony and unity of purpose with the ministry of education, which then faces problems in implementing a particular educational policy or directing activities of teaching institutions.

2. Because of the fact that different educational programmes fall within the purview of separate ministries, much duplication is often the result, and this becomes the cause of stagnation and wastage in education.

3. The administrative structure is such that a balance cannot be maintained between secretaries and directors of education.

4. The administrative unit wishes to direct educational activity in a general and normal manner but it also seeks to remain indifferent to the actual problems of education.

5. In this administrative structure, democratic values are almost invariably neglected and frequently violated.

Suggestions for Solving Problems. The Secondary Education Commission has suggested the following solutions to the problems outlined above:-

1. The Director of Education should also hold the office of the Deputy Secretary of Education so that he may, in consonance with the minister of education, be able to discharge his duties efficiently.

2. Ministers of various ministries should organise a council under the chairmanship of the education minister. This council may

then formulate policies for the educational activities of different ministries.

3. A secondary education council should. be set up, with the director of education as the chairman, for the formulation of general educational policies.

4. The Central Educational Advisory Board must make periodical studies of the problems of education in India and offer its suggestions, which should be implemented.

5. The school has an important function in educational administration. Hence, the inspectors of schools should be conscious of the problems of education. They should also have sufficient staff to carry out their functions effectively.

The Kothari Commission has put forward numerous very significant suggestions for vitalizing educational administration. These are as follows:-

1. 50% of the employees of the education ministry should consist of individuals promoted from the departments of education so that knowledge about the actual problems of education may be obtained, because these individuals will have personal knowledge of such problems.

2. At the State level, Education Councils should be created to evaluate the working of the education ministries.

3. At the national level, an Indian Educational Service should be organised, within whose cadres there should be such posts as Directors, officials of the directorate of education, district level officers, and posts of principals of the state and central schools.

4. A similar State Education Service should also be constituted. In this service, the first class posts should include the secretary of the district schools council, district inspectors and teachers. 75% of the appointments should be direct, while 25% of the appointments should be by promotion.

5. In service curricula or courses should be introduced for the non-gazetted staff.

6. It is important to enact educational laws in the states as well as union territories. In accordance with these laws, the educational administration should be restructured.
7. Staff colleges should be established for the training of administrators in education.

In this way, we can note that wherever there is laxity in administration in the educational sphere in India, it is due either to lack of adequate staff or indifference towards the problems of education. The Kothari Commission has accepted national development as the ultimate goal of education, but this goal cannot be achieved as long as the administrative structure, which frames educational policies arid implements them, is not suitably modified.

Education can achieve its objectives only if the administration is sound, because in the absence of an able administration, nothing. can be done correctly. The Kothari Commission has offered the following suggestions about administration:-

Planning. The Kothari-Commission points out that the existing mechanism of educational planning lacks many desirable elements. It has neither an adequate staff nor is this staff suitably trained. At the district level, there is hardly any educational planning anywhere in the country. The planning units in the offices of education directors are inadequate, and they are staffed by men lacking training in this field. Their work is mainly administrative and financial. It is limited to collection of educational and financial statistics and preparing reports based thereon. Hence the following suggestions are being given for making educational planning more effective:

1. Formulating a comprehensive anal effective policy for the development of education.
2. Introducing programmes designed to avoid wastage.
3. Where the budget is small, there is greater need for economy and growth.
4. Universities, professional institutions, training colleges, etc., should assist in the evaluation of work.

5. The Asian Institute of Educational planning should work upon educational planning in various states.
6. The U.G.C. should establish centres for advanced studies concerned with educational planning, administration and finance.
7. There should be cooperation and sharing of responsibility in school education, local organisations and states, while higher education should be sustained by the co-operation of states and the Centre.
8. The states must shoulder the responsibility for providing educational facilities.

Private Enterprise. The work of education and its spread has taken place more through private institutions, hence the following principles should be observed in the setting up of private institutions-(a) state governments should extend all possible aid to such institutions. (b) state governments should make available all facilities necessary for the spread of education.

Local Administration. The process of education gains momentum through local administration. The suggestions in this regard are - (i) the local administration should maintain a good educational administration, (ii) all the educational committees of schools should always maintain awareness of the process of education, (iii) local conditions must always be kept in mind, (iv) District School Boards must be established to look after the local schools, and to implement the state's educational policy; in addition, such boards should also formulate local educational policies, (v) in large cities, the municipal boards should take up programmes of the kind described above, (vi) appointments and transfers should be decided upon by a committee, (vii) the school board should, in the initial stages, not be burdened with excessive administrative load.

Work of the Central Government. The responsibility of the Central Government lies in the creation of administrative efficiency and skill. Hence, the following arrangements should be made: (a) making arrangements for education in the centrally administered territories, (b) taking the assistance of reputed and brilliant persons in the work of national development, and inspiring educational growth in the country, (c) making changes in the budget only with the consent of the Planning Commission, (d) since the direction of education has been put in the hands of the central government by the Constitution, it should maintain flexibility and freedom in conducting experiments in the sphere of education.

Ministry of Education. The administrative structure of the ministry of education should take the following form: (i) a tradition should be created for appointing a renowned educationist as the secretary and advisor of the ministry, (ii) 50% of the appointments to the ministry should be made by promotions of individuals from the state departments of education, while 50% of the posts should be reserved for well known educationists. (iii) Committees should be constituted for the performance of various tasks. (iv) The Central Advisory Board of Education should perform its functions effectively and forcefully. (v) The statistical department of the ministry of education should be restructured so as to give concrete shape to the suggestions of the Commission so that education may be planned in the most suitable manner.

National Council of Educational Research and Training. At the national level, the NCERT bears a heavy burden of responsibility for the development of education. In this context, the following suggestions have been mooted- (i) For the departments of education of the various states, the national board of education, the NCERT, etc., should function as a technical agency. (ii) The non-governmental representation on the controlling body of the agency should be taken from every class and part of the country. (iii) It should have full time directors and joint-directors, who should be employed for a period of five years, which may, if necessary, be extended. (iv) The Central Institute of Education should be handed over to the Delhi University.

Administration at the State Level. At the state level, the administration of education should be improved in the following manners: (i) Educational councils should be constituted at the state level, and these should implement evaluative programmes at regular intervals. (ii) There should be a standing committee of officials under the chairmanship of the secretary of education. (iii) The secretary of education should be an educationist, and his main function should be to reflect upon the problems of education. (iv) A statutory council of education should be constituted in each state, consisting of representatives of universities, with the minister of education as its chief. The annual report of such a council, along with its suggestions, should be put before the legislative assembly. (v) The secretariat of education should keep an eye on the financial and administrative problems of education, and implement the government policy liberally.

Indian Education Service. The introduction of an Indian Educational Service at the national level is a very fine suggestion. It has been suggested that-(1) An Indian Educational Service should bt introduced. (2) One third of its posts should be filled by direct recruitment. (3) For the remaining two-thirds of the posts, the policies of promotions and direct recruitment should be adopted. (4) Some of the posts should be reserved for teachers also. (5) This service should have the following posts- (a) A Director, and officials of the directorate, (b) Officials at the district level, (c) Principals of state and central-institutions. (6) High scales of pay should be given in universities and colleges, so that high standards may be maintained, (7) 50% of the I.E.S. officials should be allowed to remain in the regions to which they belong.

State Education Services. At the state level, too, a state education service should be established in the manner outlined below:-

1. Even in the states, an education service at the state level should be set up. 2. Kinds of Posts-

(a) Class 1

(1) Secretary of the District School Board

(2) District Inspectors

(3) Teachers

(b) Class II

(1) District Inspector

(2) Teachers.

75% of the appointments should be direct while 25% should be through promotions. It must be kept in mind that teachers must have the same scales of pay as the officials of the administration.

Training of Educational Administrators. For the proper training of administrators in the educational sphere, a staff college should be set up in the following manner - (i) the State Institute of Education should run courses with the help of colleges and universities for the training of non-gazetted staff so that this staff may be properly trained. (ii) Administrators should be given leave to enable them to study the problems of education. (iii) Administrators should also be given opportunities for improving their qualifications and skills through in-service courses. (iv) A national staff college for educational administration should be set up. (v) The staff in the departments of education should be increased.

Method. The methods of educational administration are, at present, lacking in uniformity. Hence it is suggested that (1) the attitudes of the administrators should be changed. (2) methods, work and achievements should be subject to periodic evaluation, and (3) inter-state exchange of views should be made possible.

Education Act. There are varying acts on education in the country. In order to end this confusion, an ideal act should be formulated. The following suggestions have been given- (a) Education Acts should be enacted in the states and centrally administered territories, (b) the Central government should enunciate an educational policy, and the state governments should implement it. (c) The possibility of enacting a national education act should be considered.

On the whole, we can clearly see that the Commission has given all possible thought to the total reform of education in the country.

The purpose of school organisation and the administration is to raise the standard of education. Many factors have contributed to the decline in the standards of school education in India, but the main ones among them are the administrative difficulties of inspection or supervision and survey. Hence, the Education Commission has offered the following suggestions for improving the standard of education at the school level:-

1. A common method of public education should be evolved.
2. School education should be organised at the national level, with their distinct objectives- (a) bringing all institutions to a certain minimum standard, (b) giving each institution the opportunity to develop to the highest level of which it is capable, (c) taking each institution to the ideal point within the next ten years.
3. The office of the district education officer should be made effective.
4. The state institute of education should be made more effective and powerful.
5. All kinds of programmes should be organised in the centrally administered territories.

The Education Commission has sought to solve education's administrative problems on the basis of the principles outlined above.

Common School System of Public Education. Our country lacks a uniform educational policy. Education is conducted through governmental, non-governmental institutions, schools run by local bodies, and public schools. The accomplishment, of these different kinds of institutions vary greatly. Because of this, it is essential that a common school system of public education be evolved. Its prime function is to evolve uniform educational standards at all the three levels. No guardian should feel compelled to send his child to a different school. In order to ensure this, the Commission has suggested the following steps for the evolution of such a system:-

A. All teachers without any discrimination should get the same facilities.
B. Teachers should get equal pay for equal work and similar qualifications.
C. Provisions for retirement and the corresponding benefits should be the same for all teachers.
D. Conditions of service should be the same despite differences in management.
E. Rules for the appointment of teachers should be the same.

The major feature of this system, as well as its objective, is the provision of free education. At the primary and secondary levels, all education should be free. Each institution should work for the progress and improvement of the community. The policy of neighbourhood school should also be implemented to make this system a success.

Schools Run by Government and Local Bodies. Despite the availability of all facilities, the actual achievements of government schools are common place and there are very few schools which can boast of any exceptional achievement. The main reasons responsible for this are the maximum exploitation of security of service by the teachers and their negligent attitude towards their duties. Schools managed by local bodies suffer from similar shortcomings. Hence, a change in the system of education is essential. The Commission has offered the following suggestions for raising the standard of achievements of these schools- (i) Making provisions for the construction maintenance and repair of school buildings, school gardens and playgrounds. (ii) Providing the necessary resources. (iii) Distributing books and writing materials to the children. (iv) Introducing uniformity in the award of scholarship and prizes. (v) Making arrangements for compulsory education in each region. (vi) Strengthening the relations between the school and the community. (vii) providing lunch to the students. (viii) Making provisions for the spread of school education in each region.

A School Committee, should be constituted to look after the schools managed by the government or local bodies. This committee will help bring the school closer to the community. Half the members of such a committee should be selected from the village and officials of the municipal organisation, while the other half should be composed of those individuals who are interested in education and be nominated by the District School Council.

As far as the question of this council's expenditure is concerned, (i) it should have adequate funds at its disposal, and the funds should be created by the municipal organisation and village panchayats, (ii) From time to time, the funds should be replenished by donations and collections, (iii) grants should be given by the district school council.

The council should aim at removing the laxity and indifference found in schools run by local bodies or governments.

Private Schools. Private schools are run by diverse private groups. They can generally be classified into three groups- (i) Recognised institutions which receive aid. (ii) Recognised institutions. (iii) Non-recognised institutions.

Of these, the number of recognised and non recognised institutions is much smaller than those of the first category. Despite the private management, these schools are an inseparable part of the system of public education. Most of their expenditure is borne by the government. Where scholarships are offered to students, the expenditure thus incurred is also compensated by the government. Such schools have intimate links with the community. They are free to act as they wish, and this is true even today, despite the increased departmental checks upon them. These institutions are found suffering from two major drawbacks- (i) bad financial condition, (ii) inefficient or corrupt management.

It is found that the standard in very large institutions is low while in smaller institutions it is high. Privately managed schools also suffer from the problem of arbitrary appointments of teachers, irregularities in payment of salary, misuse of financial facilities, etc. The teachers teaching in these schools do not get the same scales of pay, facilities or respect as the teachers in the schools run by government or local bodies. All these factors adversely affect the teachers.

In order to overcome these shortcomings; the Commission has suggested that- (i) The discrimination between private and governmental teachers must be ended. (ii) By the end of the fourth plan, education should be completely free at the primary level. (iii) By the end of the fifth plan, there should be free education at the lower secondary level. (iv) Necessary facilities for good education must be made available. (v) The government should inspect schools which receive governmental aid. Badly managed schools should be taken over by the government. (vi) Privately managed schools should enjoy the same facilities as the government schools.

With reference to the schools which has not been given recognition, the Commission have clearly said that these generally include the pre-schools or preparatory schools in urban areas. Most kinds of coaching classes cause more harm than good. For such institutions, the first legal step can be to compel them to seek registration. Those which fail to do so will be regarded as committing a crime. The state government should have the right to cancel the registration of any institution which it finds functioning in an unsatisfactory manner. The criteria for such a decision may be : (a) lack of proper grounds in the school, (b) improper location of the school in view of the age, ability and sex of the students, (c) absence of proper teaching arrangements, (d) the owner or teachers of the institution being unfit to hold such office.

Neighbourbood Schools. The Commission feels that our schools are found to be suffering from distance or a sense of separation. Hence, the mechanism of education should be such as to encourage social and national unity. For this purpose, the Commission has recommended the concept of "neighbourhood school". Elaborating the concept, the Commission points out that the concept of a neighbourhood school means that no student of the neighbourhood should be refused education on the grounds of caste, community, class or religion. This will have two advantages: (i) these schools will provide good education because of the normal life and atmosphere in the school, and (ii) when such schools are established the rich and powerful classes will begin to take an interest in public education. This scheme will put an end to the alienation which exists at present between different kinds of schools. For this, it is necessary (i) to bring all primary schools to the same standard, and (ii) to implement in practice the concept of neighbourhood schools.

Scholarships. All the children in the country should receive their education under the system of public education, which should give them the opportunity to develop their talents. In order to develop interest in nationhood, it is necessary to make education free and to grant scholarships to all brilliant students. Scholarships should not be available to students studying in schools which have separated themselves from the mainstream of public education.

School education is a partnership between local and state administration, since the responsibility for it falls upon the local community as well as the state government. It is directed by the District School Board and the local committee. In the opinion of the Education Commission, the entire responsibility for school education is upon the state government. There is no doubt that the local community does take interest in education, and it would be desirable if the state government helped these local institutions. Local institutions perform the function of agents in the spread of education. The department of education should perform the following tasks:

1. Formulating an intensive scheme for school development, and making periodical preparation and revisions of curriculum, text-books, teacher's guidance materials, and also improving evaluative as well as teaching techniques.

2. Determining the standards in schools with the assistance of the State Board of Education, the State Evaluation Organisation, etc., and providing the necessary financial aid for attaining the requisite standards.

3. Supervising the training of teachers, their pay-scales, their facilities regarding vacations and retirement, and also organising in-service training through training colleges.

4. Fulfilling the responsibility of inspecting and supervising schools, which may be done by the officials of the state education department or state board of school education, or both.

5. Making arrangements for a state evaluation organisation.

6. Improving the administration of local committee and institutions.

7. Organising a state institute of education.

8. Making provisions for vocational and technical education at the school level.

Many efforts must be made to give a proper form to educational administration. 'Till the present, schools have generally been found lacking in the facilities necessary for proper administration. At the local level, many deficiencies have to be made up. Administrative and organisational improvement can be achieved by taking the following steps:

Organisation of offices at the District level. The district educational officer and his assistants play an important role in the organisation of schools. In the district, he performs the same functions as are performed by the director. of education in the state. This official belongs to the class I category in many districts, while in many others, he is of the class II category. He has deputy and sub-deputy inspectors to assist him. The nature of his work differs according to the nature of the state, but in all states he has at least one common function, which is to get recognition for the schools in his district. His main function is inspection and supervision.

Nowadays, the importance of district has increased, with the increase in population. Hence, in order to strengthen the organisation at the district level, the Commission has suggested the following steps:-

(i) The district education officer should be given a suitable grade, and this can be done easily if this post falls within the purview of an Indian Educational Service.

(ii) The district education officer should be liberally endowed with rights or powers so that he may be able to fulfil his functions effectively. The district office should function as the directorate for the local schools.

(iii) The inspecting staff suffers from three defects- (i) their number is inadequate; (ii) because of their low salaries, they are usually not suitably qualified, (iii) the inspecting officials, instead of being specialists, are generalists. These defects have to be overcome. Hence, according to the Commission-(a) better pay scales should be offered to attract more talented and qualified individuals, (b) at the district level, the staff should possess specific qualifications, and (c) the number of workers should be in proportion to the number of students.

Principal. The function of inspection and supervision, as a part of administrative activity, is not limited only to the district offices. The principals of local institutions also play an important part in it. As a class, principals are being neglected at present. In this context, the Commission has pointed to the scales of pay of principals. It has suggested that special courses should be prepared for the training of principals. Principals of governmental institutions are treated with even greater indifference. The members of their staff are often transferred without their consent. Hence, it is essential that - (1) principals be given the necessary powers, (2) they should have full freedom in their work, (3) in private institutions, the management committees should give the principal the necessary freedom.

School Complex. In many schools in India, the means of teaching are not available. Hence, the Education Commission has suggested the idea of setting up school complexes through the co-operation of local institutions, so as to bring about a general improvement in educational standards. It has said that the school complex programme should be developed as a national programme and under it, conditions should be created to encourage each school to strive for the highest results which it is capable of achieving.

The Commission's suggestions with regard to 'school complex' are :

(i) Each school should be treated as a unit and assisted to move towards progress at its own pace.

(ii) There should be more emphasis upon human resources instead of upon material or physical resources.

(iii) In the next 10 years, at least 10 primary and secondary schools in each such complex should be raised to the limits of their development.

'The School Complex' is an organisation of educational institutions, of similar or different standards, in which the institution strives for their educational improvement through co-operation. It gives rise to mutual goodwill, co-operation, healthy exchange and mutual encouragement. These factors are helpful in bringing about an acceleration in the pace of progress at various levels for the better achievement of educational goals.

In the Education Commission's opinion, supervision is, in one way, the basis of educational development, but unfortunately, the supervision of schools has been neglected for many reasons. These reasons are - (a) The proportion of supervisory staff has not increased in the same ratio as the schools. (b) The functions of inspection and supervision have to be performed by the same officer, and thus, because of an excess of administrative work, supervision is often hindered. (c). Members of the supervisory staff have to engage in non-educational work as members of Block Team Work, and thus they get little time for their own real work. (d) Prescriptive methods are used for supervisory work whereas, in fact, creative or developmental techniques should be employed in this activity. (e) Inspecting officials also do not have the requisite qualifications or even abilities.

To overcome these shortcomings, the Commission has made the following recommendations—

Separating Administration from Supervision. In order to simplify supervisory work, it is necessary that the district education council should perform the supervisory function while the district education officer should function as the inspector. Both these institutions should work in consonance with each other. The advice of the district education officer can be sought in such matters as evolving new methods of teaching, guidance of teachers organisation of in-service training, organisation of extension services, etc.

Giving Recognition to Schools. Nothing would be better than making it possible for the schools to get recognition themselves. However, at present, a school is able to get recognition only when it fulfils certain conditions and complies with certain rules. This is the situation in every state. The Commission's view is that recognition is an opportunity, an achievement, which the schools should seek to attain. It has expressed the hope that every local and private group should request the government. to grant recognition to their schools. The department should grant recognition only when the school fulfils certain minimum conditions. Periodical inspections should also be carried out.

Kinds of Inspection. The existing practice is to carry out annual inspections, and they are more nominal than factual. For the future, the

Commission has recommended the following two kinds of inspections for each school:-

Annual Inspection. This inspection should be conducted by officers of the department of education. Primary schools should be inspected by officials of the district education council, while secondary schools should be inspected by officials of the state's department of education.

Quarterly Inspection. Every school should be inspected thoroughly every three or four months. The primary education officer should inspect primary schools, while secondary institutions should be inspected by a panel.

At this point, it should be clarified that supervision has a flexible base since it aims at helping and guiding schools and colleges. It should guide the general schools to improve and progress, and also provide facilities for the better schools to conduct experiments. The entire nature of education can undergo a radical change if supervision is effectively implemented by qualified and able supervisory officers. This can be achieved through the following means- (i) improvement in the abilities of inspection staff, (ii) possession of specific qualifications by them, (iii) in-service training. But the establishment of a national staff college for educational administrators is essential.

Problems related to school organisation and inspection have always had a profound impact upon the standard of education. However, it is also true that the solution to all these problems can be found through a single step, which is the proper organisation of the mechanism for administration and inspection. The following are the Education Commission's recommendations regarding improvement in school administration:-

Preparation of Institutional Plans. In order to improve school administration, it is essential that each school should prepare its own plan. The characteristic feature of our educational system has been the fact that its schemes have been thrust upon schools from above, without ever reaching the base. Some guidelines can be provided for guidance, and such schemes may be concerned with reduction in wastage and stagnation, development of teaching techniques, assistance of sub-normal children, special attention to the brilliant students, improvement in the effectiveness of the curriculum, organisation of instructional programme in the school, improvement of the teacher's qualifications under scheme of self-study, etc. They may also include schemes for the improvement of the local community and the school. Praiseworthy work in this direction has been done in Tamil Nadu.

Intelligent Planning and Continuity of Efforts. Every scheme for improvement depends, for its success,- upon skilful planning and continuous efforts at implementation. For any such scheme, it is essential to orient the educational officers at every level. The Centre as well as the States should make efforts in this direction. In the Commission's view skilful planning and continuity should be integral parts of our educational programmes.

Experimentation and Elasticity. Teachers as well as institutions should be encouraged to experiment, but the existing system of teaching does not allow such freedom to either teachers, or schools. Decentralisation will have to be introduced if we wish to try out new ideas and methods, and the government will have to accept each school as a separate entity in itself.

Classification of Schools. The success of many an educational programme depends upon the continuance of certain teachers in those institutions in which the experiments are being conducted. Hence, in order to create contact with the community and to win its co-operation, it is essential to classify institutions. This classification can be based on the following foundations-

(a) Institutions conducting various kinds of scientific experiments, such as the NCERT.

(b) Institutions which put forward the minimum and ideal qualifications for good schools, such as National Board of Education.

(c) On the basis of their achievements, schools can be classified thus -

(i) Schools with a standard higher than the expected standard.

(ii) School with a standard falling between the minimum and the maximum expected standards.

(iii) Schools with a standard lower than the expected minimum standard.

Programme for Action. Work should proceed on the basis of the following points if the programme is to achieve success: (i) Quality schools should be established at every level. The number of good schools should increase. (ii) The Work should start by first strengthening the existing good schools. (iii) At the primary level, there should be a proper distribution of schools and neighbourhood schools in the rural and urban areas. (iv) At the primary and secondary levels, an adequate programme of scholarships should be introduced. Scholarships should be distributed on the basis of geographical as well as communal factors. (v) The minimum standards should not be allowed to fall further. (vi) Students achieving distinctive results in periodic assessments should be given prizes.

State Institute of Education. A state institution of education should be established in each state for the progress of education. These institutes should do the same work as the NCERT is doing for the Centre. Their functions should be as follows:-

(i) Arranging for the in-service training of departmental officials; for this, in-service training programme should be introduced for the training of both officials and teachers.

(ii) Teacher's training should make progress, and for this purpose a state board of teacher's education should be established.

(iii) Preparation of curricula and text books, giving of guidance and carrying out evaluation should be pursued. Vocational work should be done on 'no profit, no loss', basis.

(iv) With the co-operation of universities and colleges, programmes for research and evaluation should be prepared.

(v) Work related to educational problems should be published.

State Board of School Education. The prime function of the department of education is to bring about steady improvement in the standard of education. This standard of education is of three kinds- (i) the potential educational standard which is determined by the teacher, the curriculum, the text-books and guidelines for teachers, and which the teacher aims at attaining ; (ii) the standard which becomes apparent from the achievements of the students through evaluation; and (iii) the standard determined by periodic educational planning for the future.

In order to attain these standards at the state level, it will be necessary to establish State boards of school education in each state, which will help the state to attain the national standards in the educational sphere. It will examine and evaluate the work of the existing educational councils. It must also perform the function of formulating the curriculum and granting recognition. It will also look into the working of the department of education, and organise public examinations. There should be a sub committee to look after the Board's work. The Board may also be divided into a number of small units so as to ensure that examination results are declared on time.

State Evaluation Organisation. The Commission has suggested the establishment of a State Evaluation Organisation for improving the standard of education in the states. This organisation should get the co-operation of the state's department of education. Its functions will be as follows- (i) rendering assistance to the district education officials in improving the existing modes of evaluation in primary and secondary institutions ; (ii) developing and improving the external examinations for classes 10, 11 and 12, organised by the State Board of School Education.

Thus, the programme of working of such an organisation will be as follows:

1. Collecting and preparing standardised evaluation material.
2. Emphasising the adoption of novel techniques of evaluation and examination in training colleges.
3. Acquainting the inspection officials with new techniques of inspection.
4. Conducting research into the problems of evaluation.

National Board of School Education. It is necessary to set up a National Board of School Education in order to maintain the standard of education at the national level. It should be entrusted with the following functions-(a) defining the various standards of school education ; (b) making necessary change from time to time in the national standards ; (c) evaluating the standards achieved; (d) advising the state governments about curricula, text-books, preparation of teaching materials, etc., (e) advising the state governments about improvements in the standard of education. Such an institution should be organised in the following manner- (1) Chairman. (2) Two representatives from the NCERT and the ministry of education. (3) Two representatives from the UGC. (4) Chairman of the State Boards of School Education. (5) Four teachers, of whom one must be from the primary level. (6) Three teachers from universities interested in school education. This board should have a secretariat possessing all necessary facilities, and it should perform diagnostic and developmental functions.

Programmes in Centrally Sponsored Sectors. In order to bring about an improvement in the standard of school education, it is essential that comprehensive programmes should be taken up in the centrally sponsored sectors also. These programmes can be of the following kinds-(1) development of vocational education, (2) establishment of good secondary schools in the centrally administered territories, (3) making adequate provisions for scholarships, (4) organising the public examinations for classes 10 and 12 with the national board of school examination.

The reality is that standards of education both at the state and at the national levels have to be improved. Qualitative and quantitative improvements are essential for achieving the highest objectives of national development. And this is possible only when the administrative machinery in education is changed.

Educational planning and administration lie at the root of a potential revolution in the field of education. In this sphere considerable thought has been devoted to each level of education, within the framework of a national policy. As a result, the following problems of planning and administration have come to light. Solutions to these problems have also been suggested.

Lack of harmony, dearth of able workers. For the development of education in the desired direction, it is necessary to have an effective mechanism, a fact to which sufficient attention has not been given so far. At present, all that educational planning and administration mean is-putting together the educational activities of various departments and harmonizing them. This synthesizing is done by the State Planning and Finance Department. In the context of the fifth plan, the notation of educational planning is gradually evolving in the states, but in spite of this, educational planning becomes difficult in the absence of necessary information. At the district level, there is also lack of adequate staff for planning. And, whatever staff does exist is lacking in professional expertise.

Ineffectiveness in Transmission. We are lacking in an effective mechanism for providing necessary information and thereby making possible the implementation of schemes. This mechanism, or its absence, is responsible for the failure of implementation of schemes, the reasons for which are presentation of schemes in a general way, without laying the necessary stress on their special features. The result is that the individual as well as the institution has great difficulty in implementing programmes. Hence, what is needed is that educational plans should be prepared in an intensive and comprehensive manner.

Inefficiency of the information gathering mechanism. It has also been observed that the existing mechanism for collecting, consolidating and transmitting information is inefficient. The information that is gathered is either not adequate or is unsuitable for the preparation of plans and the achievement of their objectives. Individuals responsible for collecting educational statistics also lack training, besides which they are not able to devote their undivided attention to this task. Statistical information collected in a systematic and regular manner is useful; in its absence, the best kind of educational planning is inconceivable.

Absence of a Mechanism for formulating plans. At the state level, there is an absence of any institution for the formulation of complete plans for higher education, with the result that a balance between general and technical education, in the context of enrolment, finance, etc., is not maintained. The colleges affiliated to universities do not raise any voice regarding educational planning although these colleges provide the entire enrolment for their respective universities. Besides, the state governments also do not have any representation on the Visiting Committee of the University Grants Commission. In consequence, many obstacles rise in the way of balancing expenditure and obtaining matching grants.

The Steering Group of the Planning Commission has offered the following suggestions for strengthening educational planning and making it effective-

Organisation for Educational Planning. For the implemen-tation of educational plans, it is essential to have effective organisations at the various levels of administration. Besides, there is also need for synthesis and harmony among the various governmental and non-governmental institutions working in the educational field. Hence, a Human Resources Development Board should be established at the national level. It should be looked after by the Prime Minister. A similar board, composed of the representatives of various departments, universities, colleges, private managements, industry and other professions should also be set up at the state level.

Organisation in the Education Department. The department of education of each state should have a developmental or planning wing in order to make educational planning more effective and to bring about harmony in educational and training matters. This wing should direct the institutions of school education, college education and technical education agriculture, health, labour and employment. This work should be performed at the level of the secretary of education of the state, and the planning wing should be under the charge of the director of education. The officials of this wing may have different qualifications in view of the differing needs of the states.

Planning Mechanism for Higher Education. In each state, there is need for a separate planning mechanism for higher education so that balanced growth may be achieved. For this purpose, a University Planning Board can be set up in each state, consisting of a Chairman (the Chancellor); Secretary, Director of the State Planning Organisation, the vice-chancellors of every university in the state, secretaries of the education, agriculture, health, planning and finance departments, representatives of the Planning Commission, the University Grants Commission, and the teacher representatives of affiliated colleges and universities. This body should formulate a comprehensive plan for the improvement and spread of higher education, with the help and co-operation of governmental and non-governmental agencies. The plans thus produced should not be merely repetitive or imitative, instead, they should seek for originality and benefits in hitherto unexplored regions. This body should also keep in touch with the other plans of the state.

Decentralisation of the Planning Process. Decentralisation of the planning process is very essential, because in educational planning and administration, the district has its own individual and unique importance. The Kothari Commission's suggestion for the establishment of a District Education Board is an important step in this direction. In view of this, the following suggestions have been offered:-

(a) There should be a district education committee in each district, with the district education officer as its chairman. Its members should include those representatives of governmental and non-governmental institutions who are concerned with or interested in educational planning and harmony. This committee should be responsible for implementing the state's educational policies in consonance with the needs of the district.

(b) There should be an educational planning wing in the office of the district educational officer. This wing should redefine and clarify matters pertaining to the condition of local schools, selection of teachers, teaching materials, resources and plans.

Local Cooperation. Successful implementation of educational plans necessitates the enthusiastic co-operation of local individuals. Teachers and the officials of the department of education should be allowed to perform their functions without interference from local, Panchayat-raj institutions. Institutions should also have the freedom to implement plans, though the department of education should exercise technical and administrative control. Representatives of the local unit should make use of local resources for implementing such schemes as provision of lunch, ensuring regular attendances, winning the co-operation of teachers and guardians, etc. This kind of democratic decentralisation should be evaluated with a view to introducing effective evaluation of educational requirements.

Inspection and Supervision. The main function of the department of education is the educational supervision of schools. In this activity, the attitude should now be modified. The purpose should be advice and guidance, not fault-finding. But this is possible only when able individuals are available for inspection of educational institutions. General inspection and educational supervision differ from each other considerably, and hence, for the latter, a professional method should be evolved. It is desirable that at the state, district and block level, institutions should have the services of specialists, who should remain in continuous touch with students and teachers and provide information about the latest techniques to both.

Classroom Teaching. The actual teaching in the classroom depends entirely upon the teacher. Hence, it is desirable that the teacher's teaching ability and capacity are developed and improved, something that can be achieved by giving the teacher opportunities for in-service training. The teachers should themselves be prepared for self-training for improving their abilities. For this purpose, Subject Associations should be organised.

Administration at the District Level. The administrative mechanism at the district level must be strong if success is to be achieved in the implementation of educational plans and the educational process. Because of negligence and indifference at this level, suitable individuals are not appointed to key posts at various levels. It is also essential to make the most efficient and effective use of the available fmancial resources. Through extension services, the school should be kept in effective touch with training colleges, state educational institutions and the NCERT. For this, it would be best if secondary colleges maintained contact, on the one hand, with primary schools, and on the other, with training college. The secondary school should receive help from the neighbouring college. In this way, a complex of many institutions, starting from the lowest and reaching the highest, can be created. In this scheme, work should be entrusted to the NCERT college teachers and school teachers for short periods of time.

Provisions of the Fifth Plan. The following schemes were proposed under the fifth plan -(i) Rs.13.32 crores were allocated for strengthening the school inspection and supervision machinery. (ii) Rs.15 crores were allotted for improving the planning, administration and statistical mechanism at the central, state and district levels. (iii) Rs. 63 lakhs were provided for organising state boards of teacher education. (iv) Rs. 2 crores were provided for the improvement of state education institution. In addition, a separate allocation of Rs. 15 crores was made for programmes under the first three sections.

PART ONE

STREAMS OF EDUCATION

2

Distance Education

In National Education Policy 1986, it is stated-'life long education is a cherished goal of the educational process. This pre-supposes universal literacy, opportunities will be provided to youth, housewives, agricultural and industrial workers and professionals to continue the education of their choice, at the pace suited to them. The future thrust will be in the direction of open and distance learning.' This statement reflects over the new thinking regarding the universalisation of education. Life long education and its conceptual framework is now old enough.

The system of education in India has a great historical and cultural heritage. It has been changed from time to time because of the socio-economic and cultural pressures. Many branches of knowledge and culture were the contribution of lust for it, but the concept and need of mass education and democratisation of education have a recent origin. These changes are effected by historical necessity.

Since the age of Vedas, there was learner motivation. Those who were interested to learn, approached the Guru and stayed with him in his Gurukul for few years. There actual instructions were given and the skills were developed. This type of learner-motivation was also found in Buddha Period. During this period, education was institutionalised. Nalanda, Taxshila, Vikramshila and so many others were the universities where the learners from all walks of life used to come for study.

During Muslim period, there were Pathshalas for Hindus and Madrassas for Muslims. In Madrassas Hindus, who were desirous to serve the emperors and nawabs, also secured their education. The system, recognised by the state was Perso-Arabic. Upward mobility was the aim of this system.

During British period, English system of Education was introduced. Learners from families with some educational background thronged the schools which were situated in towns. The purpose of education in British period was to prepare persons who might be helpful to run the administration.

Dr. Radhakrishnan Commission says in its report that education must be universalised and equal opportunities for all be given. Each and every citizen be given education irrespective of his caste or creed, social or economic status, motivation or aptitude.

Meaning and Definition

Peter says, 'Distance education is a method of indirect instruction, implying geographical and emotional separation of teacher and taught whereas, in mainstream education, the relationship between a teacher and student in class room is based upon social norms, in distance education, it is based upon technological rules.' Jack Foks stated about Distance education-'Distance education is a mode of learning with certain characteristics which distinguish it from the campus based mode of learning.'

These definitions explain the system of education through which one gets education but he maintains a distance ; what is that distance? Regarding this some studies have been done. We are mentioning them.

Autonomy of Learner. Wedemeyer expresses Distance education as an independent study, open learning and distance education. The three terms expressed the following meanings:-

Independent Study > Correspondence Courses.

Open Education > Open University.

Distance Education > Correspondence Education.

Wedemeyer has outlined this idea about 'Independent study' and its purpose (i) It consists of teaching/learning arrangements, and these arrangements have various forms. The special feature of these arrangements, is that, the teachers and learners stay away from each other and didatic communication takes place in various ways. (ii) Its purpose are to facilitate learning activities of both the on campus and the off campus students.

Distance between Learner and the Teacher. The learner has to learn apart from the teacher. There is a vast difference between traditional classroom learning and learning with distance. The innovations in education and technology have given a different way of learning as well as teaching. Writing made possible to record communication and transfer them over space and time. Printing broke down the monopoly of a single copy writing, telecommunication collapsed the dimensions of space and time, democratic philosophy broke down the monopoly of elites. Correspondence education was the result of needs and pressures. The development of programmed learning and teaching machines pointed to the possibility of self instruction and learner based education.

Structural System. The structural system is based on the institutional philosophy of the society. In one, society, there are many socio-economic and cultural changes which effect the structure and motivate the aspirations of the people. Therefore non-contiguous educational communication is suggested. It means that main characteristic of distance study means that the learner is physically at a long distance from the teacher for much, most or even all of the time during the teaching learning process.

Moore's Motion or Independent Study. Michael Moore expressed his views in his work 'Teaching at a Distance' about Distance Education. Distance and Autonomy are the two variables of this programme. There are three phenomenon of it -(i) Dialogues, (ii) Individualisation, (iii) Structure. Dialogue means the face to face communication. Individualisation refers to curricular components - objective, methods, material, and evaluation. Structure means that the process of instruction be maintained.

A Function of Dialogue and Individualisation. In Distance education these are as follows:-

1. Programmes with no dialogue but with structure, i.e., radio, television and audio, audio-video programmes.

2. Programmes with no dialogue and no structure, i.e., independent reading or self directed study.
3. Programmes with dialogues and structure, i.e, correspondence method.
4. Programmes with dialogue and no structure-a tutorial programme.

Learner Autonomy. The concept has an autonomy in learning and teaching. In an educational programme there must be the autonomy of objectives, methods, materials and evaluation, and these must be decided by the institute and the teacher.

Logical Basis

Philosophy of Distance Education generates the idea that each individual has the right to gain education and to crop with the development of knowledge and skill. Distance education has the idea of life long education. The age, time and place has no significant value for this programme. This is meant for adults who have left schools or traditional system of education and are busy for their livelihood. Therefore, the process of communication is more important. Use of the means of communication for educating the individual sitting on a long distance, i.e., another city, District or province, Print media, Programmed instruction and Postal Service are the basis of the Distance education.

Distance education accommodates the term correspondence education.

Evolution and Development

Distance education is a world wide phenomenon. In Africa, Distance education was spread over to train teachers and to educate the masses. Countries like Nigeria, Kenya, Tanzania, Guyana, Ethiopia and Ghana offer distance education courses. Print and electronic media and personal contact programmes are the primary means used to impart knowledge and skills.

In North, South and Central America, the following forms are found- (i) application and professionally oriented courses are being offered, (ii) print and electronic media play an important role in disseminating information, knowledge and skills.

In Asia, countries like India, Pakistan, Thailand, Sri Lanka, Philippines, China, South Korea, Indonesia and Japan adopted Distance education system and courses are based mainly on print materials which are supplemented by electronic media and contact programme.

In Australia, the university level courses are based on an integrated model-New Zealand, Papua New Guinea and Pacific Islands promote distance education in a big way.

Current Scenario

About 25 years ago, correspondence education in India was started as a pilot project in the University of Delhi. The success of this experiment encouraged other universities to take up instructions through the distance education. By 1985, 31 universities adopted this scheme. About 40,000 students at various levels were enrolled by the universities under this scheme. Though the universities are providing education through this media, but there was a great demand for an open university. As a result in 1985, the Govt. of India decided to set up Indira Gandhi National Open University. The focal points of this university are as under -

(i) to promote open university and distance education system.

(ii) to determine the standards of teaching evaluation and research in such system.

(iii) to allocate and disburse grants to colleges, whether admitted to its privileges or not, or to any other university or institution of higher learning as may be specified by the Statutes.

Indira Gandhi National Open University is providing Degrees in B.A., B.Sc. and B. Com., Diploma Courses in Distance education, Creative writing, Nutrition, Management, Local Self Government, Library Science, Banking, etc.

Separate Radio and TV channels have been started to broadcast and telecast the educational programmes.

As a measure for implementation, the programme of action has also favoured and recommended Open Universities System to provide higher education through non-formal channel. The main suggestions and recommendation of this Action Programme are given as under :

(i) Action Programme suggested the Open University System. This should be cost-effective, flexible and innovative.
(ii) Indira Gandhi National Open University has been established and is running effectively.
(iii) Non-formal education system should be structured on modular pattern.
(iv) Minimum level of learning should be objectively assessed.
(v) Separate Radio and Television channels be used for the use of distance education.
(vi) Net- work of course be framed.
(vii) Quality of programmes be ensured.
(viii) Financial Assistance will be ensured very carefully.

Good Aspects

Distance Education is a very continuing education. Rather to say it is an effective media of life long education. National Education Policy of Education (1986) has rightly explained the life long education-'It is a cherished goal of educational process. This presupposes universal literacy. Opportunities will be provided to the youth, housewives, agricultural and industrial workers and professionals to continue the education of their choice, at the pace suited to them. The future thrust will be in the direction of open and distance learning.'

National Education Policy 1986 has rightly stressed that distance education will provide many opportunities for education and will lessen the burden of formal education.. The advantages of Distance Education are as under-

Reliable. Distance education is reliable. It has the cost-effective alternative and new means of communication.

Education at Learners, Door. Distance education is the only way which provides the education to the learner at his door. It provides equal educational opportunities even to those who used to live in remote areas.

Beneficial to Adults. Distance education provides many benefits to adults. They may update themselves for the development of skills and-knowledge.

Variety of Programme. Distance education provides variety programmes according to the needs of the learners.

Co-ordination. Distance education is the co-ordination of various educational factors, i.e., general, basic, professional, technical, life-long, in service and expansion.

Minimizing Pressures. Distance education minimizes the educational pressures caused by the explosion of population.

Educational Needs. Distance education fulfils the need of society through variety of educational programmes.

Learner Centered. Distance education is learner-centered, therefore, there is no doubt in its success.

Freedom. This system provides freedom to learner. A learner, learns according to his needs, conditions and facility.

Lust for Knowledge. Distance education provides the opportunities to gain knowledge to those who are really thirsty for it.

Distance education is still in an experimental stage. Even then nobody will disagree that this system will be helpful to solve our educational problems and minimize the pressure of population over the traditional system of education.

Fundamental Ideas and Purpose

Article 45 of the Constitution of India lays stress upon providing universal education, but so far, the promise implicit in this article has not been fulfilled. As a result, we find today that the number of uneducated and partly educated, illiterates and partly literate; individuals is on the increase. It is a matter of no little shame for any country if a large number of citizens in it are deprived of the right to education. Therefore, for all those individuals who either could not study at all or were compelled. to give up education without completing it, irrespective of their age, sex or class, it is necessary to provide opportunities for education as a part of their working conditions. These opportunities have been given the name of Non-formal Education.

Education is a life-long process. In school, child receives education upto a certain age and a certain level, after which he enters society. In keeping with the time, period, environment and individual circumstances, he is compelled to modify the knowledge he has received. This modification occurs through the process of adaptation. In order to live life successfully and skillfully, it is necessary to modify one's experiences. In view of this, we consider non-formal education to be that education which, at all times, in every place, and in every situation, prepares the individual to lead life in a successful way, and which operates both formally and informally. In the opinion of Mehta and Verma, life is changing very quickly because of the rapid growth in knowledge and the high speed of scientific progress, and consequently old assumptions are becoming inoperative. New assumptions are rising on the horizon, and man is constantly becoming conscious of myriad new problems in his life. Not merely this, every child has his own individual problems due to cultural, social and psychological differences, but the organisation, syllabus, time period, location, etc., of school education have so much rigidity and formality that it limits the capacity of education to be flexible and dynamic, and to adapt itself to the needs of the individual students. It is evident from this that formal education does prepare the child for life, but it cannot fulfil the need for universal education. Hence, public needs can only be met by providing non-formal education through the medium of other means.

The following ideas have played a significant role in the emergence of the. concept of non-formal education:-

1. Because of the explosion in knowledge, the knowledge obtained through the stream of formal education remains incomplete, and so the non-formal means of propagation of knowledge can be employed for new knowledge and experiences.
2. The science of educational structure (architecture), is developing rapidly. Because of its hardware and software approach, education has emerged from the classroom and come into the community. Among the effective means of non-formal education are civic life, literacy and cultural institutions; radio, television, pocket books, magazines, libraries, correspondence courses, scientific inventions, films, etc.
3. The responsibility of imparting education is not solely of the school's ; it is the shared duty of all those who know something. Such individuals may well not be a part of the formal stream of education, but their informal functioning as educators is of the highest importance.

From this viewpoint, non-formal education is not the antagonist but the complement of formal education. Non-formal education has its beginning where formal education has its end. It is, in fact, continuing education. For this reason, Mehta and Verma have defined : Non-formal education thus Non-formal education is a system or organisation in which the nature of education is determined in accordance with the needs and convenience of the student. It tries to provide educational opportunities for those engaged in some profession, and for those who were, for some reason, deprived of education. It presents such practical foundations of education that education becomes a natural part of life and helps to stimulate society into progressing towards continuous education.

In the modern world, non-formal education is making rapid progress all over the globe. It has come to be believed that the aim of education is to make the individual useful for the fulfilment of personal, national and global needs. Useful individuals make their country useful and their nation strong.

The following suggestions were preferred for acceptance at the 28th All India Indian Adult Education Conference, (1975) held at Jabalpur - "Within the framework of adult education, non-formal education puts forward a new organisation. It is neither an alternative for formal education, nor an attempt to displace it. It offers an alternative to those who could not take advantage of formal education or abandoned their education without completing it."

In keeping with its nature, non-formal education attaches the maximum importance to the various forms of a flexible mode of operation and the environment of the individual. It is wrong to conceive of it as the second class or rung of education. Instead, it would be far better to see it as a new form of education. It possesses the capacity to help an individual derive the maximum benefit from formal education.

Thus, non-formal education finds its expression in the following programmes-

1. Education for the 6-14 age group.
2. Education for the 15-25 age group in which functional literacy is inherent. It is suitable for both rural and urban areas.
3. Increase in the skill and productivity of urban workers.
4. Education of women through useful education.

5. Continuous education organised by universities and all classes and institutions.

6. Programme of civic education.

The Government of India has decided to. rename the Department of Adult Education as the Department of Non-formal Education, and hence the following changes are visualised:

1. The name of the Board of Adult Education should be changed, it should be reorganised and activated, so that new programmes may be introduced in the sphere of non-formal education.

2. 10% of the educational budget of every state government and the central government should be earmarked for non-formal education.

3. Voluntary organisations should be encouraged to co-operate.

4. The maximum possible number of universities should introduce programmes of continuing education.

For all such programmes, the co-operation of universities, schools, voluntary organisations and other agencies should be solicited.

The UNESCO report on non-formal education, entitled "Learning to be" says that it is necessary to eliminate the artificial obstacles or barriers between the various subjects of education both in formal as well as non-formal education. Recurrent education should be promoted for those who wish to receive it in various form. In other words, this means that an individual should be able to acquire education according to his own needs and conveniences.

Prof. Philip H. Comb and C. Roy have conducted a survey of non-formal education, reported in their work entitled, "New Path of Learning". In the preface to this report, the following concepts have been accepted-

1. Education is a life long process, which cannot be tied to place, time and circumstances.

2. It is necessary for every individual to be aware of the minimum learning skills, who include (a) creative attitude, (b) creative literacy and organisation, (c) scientific attitude, and shackling of the process of nature, (d) earning wealth, civic co-operation and raising the standard of mutual exchange.

In order to make the programme of non-formal learning a success, it is necessary to provide pre-school education to prepare children for school, to make arrangements for a desirable and parallel system of non-formal education and to make these arrangements operative with complete dedication.

All these facts emphasize the view that education. should continue throughout one's life. Life-long education is a universal truth which can not be refuted. In the last three or four decades, despite the rapid rate of scientific progress, the rate of social change remained slow. But, in more recent times, scientific development and the spread of education have increased life's necessities manifold., As a result, it has become necessary for every individual to turn to non-formal education if he does not wish to fall behind others in the race of life.

The idea of life-long education sprouted from India's varna-ashrama system in which there were provisions for the return of 'akshana' (Pitra Dev, teacher and society). In the modern context, it is non-formal education alone which can keep an individual in close contact with knowledge and new skills throughout life.

School Education

Formal education possesses the following characteristics-

1. It is limited to the time of learning, not related to the daily routine;
2. Some points of entrance and progress are implicit in it;
3. It is inclined towards the impersonal goals of attainment of knowledge;
4. It is inspired by such motives as employment, appointment, winning of position and prestige, etc.;
5. It is tied to a pre-determined syllabus, comprehension and a definite subject-matter;
6. It is thrust upon the recipient (the student) by the donor (the teacher) without any interaction between the two;
7. It undoubtedly gives rise to characteristics of discipline and obedience;

8. It tends almost exclusively to avoid failure, win success and adopt the approach leading to success;
9. It works within a definite time-space frame, and hence it soon becomes alienated from special changes.
10. It encourages the status quo and discourages mobility;
11. It prepares the individual and society for a particular acquaintance (asmita), which is in fact the need of an immobile and non-developing social and cultural structure.

Good Aspects

1. It is-life-long, it is intimately relating to a working life, and it constantly enriches life with novel experiences.
2. It is free from the bondages of admission and progress. It provides opportunities for repeatedly joining the stream or leaving it. It can take place anywhere, at any time.
3. It is a process of understanding, improving and satisfying an individual needs, environment, social objectives and mutual relations.
4. It has its spring of motivation in individual development, self-improvement, and the increase of human potential.
5. It adopts a variety of flexible modes of education which are adapted to the student and his environment.
6. It is a process of mutual sharing and exchange, in which the learner fully participates in the research to obtain analytical results.
7. It shows the path to general or public success, which is both relative and general, and which possesses the virtue of providing general satisfaction by continuous learning by everyone involved in it.
8. It gives birth to free thought, self-improvement and a self-generated and self-satisfying awareness.
9. It accelerates the process of questioning, gives a healthy direction to mobility and aims at progress.

10. It works on the presumption of an unknown future, is always prepared for all possible changes, and hence, not only does it exist in parallel with society, it even influences its changes.

11. It constantly pushes the individual and society towards a continuous dynamic acquittance (asmita) - it keeps both on the path towards continuously moving forward, improving and modifying themselves.

The foregoing description of the differences between formal and non-formal education stresses the single fact that education is meant not only for the illiterate but for all those who constantly want to move forward in the race of life, and adapt themselves continuously to the explosion of knowledge taking place around them.

Major Aims

We have already pointed out that education is a life-long process. Non-formal education has the following objectives:-

1. Understanding the environment and conditions, and arousing awareness of the need to make changes in it.
2. Generating faith in science and technological knowledge and encouraging the individual to adopt their skills.
3. Creating the capacity to learn by working and to increase one's skill.
4. Utilising acquired experiences in new situations.
5. Performing the role of an agency for bringing the desired changes in society.
6. Generating a desire to participate in and contribute to the general development of the country through the democratic method of working.
7. Developing the tendency to continue for ever one's own learning and teaching others, and generating a suitable atmosphere therefore.

The Setup

It is natural to ask: for whom should non-formal education be made available? What should be its nature? It is, of course, obvious that non-formal education has no relations with formal education. Non-formal education is needed for the individuals who have been cut off from the stream of formal education, irrespective of their age group, caste, class or sex.

For the sake of convenience, these individuals can be divided into two classes : (1) 8-14 years age group, (2) 15-35 years age group.

The 8-14 Age Group

There is no dearth of students who abandon school by the time they reach the fifth class, either in order to become economic units for their parents, or because they are the victims of their parent's superstitions or the cruelty of society. In rural areas, such boys and girls become the victims of the evil ambitions of the dominant castes and are thus compelled to live a life of virtual slavery.

Children in this age group fall into two categories: (1) those who have never seen a school, (2) those who have attended school for a short time. But even these latter children soon decline to the level of illiterate children. Dr. Zakir Hussain has opined that if the country has sufficient funds to impart compulsory education for only three years instead of for eight years, he would prefer to provide compulsory education for individuals only of the 11 to 14 age group. The reason for this is that for the 11 to 14 age group, the educational requirements are the same as for the 6 to 14 age group.

For this age group, the syllabus should consist of knowledge related to Hindi, Mathematics, knowledge of the environment, and vocational knowledge. Suitable books should be prepared by skilled writers completely familiar with the conditions and environment of the community. Lessons 'should be concerned with day-to-day experiences. There should also be lessons on human physiology, the science of family, citizenship, etc., to promote the qualities of citizenship. The syllabus should be so structured that, if the child so wishes, he may be able to continue his education through its medium.

Children belonging to this age group should be subject to continuous evaluation. There should be no formal examination. Instead, progress should be based on an evaluation of the progress in the child's performance.

The 15-35 Age Group

The second group of students in non-formal education falls in 15 to 35 age group. For educating this group, it is essential to complete non-formalisation of time, place and means or tools of education. For them, the purpose is not merely to provide the learner with the tools of reading and writing, but also to bring about an improvement in his efficiency and vocational skills. It will be necessary to provide various forms of education for individuals in this group. This stage has been called Creative Literacy. Learners in this category have fully developed minds and bodies, and hence, economic self-reliance must be a necessary element in their education.

The syllabus for this age group should comprehend the following programmes.

1. Teaching the adults about the means of developing better methods for reducing the labour and maximising the profit in the profession in which they are, engaged.
2. Giving knowledge and developing the necessary skills of other associated professions.
3. Giving knowledge of health sciences, dietary and nutrition.
4. Improving their knowledge of general social, religious and civic matters.
5. Teaching, reading, writing and arithmetic needed for general use in daily life.
6. Developing an attractive and useful syllabus.

From this viewpoint, the knowledge of language, mathematics and environment should be imparted in such a manner that it provides the learner with many alternatives for slipping into real life.

Infrastructure

The organisation of non-formal education should comprehend the advisory and administrative functions at the centre as well as practical teaching in training centres. In the sixth plan, the major emphasis falls upon non-formal education, a part of the movement for adult education.

Non-formal education should be organised through centres which should be set up whenever they are needed. They should be subject to periodical inspections. Since the programme is intended to educate the masses, it is necessary to obtain the co-operation of the people. The following factors should be kept in mind with reference to setting up such centres:

1. Thought should be given, in selecting a place for such a centre, to the number of illiterate people, the interest of the local population, and the density of population in the area.
2. Centres of non-formal education may be set up in some school building, panchayat house, the village centre, labour welfare centres, towns, etc., depending upon the convenience of the learners.
3. In selecting instructors of these centres it is necessary to ensure that they do actually possess the ability to direct and implement non-formal educational programmes. They must be possessed of interest, enthusiasm and dedication for the task in hand. They should have organisational talent as well as the skills necessary for educating adults.
4. Instructors of centres must also undergo training. They should be encouraged to teach through discussion rather than lecturing, by reflecting upon problems, and adopting other means of non-formal education.
5. Instructors of centres should be trained at the district level. The district education officer, the senior deputy district education officer, the planning officer, inspector, etc., should join hands to give the right direction to training, inspection and planning.
6. Instructors of centres will make a study of local problems and plan their working according to the local conditions obtaining in their areas.
7. Greater attention must be directed towards the teaching of reading, writing, calculation and knowledge of the environment.
8. People should be encouraged to visit the centre and obtain training after establishing formal contacts with them.
9. Inspectors must also be appointed so that the centres are inspected regularly and at the right time.

10. The centres should also be given the benefit of an administrative system and all necessary assistance.

11. The entire programme should be evaluated regularly.

Kothari Commission Report

The Kothari Commission has defined non-formal education in the context of education. As is the case with innumerable other thinkers, the Kothari Commission also sees education as a life-long process. It has laid stress upon the following programmes for non-formal education:

Education of Illiterates. It is necessary to put a stop to the rise in illiteracy, as a proportion of the increasing population, if we want to bring about the welfare of the nation. Democracy can succeed only if illiteracy is eradicated. hence, it is essential to adopt education based on work experience. For this purpose, it is necessary to make arrangements for universal or full-time schools for the 6 to 11 age group, part-time education for the 11 to 14 age group, either full-time or. part-time general as well as vocational education for the 15-30 age group. And, to achieve success in this programme, it will have to be implemented with the cooperation and dedication of all institutions, individuals and agencies as well as leaders. It will be necessary to win the confidence of the illiterate masses and also to make the fullest use of television, radio, films, lecture and all other teaching aids.

Continuous Education. For the development of non-formal education, it will be necessary to evolve education as a continuous process, and for this it must be linked with employment. It will be necessary to impart vocational education which possesses the potential for future development. Such institutions as the Shramik Vidyapith and Gram Vidyapith will have to be set up.

Correspondence Courses. Correspondence courses will have to be introduced for those persons who want to continue their education after having left school. Students enrolled for such courses should get opportunities at regular intervals to meet their teachers in 'contact classes'. Lessons should be broadcast through the medium of radio, television, magazines, etc.

Correspondence Courses should include, apart from the general courses, courses on agriculture, industry and professional training so that national production may be stimulated. A policy of granting recognition to institutions running correspondence courses should be adopted and encouragement should be given to new experiments conducted in this sphere. In addition, facilities should be provided for individuals who wish to appear in university or formal examinations as private or non-institutional examinees.

Libraries. The Kothari Commission has recommended the setting up of libraries all over the country, and the use of school libraries for public benefit. These libraries should make available simple, interesting and useful literature for the reading public.

Contribution of Universities. Universities can make a valuable contribution to the proper development of non-formal education. Each university should have a department of adult education, similar to the Rajasthan University's department of adult education. Our universities can take on the role of Open Universities, and thereby grant education to those who want to satisfy their desire for knowledge. In this context our universities should perform the following functions-(1) Social, economic and cultural development. (2) Transmitting to society the advantages of new scientific conclusions. (3) Re-educating workers in various professions. (4) Re-education of teachers. (5) Developing new methods and skills of teaching. (6) Creating awareness of hygiene, cleanliness, population control, etc. (7) Providing training in leadership.

3

Open University System

To universalize higher education open university system is a unique experiment in India. Since 1958 to 1985, an individual had to go-through the formal stream of education to get the entry into the gateway of university. If any person deviated from the stream, he had to face a lot of difficulties to regain the same. The first step was to give permission to the individual to appear as private candidate for university examination. Second step was - correspondence courses for the various subjects and standards. Finding increasing craze for getting higher education, India felt the need to establish open university on the lines of England.

The Concept

Open university is an experiment recently introduced to universalize higher education in the world. Through this system an individual wants to keep himself upto-date in the process of emerging new knowledge. An Open University is meant for those who want to gain higher knowledge and develop higher learning skill. Following are the main characteristics of an Open university:

(i) There is no need of any qualifying examination to get admission in the university.

(ii) There is no age limit for selecting admission.

(iii) Individual belonging to any State or region may seek admission.

(iv) There is no time limit for examination.

(v) There is no formal campus for study.

It is to be noted that Open university has curriculum, study and examination just like traditional universities.

The Evolution

The pressure is regularly increasing on the universities. To solve this problem, in 1979 the first opened university was open in Britain. There 25,000 candidates were registered in the first year. By 1985, there 1,00,000 candidates had been registered. This number is increasing day by day. This university uses 300 study centres, Radio, Television and other means of communication for conducing studies. Now a days, there are Open universities in China, Japan, Thailand; Korea, Spain, Netherland, Pakistan, Sri Lanka and India.

Since 1970, the efforts were made to open Universities. In 1982, the first Open university was started in Andhra Pradesh ; the name of this university is Annamalai University. This university imparted instruction for B.A., B.Sc., B.Com and Post-graduate degrees in various subjects as well as B. Ed., M. Ed., and LL.B.

The first open university in India was S.N.D.T University, Bombay. Formerly it was a university for women. Later on the structure of this university had been changed. Many useful curricula are being run for women by this university through distance education. Seeing the achievements of Open universities Homeberg has rightly said that real study is basically an individual effort. This effort comes out through inner urges. Open universities were called Air Universities. Later on, these universities were renamed as Open Universities.

Open Universities are becoming popular and this experiment is quite successful. The achievements of this experiment are as follows:-

1. This is a successful experiment to universalize higher education.

2. There is no need of any qualifying certificate to seek admission in it.

3. Radio and Television are frequently used to impart education.

4. Every individual who wants to seek admission, may get opportunities for the same.

5. Individual is free to select the lifestyle and way of progress of this media of higher education.

6. Through correspondence the teaching material along with complete instruction is sent to the candidates. They send it back to the office for evaluation.

7. This university has complete structure - Academic and Administrative. There is a central body to control over the functions of the university.

8. There are university study centres in States.

9. In each district, there is an arrangement for study centre.

The Setup

In an Open university, there is a three tier system of evaluation (i) self-education, (ii) education by the tutor, (iii) education by the university. After completing three stages a certificate is awarded to the candidate.

Significance of New Education Policy

New Policy of Education, stressed over the need of Open university. There is 4.9% higher education in our country. Therefore a policy is adopted to universalize higher education and keep the individual upto-date with knowledge. In the policy following points have been stressed:-

(i) Open university system has been introduced to democratise education and increasing educational opportunities for the common man.

(ii) Indira Gandhi Open University established in 1985 will cater the needs of learners.

(iii) The development of this powerful educational media will be done with great care:

The strategy of an open university is as follows:-

Evaluation Structure. Evaluation will be done by the candidate himself, by the tutor and by the university.

Execution. This programme has been started since 1987 and new curriculum, have also been started since 1988. A separate channel on TV is introduced for educational programmes. Orientation Courses are being introduced for men and women. This programme is framed on the pattern of Modulus are credit system. University Grant Commission will give sufficient grant for the promotion of this programme. Courses for Agriculture, Industry and many other fields, National norms for curriculum and evaluation will be developed. State open universities will seek guidance from the National Open University.

Model of I.G.N.O.U.

In 1985, Indira Gandhi National Open University had been established through an Act passed by the Parliament. President of India is a visitor of this university and head of the university is vice-chancellor. For his assistance there is an Executive Council, Academic Council, Planning Board, Finance Committee and Board of Recognition. There is Pro-vice chancellor and Directors for assisting Vice-chancellor. There is a Registrar who is Administrative head and a Finance Officer. Its headquarters is at New Delhi.

Structure. There is a different structure for Open University. There is no boundary for learners. Audio-visual aids, audio equipments, Television, edited teaching material and contact programme are used in place of teacher. Guidance programme is introduced in contact place. Co-ordinates of study centres are responsible for conducting the contact programmes.

Teaching Programmes. Diploma in Management, Diploma in Distance Education, Nutrition, Creative writing and B.A., B. Com., B. Sc., etc., have been started in 1987. Besides these Diploma in

Management, Studies, Local Self Government, Energy Resources, Horticulture, etc., have been planned. Qualifying examination for the admission is Intermediate or its equivalent. There is an admission test for those who are not Intermediate.

Regional Centres. There are Regional Sectors to run the programmes of university smoothly. Head of the Sector is called Director. State Governments provide this sector building and other facilities. These sectors are co-ordinating units. There are libraries and other teaching material in every sector.

Curriculum. B.A., B.Sc., B. Com. courses under Three years degree scheme have been started by Indira Gandhi N.O.U. The student is expected to complete this degree within eight years.

Review

Homeberg has rightly said that this system influenced the outlook and perspective of the learner. This system has made them a critic and has removed their doubts. The feeling of co-operation is developed. There is a solution to remove unemployment by providing them up-to-date knowledge and skill, fine behaviour and impressionistic discipline.

Open university is a vital organisation to meet the demand of the growing higher levels of learners. Those, who have not enjoyed any opportunity for colleges and universities, may get the chance to fulfil their ambitions. The persons, who are working on the basis of old knowledge and skill may also keep themselves up-to-date.

Open universities are trying their best to minimise pressures of the regular system of higher education by using the means of communication. In new education policy, it is said that modern technology of communication has controlled over the time and space. This technology has opened new dimensions in the field of teaching, learning and national development. To improve the quality of teachers' training, in service programmes, consciousness towards art and culture, developing permanent human values, this system will be a boon.

It is hoped that open universities, to be opened under New Education Policy will cater to the need and aspirations of the masses.

The objective of New Education Policy is to prepare the manpower for national development ; such type of manpower is not merely a degree earner but in real sense curious and keen thinkers. We need such type of education which caters to the real knowledge and skill among the learners instead of spoon feeding by the teachers. There must be development of thoughtful-process which is responsible for the exposition of the inner self. India is committed for the exchange of knowledge and national development; therefore it is necessary to provide the maximum opportunities of fast growing and emerging knowledge to the citizens of India.

4

Vocational Education

Origin and Growth

The Rigveda indicates that, since the very emergence of Indian culture and civilisation, the people of that ancient period had learnt to make dams for irrigational and other purposes. The ruins of Mohanjodaro and Harappa are concrete proofs of the fact that India had always been the leader in the technical and vocational spheres. Even Alexander the Great took many objects made of iron from India, a fact that proves the excellence of this industry. Not merely this, concrete products of the Indian industry and profession are to be found in every part of the world. However, with the passage of time, India fell behind in the race for progress, and, as a result, the countries which used to be considered backward in cultural terms, are today giving advice to India in the technical and vocational fields.

The modern period in the history of technical education has its beginnings in the administration of the East India Company. It began when the company felt the need for some workers and technicians. A few schools were set up to train skilled workers for; certain specific tasks. Although the Christian missionaries repeatedly emphasised upon the company administration the need for setting up technical education institutes in India, the company failed to pay much attention to it.

The history of technical education in pre-independence India can be divided into three periods.

From 1800 to 1857. It was proposed that in the educational field, the organisation should be such as to offer practical benefits to the people of India. The administration did not attach much importance to this statement, but the Roorkee Engineering College did come into existence in 1847. Later on, in 1857-58, two engineering colleges were established at Madras and Calcutta. A mechanical school came into existence in Poona in 1854, but considering the situation of the country during this period, this progress can be termed negligible.

1857 to 1902. Although Mr. Wood was deeply influenced by the-arts and sciences departments in England in the preparation of his famous despatch, he did lay very deep emphasis upon vocational education. He proposed the introduction of technical education in his Despatch, but the British government, adopting the policy of laissez faire, unburdened itself of this responsibility. Only such institutions were set up as could be of use to the administration. In consonance with this policy, the Poona Engineering College (1886) and the Victoria Jubilee Technical Institute (1887). Bombay, were established. Most of the work was done by the Christian missionaries because it was necessary to provide employment to the new converts to Christianity. In their schools, the apprentices were trained in wood-work and smithy (iron-mongering). By 1902, the total number of students studying in technical schools was 4105.

On the 18th of June, 1888, the government published a proposal, pointing out the need for and importance of technical and vocational education, along with literary or liberal education. Besides, it made clear the fact that such education should be specialised according to industries, for instance, the cotton textile industry etc. It was stressed that this kind of education should be organised with the help of the local administration, and according to local needs. Besides, some thought was given to providing technical education in colleges and universities.

From 1902 to 1947. During this period, the Indian National Congress took birth, and it soon pressed the government to make prompt arrangements for technical education for the development of the country. In addition, it suggested that students should be given scholarships for studies in America and the Commonwealth countries. It was with this object in view that in 1904, the Association for the Advancement of Scientific and Industrial Education was established. By 1905,103 scholarships were granted to Indian students for studying abroad. These scholarships were meant for training in such industries as consumer goods manufacture, mines, pottery, tanning, match-making, glass-work, pencil, paper, etc. At the same time, an Institute of Mines was set up at Dhanbad, and an Institute of Textile Industries at Kanpur, and an Engineering College at Bombay were also established. This progress, of course, touched only one aspect of the advance in technical education, and hence it never became available to the masses in general, despite the fact that the College of Engineering and Technology, Jadavpur, the Tata Institute, Jamshedpur, and the Banaras University had already come into existence to provide technical education.

Out of many other, two factors in particular have influenced technical education- (1) the unemployment resulting from the spread of education, and (2) the need for skilled workers after the World War I, and in preparation for the World War II.

Both these factors were responsible for bringing technical education to India. After the World War I, the British government had come to realise that it could not fight another: war successfully by confining itself and its resources to Britain alone. Consequently, it set up Ordinance factories at a number of places. In 1941, a polytechnic school was set up at Delhi, and, in 1945, a committee was constituted to' study the possibilities of technical education in India, based on the working of the Massachusetts Institute of Technology, England. This committee was referred to as the 'Government Committee'. On the basis of its suggestions, institutions were set up in all parts of India, though these institutions were set up primarily to meet the requirements of war.

On 30th November, 1945, the government set up the All India Council for Technical Education, while in March 1947, the Scientific Manpower Committee was constituted, and entrusted with the task of estimating the need for scientifically trained manpower in various spheres in the coming years. This committee projected that 54,000 engineers and 20,000 technicians would be required by the end of 1947.

After Independence

In 1947, after independence, India possessed 38 technological institutions providing education to 2,940 students annually. There were 53 polytechnic schools educating 30,670 students every year and giving them diplomas. These educational institutions were made capable of playing a constructive role in the country's five year plans. In the First-Five Year Plan, many new courses were introduced at the degree level, particularly the courses which the country was in dire need of. The following was the nature of technical education in free India:-

Administration. Technical education has generally been directed jointly by the central and state governments. The All India Council for Technical Education, set up by the central government, has done much to encourage it. The centre's purpose is to provide for the technical development of the whole country, to make arrangements for higher technical education, to provide finance for these institutions, to give grants to universities and states, and supervise the functioning of all these various institutions. All these functions come within the jurisdiction of the ministry of education. The aforementioned council created four regional councils, and entrusted them with the tasks of constituting boards of studies,- introducing national diploma courses, part-time courses and post-graduate courses. At the state level, too, technical education is supervised by the relevant departments within the departments of education. This department provides for technical education through a council consisting of 17 members and the education minister as its chairman.

Institutions. Institutions providing technical education can be divided into three main categories-

A. These are institutions which provide education through degree and post-graduate courses as well as research. The subjects covered by them include Mining, Metallurgy-cum-Engineering, High-way (Roads) Engineering, Irrigation, Soil Mechanics, Foundation Engineering. Production Technology, Chemical Engineering, Electrical Communications, Advanced Electronics, Geophysics, Petroleum Technology, Textiles, Architecture, Leather technology, Aeronautical Engineering, etc.

B. Institutions of this category include those which conduct diploma courses, and they provide training extending from 1 to 3 years in a variety of courses. They are called polytechnic institutions. Some of them have been established primarily for girls.

C. Institutions of the third kind provide vocational and industrial training. They conduct two kinds of courses-

(a) The first include courses connected with art and handicrafts, such as - domestic industries, weaving, dyeing, printing, metal-work, leather dyeing, leather working, metalwork, iron-mongery, jewellery making, carpentry, pottery, utensil making, weaving of cane furniture, etc.

(b) The second kind of courses are intended to produce partially skilled and semiskilled workers, and for admission to them students require knowledge only of reading and writing. In 1947, the country had 53 schools and 38 colleges of this nature, providing diplomas to 3670 students, and degrees to 2940 students. By 1962, these numbers had swelled to 221 schools and 114 colleges in which 38,826 students received diplomas and 17,074 degrees. For the third five plan, it was proposed that the engineering profession should be expanded. Consequently, Regional Engineering Colleges were established at Warangal, Bangalore, Nagpur, Bhopal, Durgapur, Jamshedpur, Allahabad, Delhi and Srinagar.

New Schemes. Among the new schemes was the provision of post-graduate education and research at the Indian Institute of Science at Bangalore, while the institute at Kharagpur was converted into a research institution, conducted on the lines of Massachusetts. Besides, Indian Institutes of Technology were established at Bombay, Madras, Delhi and Kanpur, in which education in a variety of courses is provided, with the purpose of developing technical education in the country. In the technical field, new courses in publishing, printing, town and rural planning, printing technology, and diplomas in management were introduced. The Council has also made arrangements for providing scholarships ranging from Rs. 50,75,150 and 250 for students studying under various courses.

Temple of Science. By 1964, the ministry of education, with the cooperation of the ministry of community development had set up 'temples of science' in various parts of the country. In these, students residing and studying in rural areas were kept in touch with the latest scientific information. However, for a variety of reasons, the government has now closed down these institutions.

Research. The Council has given even more encouragement to the existing institutions to encourage research in the technical sphere. These researches have proved fruitful for technical education in such matters as progress, improvement guidance and maintaining liaison. The Council has also sought to ensure that the knowledge produced by these researches should find actual use in workshops. For this, there are provisions for attractive scholarships.

In the light of the progress of other nations, we, find that our country is quite backward. Even today, our country stands in great need of vast developments in technical education, and the need will be met only when the government decides to spend at least 7 per cent of the national income upon education.

Major Issues

While the British government failed to take adequate interest in the spread of technical education in India because of its own vested interests, the government of free India has come to feel need for it. The existing government wishes to put India on the path to progress through five year plans, proof of which lies in the various technical schools polytechnics and engineering colleges, etc., established in various parts of the country. The skilled individuals produced by these institutions have played some role in the country's development, but, the sphere of technical education is riddled with certain problems which are preventing the desired progress. The main problems of technical education are outlined below:-

Need for Technical Manpower. India has generally suffered from the lack of mobility of manpower. The rising needs have necessitated an increase in the demand for both quality and quantity in technical education. But, because of hampered mobility, our trained. manpower has not developed as rapidly as in other countries. Wood's view was that it was India's great misfortune that, despite receiving technical education, an Indian does not get the opportunity to apply it in practice, and consequently, he lags behind individuals of other countries. The people of India begin the chapter of their development at which the people of other countries complete the process of their growth.

The conflicts with China and Pakistan, too, have further highlighted the dearth of technicians. Today, apart from the other spheres of activity, the work of security and defence also requires skilled technicians, but their shortage can be overcome only when condensed courses are introduced.

Demand for New Institutions. Another reason for the shortage of trained individuals is that we could not establish a sufficient number of such training institutions. At present, the country has 120 such colleges. The setting up of one college means that Rs. 4.15 lakhs are needed for buildings, Rs. 0.08 lakh, for recurring expenses, and Rs. 3 lakhs for materials, but unfortunately our country cannot afford to spend so much in this one sphere alone. Hence, the Technical Education Council set up 9 Regional Colleges and 27 Polytechnic Colleges, which provided a variety of courses. Even today, continuous efforts are being made to procure more and more trained individuals.

Dearth of Technicians at the Lower and Middle Levels. In technical education, it is possible to obtain individuals at the middle and higher levels in adequate numbers, and, unfortunately, most of them get into the habit of getting the work done by mechanics. The outcome is that, when there is a dearth of mechanics, these individuals just sit idle. Hence, it has become necessary to provide training for semi-skilled technicians also. Such individuals can develop skills for working in various spheres, such as starting an engine, fitting machines, carrying out electrical repairs, etc.

Efficiency of the Administration . In India, it is being increasingly felt that if an administrative department takes interest in its work, it usually shows satisfactory progress. Administrative departments face two major obstacles- (i) in some spheres, individuals have an excessive workload, which prevents them from increasing their efficiency; (ii) in some cases, more than enough staff is provided for a single piece of work, with the result that they pass the responsibility to the next man, thus ensuring that nothing actually gets done. Hence, the Planning Commission has suggested that, in the entire sphere of technical education, the work-load and the responsibility should be collectively and individually put upon the workers. Statistics show that, in the administrative sphere, the real need is for workers actively working in the field rather than in the office. Hence, the administrative departments should be revamped in such a manner that the emphasis shifts to the creative work in the field. There should be more creative and active workers in every department.

Narrow or Limited Curricula. So far, people have generally assumed that the purpose of technical education is to produce an educated manual worker or labourer, while in reality, technical education induces profound respect for labour, and awareness of the dignity of labour. Hence, it is necessary that, technical education everywhere should be accompanied by general education so that the curriculum of technical education should not remain rigidly stuck to training in a particular field of technology. The Council too has been making efforts to overcome this narrow approach, and also to achieve an increase in the number of skilled and semi-skilled technicians.

Medium of Education. Pandit Nehru had recommended that English should be the medium of technical education, since he felt that almost all the literature in this sphere was available only in English. But, the question, is, how many Indians know English? Not very many. The result has been that the common man has been kept away from technical education. It is possible to evolve a technical terminology in the various Indian languages, and it can be argued that rapid progress can be achieved in the sphere if technical education is available in Indian languages, just as education in law is available in them.

Lack of Teachers. There has usually been an acute shortage of teachers in technical and engineering education, because of the fact that the demand for engineers and technicians is very high in the country. Teaching does not offer very attractive scales of pay, and besides, it offers very little scope for working with one's own hands. Besides, the teacher does not enjoy a very high social status. For instance, even at the national level, the engineer is given more importance than a teacher, although the former is the product of the teacher. The dearth of teachers can be overcome if teachers are given better scales of pay, more attractive facilities, more importance than engineers, and importance at the social, economic, cultural and national levels.

Proper Arrangements for Practice in Workshops. The absence of well equipped workshops in engineering and technical colleges has, for long, been a sore point. This problem manifests itself in two ways -(i) lack of good workshops, (ii) presence of excessive trainees in the workshops. Thus, even if the workshop is itself satisfactory, the number of trainees is so large that the workshop cannot achieve its real objective. If workshops are organised on the following bases, technical education can progress more rapidly- (a) workshops should not depend upon imported machines. (b) New workshops should be established and equipped with Indian materials and machines. (c) Industrialists should be induced to cooperate in this collectively. (d) As in the case of the USA, cooperative programmes should be taken up, and students learn to produce the maximum quantum of goods through the most modern technology.

Post-school Education. After emerging from the engineering school or college, the student finds himself backward when confronted with the real work situation. His knowledge once again takes a backward path. In order to confront this problem, it is necessary to introduce morning and evening classes to provide the latest information. The benefit will be that the students will keep in touch with the latest progress in their field, and also make the best use of their time. In-service training courses should also be organised at regular intervals.

Research. India spends only 0.2% of its national production upon research, whereas Russia and America spend as much as 2.8%. And, in fact, it is India which has the greatest need for research into such spheres as improvement in the quality of goods, production of new goods, re-cycling of waste products, reduction of costs, reduction of the risks in productive processes, overcoming difficulties, and determination of basic standards, etc. For this purpose, through engineering design, structure, method of working, etc., research can be made capable of developing techniques which will help the country to create international markets for its goods.

Absence of Co-operation between State Industries and Technical Education. Occasionally, our newspapers report that thousands of overseers are unemployed in a particular region. In planning for the spread of technical education, the state must keep in mind its manpower needs, since it is being observed that engineers and overseers are being produced without any planning. It would be far better if the state first conducted a survey of its manpower needs and then made arrangements for the training of a sufficient number of engineers and technicians.

Kothari Commission Report

After reflecting upon the problem of unemployment, the Kothari Commission has expressed its view on technical and vocational education in the following terms-

1. By 1986, 20% of the lower secondary students and 50% of the higher secondary students should receive vocational education.
2. Vocational courses should be introduced at the school level. Brilliant and talented students must get adequate opportunities in this sphere.
3. Arrangements should be made for training skilled and semi-skilled workers. For this, the following kinds of institutions should be established:-
   (a) I.T.I.
   (b) Junior Technical School
   (c) Technical High School.
4. In the courses for skilled workers, the courses below class 10 should be included in the polytechnic.
5. The rigidity of the present curriculum should be abandoned.

Technician Training. According to the Kothari Commission, in our educational system, the second level of skill which exists at the secondary level produces a middle level specialist whose functions are understood very little in our country. Hence, the following suggestions have been offered:-

1. Technician training should be restructured in the light of modern knowledge, and training should be based upon professional differentiation and specialisation.
2. Diploma training will be particularly useful for institutions.
3. Polytechnics should be established in industrial areas.
4. Teachers in polytechnics should be recruited from the industries, and there should be flexibility in evaluating their academic or educational qualifications.
5. There should be different kinds of courses for girls, including diploma as well as certificate courses.
6. In polytechnic schools, wastage and stagnation should be prevented, in view of the labour and power involved in training students.
7. Some selected polytechnics should provide post diploma courses also.
8. Keeping in mind the mobility of labour in the country, polytechnic schools should have courses based on local needs and available resources, but special emphasis should be given to the teaching of science and mathematics.

Other Vocational Education. Today, an almost unaccounted variety of vocational courses have emerged. For their best development, it is necessary to be cognizant of the following facts:-(i) Commercial, clerical, and scientific education should be imparted in classes 11 and 12. The interests and aptitude of girls should be kept in view. (ii) Students emerging from polytechnics, etc., should be encouraged to set up their own enterprises.

Engineering Education. In the opinion of the Kothari Commission; the progress of industrialisation depends upon the proper understanding of science, and, it also necessitates the best possible training for engineers. It is suggested, therefore that- (i) in some subjects of engineering, students with B.Sc. degree, for instance, in electronics, should be granted admission. (ii) The differences in the pay scales of teachers in various institutions should be eliminated. (iii) Practical training should be given for one full year, after the third year of education. (iv) Mixed courses should also be introduced. (v) More productive work should be done in the workshops. (vi) There should be variety in the courses so that they may meet the changing needs of changing times. (vii) The curriculum should be edited and reviewed from time to time, and the various subjects should be given a progressively more scientific shape.

Teachers. The attractions in the engineering professions are so powerful that hardly any engineer is attracted towards teaching. Private firms offer better scales of pay as well as better working conditions and facilities. To overcome this difficulty, the following steps should be taken- (i) Teachers should be allowed to take up consultancy work for industries. (ii) Summer courses institutions should be introduced. (iii) The scale of pay should be made more attractive. (iv) Teacher training courses should be introduced to overcome the present shortage of teachers. (v) The policy of transferring teachers should be suitably modified.

Resources. The best possible education in engineering depends upon the availability of necessary resources. For this, the following suggestions have been offered- (a) Facility of utilising foreign exchange should be given. (b) Machines of the best quality should be installed so that they may be utilised for longer periods. (c) Post-graduate courses should be introduced. (d) The training and education should be practical (e) There should be close co-operation with industries.

Medium of Education. At the secondary, polytechnic and other levels, the medium of instruction should be the regional language. It is suggested that (a) vocational education should be given via the regional language, and hence the literature needed for the course should be prepared in the regional language. (b) Postal coaching or teaching should also be introduced so as to spread vocational education rapidly.

Administration. Good administration is needed for the proper running of engineering institutions. For this, it is suggested that- (i) There should be an organisation similar to the UGC for technical education. (ii) IIT etc. should be granted the status of universities. (iii) Technical education boards should be set up at the state level. (iv)

Principals of institutions should have complete powers regarding administration.

The Kothari Commission has thought extensively and deeply about engineering and technical education, and as a result, it is hoped that our country may soon be free of the spectre of unemployment. This Commission has made complete provisions for manpower planning for vocational education. It has also stressed specialised studies. However, what we have before us is only a plan. This alone will tell us how much success it has attained.

Role of Five-Year Plans

First Five-Year Plan. Rs. 23 crores were spent upon the development of technical education. In this plan, the Indian Institute of Science, Bangalore, was enlarged and arrangements were made for imparting training in crafts, Polytechnic, technical, high schools and industrial training schools were increased and enlarged, while more scholarships were also provided.

Second Plan. The allocation for technical education in the second plan rose to Rs. 48 crores. During this period, the number of institutions offering degree and diploma courses was doubled. New institutions were set up and more scholarships provided.

Third Plan. In this plan, Rs.142 crores were provided for technical education. The new institutions were set up, while the curricula of 12 institutions were reconstructed and enlarged.

Fourth Plan. A sum of Rs. 253 crores was allocated for technical education in the fourth plan, and arrangements were made for the appointment of teachers; creation of hostels, establishment of new institutions, and introduction of correspondence courses.

Today, our engineers are faced with unemployment. This is obviously a very grave problem, and it is reflected in the fact that the enrolment in technical institutions fell to 64%. In the fourth plan, emphasis was laid upon the consolidation of the existing institutions. Besides, the curricula of technical education was remodelled in the light of the requirements of our industries.

Differences in the Rate of Progress. The pace of progress of technical education has continued to vary. The work in technological institutions was started after delays, besides which, the state governments, too, showed little interest in the consolidating and strengthening the existing institutions. The outcome was that even the allocated sums were not fully expended.

Difference in Certificates. Many states committed the folly of issuing different kinds of certificates. Sandwich courses were initiated. The polytechnic method was revaluated, and efforts were made to see how these courses could be made more practicable.

Educational Plan. The need for an educational plan for post-graduate education and research was soon felt. At the same time, management studies were also introduced. The consequence of this progress has been that technical institutions are now capable of offering enrolment to 74,000 students, while this figure was only 2000 a few years agro.

In view of the existing facts, an effort should be made to formulate a plan for the next 15 years, with the object of creating a technical society. For this, the objectives should be clearly defined, so that the necessary flexibility in the method of education may be maintained. In the fifth plan, the following aspects were considered, in the light of the need for rapid development in this sphere - (i) Technical education should be directly linked to economic development. (ii) The curriculum should be restructured so that primacy is given to the generation of skills in addition to imparting of knowledge. It is also necessary to develop practicability and enterprise. (iii) Technical extension services should be introduced, because these services will bring about co-ordination between the masses, the institutions and industries. (iv) For the growth of technical education, state, regional and institutional plans will be prepared. (v) Provisions will be made for the Continuing Education so that, even after the completion of training, the trainee should maintain his contact with knowledge and new skills. (vi) Provisions will be made for every kind of technical education in the light of the need for technically skilled manpower. In this context, thought is being devoted to (a) joint centre state responsibility, (b) blue-print of a plan, (c) an enrolment policy, and (d) Multiple Entry Points.

In the fifth plan, the following provisions were made for technical education, keeping in view, the points elucidated above:-

Programme. Thought has been devoted to various programmes with a view to achieving long-term goals and objectives. Every technical institution was consolidated in terms of its needs for buildings, resources, aid, etc. A detailed plan was prepared for the reorganisation of polytechnic education.

Qualitative Development. Efforts were made to bring about a qualitative improvement in technical education through the development of faculties, curricula and preparation of teaching materials. It was opined that the workshops and laboratories. should be equipped with the latest machines and tools. Besides; such varied courses as practical art, commercial conduct pharmacy, etc., were also developed.

Training of Teachers. The training necessary for teaching technical courses is in itself a serious problem, and hence much thought was given to the training of teachers. According to the recommendations of the All India Council for Technical Education, it is necessary to provide at least short term training to teachers.

Post-graduate Education and Research. For the fifth plan, arrangements have been made to ensure that, in the various institutions, advance study centres should be set up and activated in a planned manner. In the Regional Engineering Colleges, practice workshops and industrial orientation courses have been introduced, with the co-operation of local industries. It was also proposed that in certain selected institutions, there should be arrangements for higher studies and research.

Management Education. It was proposed in the fifth plan, that management education, instead of being limited to merely four management institutes, should be made available through university departments also. Besides, there should be provisions at many centres for training of foremen and supervisors.

Establishment of Specialist Institutions. Institutions related to specific industries should be established, along the lines of such existing institutes as the National Institute of Foundry and Forge Technology, the National Institute for Training in Industrial Engineering, the Central Institute for Industrial Design, etc. The Regional Training Institutes should introduce courses for the training of teachers of training institutions through such courses as pedagogies, creative programmes and industrial experience.' Teachers of polytechnic institutions must also be trained.

Scholarships. The number of scholarships based on ability and resources was increased in the fifth plan. It was suggested that the Apprentice Act should be amended and individuals holding certificates should be taken within the purview of this Act. Archives would be set up in selected institutions while text-books of a superior standard would be produced, and thus science will be brought close to technology.

Administration. It has been felt that there is need for a good administration for effective planning and organisation at the state and national levels. It was suggested that boards of technical education should be set up in state by legislative acts, and in addition, the ministry of education should set up a department for manpower planning, monitoring and evaluation.

The Economic Aspect. Rs. 300 crores were allocated for all these programmes. 2200 crores were provided for all educational programmes, but it was not possible to accommodate technical education within the general education budget. The Working group suggested reconsideration of the plan, pointing out that the expenditure on construction could be reduced. Thus, it suggested the allocation of Rs.190 crores.

The Sixth Plan. In the sixth plan (1978-83), the emphasis was mainly upon a continuation of the programmes of the fifth plan. It was felt that the existing system of technical education was adequate for the forthcoming decade. At present, 25,000 students gain admission to degree courses and 50,000 students to diploma courses. The sixth plan provides that technical education may be revaluated in case of need. Five centres for advanced studies into energy, materials, oceans, etc., will be set up. The plan provides Rs.150 crores for this purpose.

Some of the proposed programmes are - (i) Setting up institutes of management at Lucknow and Bangalore, to be run by such institutions as the NCERT and UGC (ii) Establishment of a national council of science education, similar to the NCERT and UGC (iii) Introducing R & D projects. (iv) Providing for Apprenticeship. (v) Modernizing the new programmes such as Archives and Laboratories.

5

Population Education

The population explosion is the most potent cause of the crisis which the world is facing. This explosion has come about through a natural and automatic process, but it has been implicit in its very farreaching consequences. The increase in material resources and every individual's right to live have created an upheaval in the world of education. When we forget the international arena, and think of this problem in the context of India, we find the situation even more pitiable and disheartening. In every five year period, the addition to our population is more than the existing population of England, and if this situation continues, there can be no reason to doubt that problem of foodgrains will assume truly alarming proportions.

The Ingredients

The notion of remaining constantly aware of the increase in population and its future consequences arose in 1960. Efforts were then made to define and clarify the concept to relate it to education. Stressing the importance of this, Philip M. Hauser remarked that "It is about time for twentieth century school curricula to comprehend and understand twentieth century demographic findings in the context of their 20th century implications."

In India, it was Prof. Sloan Wayland of Columbia University. who gave concrete shape to the notion of population education. According to him, irrespective of the nomenclature, we are concerned with the fact that the public policy on family planning, nation and family, the desirability of family planning, etc., should be comprehended under the counselling system in formal education. At the same time, studies should be conducted into the economic and social development of education, size of the family, and the dynamism of the qualities of a nuclear family. Hence, it is necessary to develop a special method of education at the school level under the linguistic provisions in a particular society.

Burleson has conceived of population education as population awareness. In his view, the increase in population brings about an increase in the already increasing expenditure on education. Education can modify the problem by arousing a population awareness among teachers and students. Population education is the awareness of knowledge relating to population. It has two objectives(1) Educationists and others concerned with them should understand the importance of population, the disadvantages of its nature. (2) Teachers and students should understand the nature of their own tendencies.

Major Aims

Population education is essential for the reconstruction or restructuring of our modern, rapidly changing society. The NCERT has set up a special wing entitled Population Education. It has set out the following objectives of population education-

1. Orientation of the school teachers towards preparing training units on which students will obtain information about the increasing population and the problems created by it and also take interest in finding solution to the problem.

2. Conducting experiments in extra-curricular courses in selected schools, and implementing similar experiments on a larger scale if successful.

3. Preparation of suitable teaching material for population education in schools.

4. Making provisions for research and study concerning population education in schools and making the programme more effective.

5. Evaluating the productiveness of students covered by the programme and developing the necessary skills.

It is evident from these objectives that in the programme of population education, it is necessary to keep in mind the ecological complex. According to Duncan, Ecological complexes are built up out of changes in the environment, changes in the structure of population measures for fighting the problem of population and the mutuality of factors, and an account of these complexes amounts to population education.

In the same way, Chauls has expressed the following opinion on population education. He says that population education should comprehend the culture of the students, the population situation of their society, their own views about the existing situation, their logical, reasoned and organised ideas on the situation of the population and its effects.

The UNESCO workshop defined population education in the following terms- "Population education is our educational programme which provides for a study of the population situation in family, community, nation and world with the purpose of developing in the students rational and responsible attitudes and behaviour towards coping with the situation."

The Purpose

It is only natural to ask why we should have population education. The answer is very obvious. Today, population is increasing at such an alarming rate that material resources have completely failed to keep pace with it. There is a complete imbalance between material resources (food, clothing, housing and the size of the population. The existing situation naturally encourages exploitation and misery, thus leading to increasing social injustice.

In order to face and overcome these conditions, educationists and demographers have come to feel that the problem must be given the form of a revolution in ideas. This implies that the problem of population must be given the form of a revolution in ideas. This implies that the problem of population must be integrated with education. In India, the task of educating people about the problems of population is being done by the governmental agency, NCERT, and the informal agencies- Family Planning Association, All India Federation of Education Association, etc. These programmes are directed at - (1) schools, colleges and other educational institutions, (2) those who have left school or have not received any education, (3) those imparting training to teachers, teachers themselves and those who impart education through training, counselling and guidance.

Present Scenario

In India, the concept of progress means industrialisation, exploitation of resources, improvement in the standards of living through material progress, and acceptance of education as the medium of the foregoing. Population is the focal point of the fulfilment of these objectives. The co-operation of all possible agencies is essential for understanding the problems likely to arise in the future and for promoting this programme of population education.

Programme for Action

The Family Planning Association of India has prepared the following for population education -

1. Family and the individual focal points of population education at these levels, determination of scope and syllabus.

2. Nation

3. The World

The following elements will be comprehended under these objectives-

Population, Factors and Results. (Rates of birth, death, life and increase).

Human, Situation and Environment. (Population, reduction in consumption and production).

Social, Economic and Development Aspects. Production, national production, health, education, housing employment.

Family Life and the Individual Aspect. (Family and social institutions, education for family life, sex education, position of women).

Fundamental Values and Qualities of Life. Objectives of society, techniques, a consumer's society, utilisation of resources.

These programmes will be implemented through studies, discourses, regional schemes and research.

Introduction and Sensitivity of Groups

1. The objectives outlined above will be achieved with the help of the ministries of education and health and other ministries, administrators; educationists, principals and teachers.
2. Arrangements will be made for discourses, contact with the people, publication, guidance cells, training syllabi, etc.

(Syllabi, extra-curricular activities, etc., in village/city).

1. This programme will be implemented through the medium of schools, colleges, social education classes, adult education classes and classes for the employed.
2. For this purpose, arrangements for reading class units, context books, hand-books, audiovisual material, information centres and library facilities will be made.

Higher Studies

1. Studies into marriages in villages and cities, sex, family life, population problem, awareness of the population problem and the attitudes towards it.
2. A survey of guardians of school-going children for an understanding of begetting of children, sex, family life, population awareness and study of problem.
3. A study of the knowledge of teachers with a view to introducing population awareness, marriage, family life, sex relations, begetting of progeny, etc., into the syllabus.
4. A study of the leaders of education in the contexts outlined above.
5. Active research into teaching methods and techniques, pertaining to sex, family planning, population education, problems, etc.

For all these programmes, close contacts will be established with educational research institutions, teachers' training institutions, social welfare institutions and voluntary agencies so as to impart speed to the programme.

At present, the Population Education Department has taken the following steps under the Fore mentioned programme- (1) preparation of context books, hand-books and publications, (2) preparation of teaching material, (3) publication of a monthly magazine, (4) establishment of libraries and information centres, (5) issue of teaching materials to schools at low prices, and (6) preparation of kits for population education.

Further Prospects

At present, all of us are being swept onwards by the inexorable flow of an ever-increasing population, but we must try to escape from this flood and also forestall it for the sake of our own existence. Today, the crowds in universities are growing larger, colleges lack even an inch of spare space. Our population annually increases by 13 millions, which is equal to the entire population of Australia. In the next twenty-five years, our population will double itself. In order to solve the problem of the future, we should adopt the following programmes:

1. Departments of education should make arrangements for in-service training, research and programme implementation.
2. Various departments of universities should conduct research and prepare desirable literature.
3. Departments of science should conduct factual experiments into the evil consequences of rise in population.
4. Various programmes of population education should be implemented through seminars, discourses, exhibitions, etc.
5. This programme should be made a part of education at every level.
6. The United Nations Fund for Population Studies has been set up at Bombay with the co-operation of the World Health Organisation and the United Nations for the purpose of combating the problem of education at the international level.

It is hoped that through the implementation of this programme, the increasing population will be brought under check, and our future generation will be freed from the spectre of a gigantic problem.

6

Social Education

Origin and Growth

Education is a life-long and a never-ending process which continues throughout life. As time passes, changes keep on occurring, and every individual has necessarily to pass through these phases of change. The criterion of success for any individual is the extent to which he can adapt himself to changing circumstances. Keeping in mind this viewpoint, the Education Commission has opined that, in a democracy, the function of adult education is to give to every individual the opportunity for obtaining the kind of education he wants, the kind of education which can contribute effectively to his individual prosperity, professional progress as well as his social and political life. The Education Commission has greatly enlarged the scope of adult education by saying that the field of adult education is as vast as life itself.

India has, for a long time, suffered from a very low percentage of literacy. During the British period, Lord Macaulay's educational policy did much to alleviate this illiteracy, and though, during this period, the British government did, in theory, accept the importance of public education, in practice it did little to achieve this goal. Whatever little was actually achieved was the result of the following three forces- (i) Rise of a middle class in urban areas. (ii) The cooperative movement in the villages. (iii) Growth of political consciousness among the people.

Of these, it was the third factor which contributed the most, and it is. the same political consciousness which has made the future of adult education bright. Till the end of the World War I, satisfactory progress was made in this direction. Adult classes were run exclusively as night classes, and the teacher working in these classes was given an additional allowance.

The co-operative movement was started in 1905, and people felt that it was impossible to make it successful without becoming literate. Hence arrangements were made for creating libraries, and stress was laid upon the reading of newspapers. Gradually, universities set up adult education sections in their extension departments.

The growth of adult education can be divided into four periods:-

First Phase

During this period, adult education suffered a blow because of the economic depression. The political movement raised the demand for adult franchise. The soldiers in the army were also infused with a strong national spirit when they returned home occasionally from their duties. By 1926, the number of cooperative committees had risen to 80,182. They conducted 100 night schools. In the Punjab, there were 3,784 adult schools in 1926-27, in which 98,414 students were enrolled. In Bombay,. there were 27 schools in 1922 while in Uttar Pradesh, 6 municipalities managed night schools for providing adult education. Similar efforts were being made in the other provinces also.

Second Phase

This was a period of political turmoil, but many new schools came into existence during the time. Some missionaries, such as Dr. J.J. Lucas, Dr. J.J.H. Lawrence and Mr. Daniel prepared new books for adults in the Roman script. During this period, not much progress could take place in Punjab, because in 1936-37, it had only 189 schools with an enrolment of 4,988 students. Two experiments, however, were carried out in Punjab. (i) Normal school teachers were inspired to organise libraries in villages for adult education ; and (ii) Cultural centres were set up in villages.

Similar experiments were also carried out in Bombay, Madhya Pradesh, etc., and many new institutions took birth, among them the

Rural Reconstruction Association, Adult Education League, Literacy Association, Seva Sadan Social League, etc. The Travancore University began to send sets of books to rural libraries from its own collection for the purpose of adult education.

Third Phase

During this period, nationalist governments were set up in the provinces. Dr. Sayad Mahmood, the education minister of Bihar, himself went to villages, equipped with a blackboard and chalk, to educate the villagers. Dr. Rajgopalachari himself wrote text-books and ran a strong movement for literacy over a period of three months. Teachers of primary schools made valiant and commendable efforts to spread literacy in villages, and as a result, 12,000 people were made literate within these three months. In this way, for the first time the responsibility for adult education was grasped by the Indian mind, and the government took this onerous task into its own hands. New curricula were formulated. The medium of teaching was changed. Books, posters, film shows and other things were recognised as instruments of adult education.

At this time, literacy movements were launched in Assam, Bengal, Bihar, Uttar Pradesh, Orissa, and Jammu and Kashmir, keeping in mind local conditions and needs. New text-books were prepared for the neo-literates in regional languages, and a separate department for adult education was formally created. After 1942, the urge towards education and literacy grew even stronger in the country, the outcome of which was that by 1947 as many as 9,50,002 adults were made literate, and 6,33,896 books were distributed among them. The Talukka Library and the Bombay City Adult Education Committee were set up in Bombay, An Education Expansion Department was established in Uttar Pradesh, while comparable organisations quickly sprang up in other parts of the country also.

The period 1942-47 was a very difficult one for adult education because it was buffetted on the side by the nationalist movement, and on the other by the instability and indecision of the government. Despite this, the movement continued because the people were keen to receive education.

Education for Adults

After independence a central education advisory committee was constituted. The committee then set up a council to reflect upon the potential for adult education. This council took adult education out of the limitations of a knowledge merely of letters and raised it to the level of authentic knowledge, and, as a result, adult education was rechristened social education. A plan for social education was put before a committee of State ministers of education on February 19-20,1949, and the Government of India distributed Rs. 60 lakhs to the States for adult education.

Social education centres were established in Bihar, where, in order to speed up the pace of social education, such programmes as touring drama troops, troops of folk dances and hymn singers, etc., were organised. In Madras, libraries were developed, and a training camp for teachers was organised under the auspices of social education. Similar work was also done in Bombay. In Madhya Pradesh, literature was prepared in Hindi and Marathi. In Uttar Pradesh, Etawah a project was initiated. It was later assimilated with the development programme and social education officers came to be appointed. The Government of India, too, has played an active role through such organisations as the Institute of Audiovisual Education, the All India Radio, the Institute of Social Education, which became involved in preparing literature and discovering new techniques of adult education as well as the training of teachers.

The Kothari Commission, in particular, is extremely cónscious of the need for and the importance of adult education. In one of its statements on this subject, it says that though, to its observation, the history of adult education in India is not an old one, literacy had risen to 29.3%, a fact which clearly implied that the movement should be suitably accelerated. In the sixth plan, the programme of adult education is being implemented on a national scale.

The Objectives

Adult education must be looked at from a new perspective. In planning for education in backward areas, it must be remembered that the adult has already gained experience of life but in receiving education he consciously regresses to his childhood stage. At the same time, he has many memories of family responsibility and of his contribution to the economy of the family. He has to discover and form social, political, constitutional and mutual relationships. Though he may be illiterate, these elements form his background. He does not possess extensive knowledge of society, but he has the requisite ability to learn all this. He can easily learn reading, writing and counting. Hence, it is essential that the adult should be properly understood before an attempt is made to teach him.

Social education is corrective or remedial education. Those who never got a chance to go to school, or could attend school only for a short period, find that their social education has remained incomplete. The deficiency can be made up through social education.

Today, many terms have become prevalent in the sphere of social education:- Adult education, social education, informal education, continuous education, etc. Each one of these terms is indicative of adult education, but they differ conceptually from each other. The general and obvious meaning of adult education is the teaching of adults. Bryson has said that education, in every situation and in every condition for the individual is what constitutes adult education. Organ and Bundy define it as the adult individual's conscious attempt to learn. Rheins, Fenster and Hadley believe that adult education implies the education related to the individual's professional, individual and social life. The concept of a social education is a more comprehensive one in as much as it comprehends reading, writing, counting, etc., and even more, becoming a skilful and useful citizen. The term social education has been coined because the purpose is to arouse civil awareness in the individual. Humayun Kabir believes that it is a means to develop civic consciousness and social solidarity. In it, attention is paid to literacy, the creation of an educated mind, and the growth of a powerful citizenship for the nation.

S.N. Mukerjee. Social education is roughly inclusive of all the informal education that is given to adults. In India, it has two aspects- (i) adult literacy, i.e., the education of those adults who have not received any kind of education in schools, and (ii) continuous education for literate adults.

Barker. His view is that adult education constitutes that education which an individual receives on a part-time basis while continuing in his occupation.

Bryson. According to him, adult education comprehends all those activities which are related to the normal life of the individual, which have some importance for education, in the doing of which the individual has to utilise only one part of his total intellect.

K.G. Sayyidain. He sees adult education as inclusive of education of politics, of citizenship and also of morality.

Humayun Kabir. His opinion of adult education is that it aims at the development of an educated mind in an illiterate individual.

Implied in the concept of social education is the fulfilment of the needs of adults-economic efficiency, increased knowledge and the growth of cultural possessions. The objectives of social education can be pinpointed as follows:-

Remedial. Here, the purpose is to increase the individual's original or innate talent.

Vocational. In this case, the purpose is to impart commercial and industrial knowledge in urban areas and knowledge pertaining to agriculture and domestic activities in rural areas.

Health. Social education aims at acquainting adults with the basic principles of good health and the various means of maintaining hygienic conditions.

Social Skill. The objective of social education is to train the individual in maintaining harmonious relations with friends and companions, leading a satisfactory family life, and becoming conscious of one's rights and duties in society.

Recreational. In order to raise the mental level of adults, adult education seeks to develop the habit of healthy recreation. The varied means of entertainment available today have not had a desirable impact upon the minds of the people, but healthy recreation helps the individual develop his life along the right path.

Self Development. Social education aims at enabling the individual to bring about his own harmonious development by developing a thirst for knowledge, forming an individual philosophy of life and evolving a creative and aesthetic approach to life. Thus, it becomes apparent that the foregoing objectives of social education fulfil four important goals of our- national life:-

Growth of Civic Sense. Through social education, those who have been left behind in the race of progress are enabled to overtake others and to march in step with them, thus, being enabled to perform their tasks with the cooperation of others.

Utilization of National Resources. Having been influenced by adult education, adults are enabled to fulfil national objectives in their own respective spheres. Lenin said that socialism can never come through an illiterate populace because the illiterate is isolated from politics. Lenin's opinion may, or may not, apply truthfully to socialism, but it is certainly an axiom in the field of good citizenship.

Creation of Cooperative Associations. Through social education, the adult individual achieves economic as well as social progress, and thus becomes enthusiastic about the creation of cooperative associations.

Growth of a Social Viewpoint. Society as a whole cannot evolve a particular social viewpoint if its members are uneducated. For instance, the realisation that "we are Indians" can be developed and rooted deeply only when the people are educated.

On the whole, it can be said that our country needs adult education for a social and political revolution. It can, on the one hand, develop emotional and national unity among the people, and on the other, develop self-confidence, fearlessness and skill in the individual. In fact, the success of democracy depends, to a very large extent, upon social education.

Various Agencies

Social education is the responsibility of society. In a democracy, every educated individual contributes to the shaping of society in his own individual way. And, the greater the extent to which society shoulders this responsibility, the better is it for society itself. Thus, (a) the government, (b) private institutions, and (c) universities and training institutions contribute to the spread of social education. At the governmental level, many ministries perform this task through a variety of programmes. Social education is imparted to the masses through (i) correspondence courses, (ii) vocational adult education, (iii) training of adult educators, (iv) agricultural and other professions, (v) public libraries, and (vi) museums, etc.

The Field

Social education is an educative process that continues through life, and hence its field is very vast. It is inclusive of spread of literacy, knowledge of rules pertaining to the safeguarding of health, vocational training for improving economic condition, feeling of citizenship, awareness of rights and duties, and healthy entertainment. In determining its scope, the following points are kept in view:-

1. Social education comprehends those subjects which are not taught in schools or those which are neglected.
2. It brings about a change in human attitudes.
3. It either reduces or eradicates the differences in social and individual progress, something which should be done through (a) knowledge, (b) deeds and (c) determination.

The Importance

Every individual today is a useful part of society. The purpose of social education is that the adult population should be educated in such a way that it may be able to improve its own life, develop the desire to create a better and a modern society instead of adhering to the traditional society, and also have faith in, the future of its nation. The responsibility for the field work in social education, including adult education, rests with the state governments and the administration of union territories.

In view of this, the importance of social education can be specified in the following terms:-

1. Social education provides the foundations for the success of democracy.
2. It is the lamp of hope for the uneducated.

3. It brings about the political, intellectual and social development of adults.
4. It inspires the aesthetic development of adults.
5. It strengthens the cultural aspect of community life.
6. It prefers new media of expression and forms of recreation.
7. When all other facilities are available in society, the existence of illiteracy is a blot.

Role of Five-Year Plans

First Plan

In the first five year plan, the education ministry provided financial aid to various projects to ensure the progress of the social education programme. Ideal community centres were set up and some special primary schools were given the form of School cum-Community Centres. Under this scheme, 116 Modern Community Centres and 454 School-cum-Community Centres were created, in addition to which many libraries, rural libraries, service centres and public colleges came to be established.

Second Plan

During the second plan, the National Fundamental Education Centre was set up with the assistance of UNESCO. Its objectives were the following:-

(i) Training workers of noteworthy importance for social education, for example, district social education organisation.

(ii) Conducting research.

(iii) Creating audio-visual aids and teaching materials.

(iv) Performing the functions of an information centre.

At the same time, the Social Education Institute was established at Indore. New literature was produced for the neo-literates and literary camps were organised. The Delhi University and the National Book Trust undertook the task of training librarians to man public libraries.

Third Plan

By the third plan, literacy had risen from 16.6% to 24.0%. In different states, different kinds of programmes of social education were implemented. In addition to the public or Janata colleges, six Vidyapeeth institutions were set up in Mysore State. A social education department was set up in Rajasthan University. 205 district libraries were created in 13 States, and States also gave financial aid for distributing books in rural areas.

Fourth Plan

The three preceding plans had not given requisite importance to social education. In the fourth plan, a sum of Rs. 3.6 crores was allocated by the Central government for this purpose. The sum was invested on the following activities:-

(a) Organising and strengthening the social education administration.

(b) Establishing labour Vidyapeeth institutions.

(c) Creating suitable literature for the neo-literates.

(d) Developing and expanding the library service in Delhi.

(e) Developing a central institute of library science.

(f) Training librarians.

(g) Implementing other services related to libraries.

(h) Giving aid to voluntary educational institutions.

(i) Initiating practical schemes, setting up Janata colleges, and organising continuous education and adult schools.

(j) Developing social education institutions for the workers.

New literature was got prepared for the neo-literates with the assistance of UNESCO. 419 books were given awards, and an adult encyclopaedia was published under the title *'Gyansarovar'*. A book entitled *'Hindi Vishwabharati'* was published in ten volumes. Workshops were organised as a part of literary camps. Among the non-governmental organisations which do praiseworthy work in the sphere to social education are Indian Adult Education Association, Social Adult Education Committee, and the State Adult Education Council.

The Central Education Advisory Council, at its 31st meeting, laid down the following standard or criterion for adult education:-

(i) Recognition of about 350 words.

(ii) Ability to write numerals upto 100.

(iii) Ability to read simple charts, posters, etc.

(iv) Knowledge of objects of daily utility.

(v) Ability to write simple sentences and names.

Fifth Plan

Again, relatively less importance was attached to social education in the fifth plan. The movement that was initiated in 1937 for the total eradication of illiteracy among the masses remained a failure then, and because of this, adult education came to be modernised in the form of social education. This programme was implemented throughout the country through the medium of community development programmes, but, for a variety of reasons, even this programme remained ineffective. As a consequence, the social education programme continued to function primarily through local institutions, with the assistance received from the State and Central governments. However, many important ideas and schemes came to light. The Vidyapeeth of Mysore, the Gram Shiksha Mohim of Maharashtra, the Bombay City Social Education Committee, the Literacy House of Lucknow, and the Rural Library Movement of Lucknow, etc., are the main forums of social education. The Farmers' Education and Creative Literacy Movement initiated in 1961 has proved of great significance. By the end of the fourth plan period, it was expected that ten lakh farmers in 100 districts should have benefited from this movement. In addition, departments of adult education were set up in some universities for giving impetus to continuing education. Through social education, efforts were made to provide information about the various aspects of life through programmes concerned with agricultural extension, handicraft training, family planning, child and family welfare, nutrition programmes, etc. However, the total impact of these programmes has not succeeded in bringing us near to the national goal of eradicating illiteracy.

With the expansion of primary education, the percentage of literacy, which was 24 in 1961, rose to 29.6, but the equally bitter truth was the fact that the number of illiterates rose from 333.6 million in 1961 to 386.7 million in 1971, which was obviously due to the rise in population. However, if the age groups 15 to 25 years or 25 to 45 years are taken into account while considering the above statistics, the situation appears to be a little better.

For the fifth plan, the allocation of funds for adult education is illustrated in the following table:-

Adult Education Plan

	Plan	*Expenditure Rs. in Crores*
1.	State Adult Education Council	1.00
2.	Literature for adults	2.00
3.	Functional Literacy	4.00
4.	Aid to Voluntary agencies	1.00
5.	Research and Experiments	2.00
6.	Capable Schemes	10.00
7.	Continuing Education	30.00
	Total	50.00

Continuing education is that form of adult education, or social education in which educational opportunities are provided to those who have given up education prematurely. In the sphere of higher education, continuing education is required most in the sphere of technical education, a fact indicated by the surveys and conclusions of the Scientific Manpower Committee (1949), Engineering Personnel Committee (1956), the Working Group on Technical Education and Vocational Training (1960), and the Technical Manpower Assessment Committee (1966), etc. Technical education points to the path for the future plans.

Hence, it becomes necessary to provide opportunities for education through correspondence courses, part-time courses or self study courses so that abilities may be developed and people may remain in touch with the latest addition to human knowledge. For this purpose, it is desirable to formulate a general policy.

Considerable thought was given to bringing adult education into the list of the nation's priorities. In the first place, social justice cannot be made available, and democracy cannot succeed in the absence of training in productive techniques, knowledge of fundamental economics and creation of the right attitudes. And, the success of democracy and social justice were the foundation stones of the fifth five year plan. And it was generally accepted that even the success of such a vital programme as the Green Revolution depended upon the success of adult education.

The various experiments conducted so far in social education have brought to light many important activities and ideas. All such programmes must have the in-built quality of attracting adults towards themselves. There is necessarily an intimate relationship between the adult's routine activity and social education. It should be closely related to introductory education, expansion of agriculture, cooperation, etc. Social education must be linked with the national service scheme, and even the predetermined curriculum will have to be linked to national as well as local requirements. It is also inseparably related to research and the creation of suitable literature. We must lay down a variable network of libraries in rural areas, and our aim should be to make illiteracy a thing of the past within the next few years.

1. Linking creative literacy with such nation-wide and productive programmes as the extension of agriculture, animal husbandry, reclamation of land, irrigation and drinking water schemes.
2. Linking creative literacy with such important national programmes as family planning, child and family welfare programmes, etc.
3. Initiating programmes for health and nutrition, literacy, recreation, social organisations, etc, wherever the density of population is high.

4. Laying stress on the programmes that proved successful in the past ; organising adult schools and polytechnics, etc.

Of the allocated sum of Rs. 28,750 crores for social education, 20 per cent was spent upon these programmes. Rs. 580 crores were to be spent upon the training of employees. According to the plan, the States and the Centre could make provisions for Rs.100 crores, while Rs. 20 crores were set aside for setting up departments of continuing education in various universities. At the same time it was also true, that, of the total educational budget of Rs. 2,200 crores not even Rs.120 crores could be set aside for social education, and hence a provision of only Rs. 50 crores was made for this purpose.

Sixth Plan

Adult education has been given national importance in the blueprint of the sixth five year plan. In India, about 20 crore people are illiterate. In addition, about 70% of the children opt out of schools by the time they reach the fifth class, and so they also fall within the categories of illiterates or semi-literates. For this reason, the sixth plan lays special emphasis upon the eradication of illiteracy, and creation of universal primary education and industry-centered education. There is a scheme for introducing a nation-wide educational programme for the illiterates in the 15 to 35 years age group. For this, it is intended to seek the cooperation of universities, labour unions, public service planners and voluntary organisations. It is hoped that the scheme will benefit 10 crore individuals.

Under this plan, importance has been given to the speeding up of earlier programmes, which include - (i) creative literacy of farmers in rural areas, (ii) setting up of labour schools and multipurpose adult education centres in urban areas, (iii) search for adult education centres in universities, setting up of Nehru Youth Centres, (iv) national service scheme. The plan aims at activating all these schemes, and it is hoped that literacy will be brought to 15 lakh people in the first year, 45 lakhs in the second year 90 lakhs in the third year, 180 lakhs in the fourth year, and 320 lakhs in the fifth and final year of the plan. This objective can obviously be achieved only through a powerful, effective and committed administrative mechanism. Some of the special features of this plan are as follows:

Attention to Weaker Sections. The plan provides for the education of the weaker sections in rural as well as urban areas, with special attention to providing literacy to the people in the 15 to 35 age-group. Special attention will also be given to women, Scheduled Tribes, landless labourers, farm labourers and other weaker sections of society.

Society and National Development. The plan envisages that special efforts should be made to ensure that the poor and illiterate individuals develop the necessary awareness about themselves, become conscious of the social reality surrounding them, organise themselves to overcome the difficulties of daily life and become partners in the process of social and national development. Apart from literacy, attention will also be paid to the fact that mixed programmes catering to the needs of the poor are initiated, comprising of general education, health education, family planning, development of vocational skills, science in relation to daily life, knowledge of technology, physical education and cultural activities.

Inspiration to Adults. The success of the adult literacy programme depends upon the motivation of the adults, and for this purpose particular attention is to be devoted to the selection and training of workers, production of good quality teaching materials, introducing developed methods of learning through the medium of doing and living, surveys and facilities for guidance.

Co-operation of Voluntary Organisations. In order to make the plan a success, the co-operation of voluntary organisations, youth and others interested in social service activities as well as organisations engaged in commercial activities will be sought. Labour unions, retired teachers and those engaged in formal education will also be made use of as far as possible, and adult education will, again as far as possible, be linked with other developmental activities envisaged in the plan.

Stress on Decentralisation. In order to make adult education a success, emphasis has been placed on decentralisation in the sixth plan. A National Board of Central Education has been established at the centre, and it is planned that similar agencies will be created at the state, district, block and local community levels.

Programme. In the sixth plan, the programme for adult education is spread over the entire plan period. The first year is to be devoted to preparation. It is hoped that this programme can be given suitable momentum by making schemes at the block and district level after consulting all related agencies, motivating voluntary youth workers, retired employees, other agencies, the adults themselves, establishing resource centres in every region, preparing suitable curricula, preparation of teaching materials, devising methods and materials for training, training of instructional personnel at the district and project level, etc. All these activities can be regarded as preparation for the programme.

Co-operation Schemes. In this programme attention has also been paid to the state agencies, centres for national development, industry, service planners, entrepreneurs, labour organisations, and the specific qualities of particular areas and groups. The programme has been kept free from the formal modalities of the department of education. In order to achieve the desired progress, the administration, cooperative units and the inspection machinery have also been mobilised.

Finance for Adult Education. In view of the national importance of the problem of adult education, a sum of Rs. 200 crores has been allocated to it. This amounts to 10% of the education budget, whereas in the fifth plan, the allocation for adult education amounted to only Rs. 18 crores, or 1% of the education budget. This budgetary provision is only one source, and it is planned that other resources will also be exploited for this purpose. For example, the various service planners and project officers will provide finance for their own adult education programmes. In the tribal regions adult education will also be financed from the budget for the agricultural and rural development, there will be provisions for providing functional literacy to the agriculturist. Thus, the provisions for adult education within the total educational budget is only one of the provisions. Once the scheme is implemented and experience gained, more funds will be made available, as need arises.

Major Problems

The National Education Commission has opined that education does not end in the school. It is a life long process. The adult today seriously needs to understand the rapidly changing world and the increasing complexities of social life. Even those who have obtained considerable education should start learning once again because its alternative is isolation from the present reality. The objective of reconstructing our nation can be fulfilled only when each individual continues to receive the latest education so that he may use his intellect skillfully and determinedly in order to bring about economic development, social change and social security. The Education Commission has rightly pointed out that the farmer who turns over the soil or the worker who manipulates machines must understand the nature of the soil or the machine. He must be aware of the scientific process inherent in productive activity so that he may be able to make full use of new achievements and bring about progress.

Maulana Abul Kalam Azad expressed his views on the importance and function of social education by saying that social education means total human education. It grants the individual literacy so that the knowledge of the world may be available to him. It teaches him how to adapt himself to his environment. This implies giving him education in advanced skills and modes of production so that he may achieve the highest economic level. Its purpose is also to give knowledge of the basic principles of hygiene so that our domestic life may be healthy and prosperous. This will benefit the individual as well as society. Through this education, we should impart to him the lesson of citizenship so that he may obtain some knowledge of the world and also be enabled to participate in those decisions of the government which are conducive to peace and progress. However, the path to adult and social education is littered with many concomitant problems, that is, those problems which always raise obstacles in the path of social education. These problems are described in the following paragraphs.

Vague Policy on Adult Education. Ever since the achievement of independence, our policy on adult education and the programmes formulated for it have invariably been vague and undefined. An effort was made to achieve clarity in the community development programme, but even that was partial or biased, since it was intended only for rural adults. It has no provisions for adults in urban areas.

Lack of Finance. The finance so far invested in adult education has proved inadequate, with the result that this programme, which should have been given the highest priority in national development, fell behind. At least Rs. 27 crores should be spent annually upon this programme.

Absence of a Comprehensive Plan. This programme was accepted in principle, but it was never implemented in a suitably comprehensive manner. Had this been done, the problem would have been over come a long time ago. Dr. Frank went as far as to say categorically that if one literate Indian makes another Indian literate, the problem will be overcome within five years.

Problem of Curriculum. The curriculum of adult education has itself proved a problem, because adults were imparted a certain amount of literacy, but no knowledge of anything else, though this can be done. The method adopted for adults is the same as the one used for teaching children, though the needs, attitudes and abilities of adults are completely different. The curricula designed for them must necessarily take into account their particular needs.

Methods of Teaching. The curriculum should fulfill the needs of adults while the methods of teaching should be such that they help in the achievement of this goal. For the spread of literacy, sentence-charts, diagrams, stories, simple words, radio, television, libraries and the drama stage, etc., can be used successfully. But, in reality, because of a paucity of resources, the techniques of adult education are not brought into use in our country to any noticeable extent.

Problem of Teachers. The problem of teachers for adult education has existed from the very beginning. Under these circumstances, an experiment was made by using teachers of primary schools for this purpose, but it proved a failure because the additional allowance given to the teachers was too nominal. In addition, the extension officers, social educators and rural service workers exhibited complete indifference.

Problem of Continuing Education. Continuing education obviously refers to an educational process which always goes on, and in the sphere of adult education, it refers to the education imparted after literacy has been achieved. If facilities for such education are available after literacy has been imparted, some benefit can be derived from it.

The Agencies of Social Education. Apart from the official agencies involved in social education, some voluntary agencies, are also usually, engaged in this programme, but in India, there is a dearth of such agencies. However, the Literacy House in Lucknow and the Adult Education Council in Delhi are doing this work. These institutions aim at producing trained social educators. Only when there is a growth in the number of such agencies can we hope that social education will make rapid progress.

Administration. Social education has a very vast field and there is no uniformity in administration. The various ministries of the government of India have made efforts to train and educate their employees. The Central Education Advisory Committee has organised conferences and seminars from time to time.

Social Education Institutions. Institutions engaged in social education do not get help at the right time and consequently their enthusiasm dies out prematurely.

Training of Workers. There has also been, in general, a dearth of trained workers in the sphere of social education, because of which the Education Advisory Committee has recommended that such workers be trained

Post Social Education. It is necessary to make arrangements for further education of adults after making them literate.

The Education Ministry of the government of India has suggested the following measures for overcoming the difficulties:-

(i) For individuals of 13 or 14 years of age, primary schools should arrange classes of two hours each at least three or four times a week. This work should be apart from the regular teaching programme of these schools.

(ii) Teachers should be trained for imparting education to the 14-15 age group. The following programmes should be taken up simultaneously:-

(a) Regular classes should be arranged for men and women over a five month period.

(b) The Neighbouring Group Method should be adopted, under which the teacher should educate groups of people in his neighbourhood. Experience has shown that adults show laziness and unwillingness in coming to teaching centres, and hence, it may be more practicable for the teacher to go to their centres instead.

(c) A Home Class movement must be initiated for the education of women, which can be made an integral part of the Rural Education Programme. Students and teachers should offer their co-operation.

(d) Teacher training establishments should formulate and implement programmes of adult education in their respective communities.

(e) Voluntary organisation should organise adult education schemes.

In the opinion of the Indian Adult Education Committee, the important work of literacy must not be lost sight of in the broader perspective of social education. Literacy should remain an important element in social education because, through the written and spoken work, it affords the adult a powerful medium for becoming educated.

What is needed today is that the various programmes of social education must be organised and harmonised. The objective, should be clear, and the adults must be strongly motivated to receive social education. Success in this endeavour depends upon local leadership and local agencies.

Programme for Action

Gandhiji said that illiteracy was a blot upon India's fair name. This blot must be wiped out with all expediency. The objective of adult education is not merely literacy, it must be linked with the daily life of adults. From this view-point, the literacy programme must have three elements- (i) it should be based on work so that it may impart skills to the learner, (ii) illiterate individuals should be able to think about the nation's problem, and (iii) adequate skills in reading, writing and mathematics should be developed so that informal education can then be continued indefinitely.

The Four Point Programme for social education is as follows-

Literacy Classes. By 1953, 400,000 individuals were made literate through 40,000 classes. By 1955, 7,000 classes provided literacy to 89,000 individuals. In community development centres, 85,000 classes helped to make 600,000 individuals literate.

Community Centres. Community centres perform the functions of providing literacy, recreation and information.

Youth Clubs. Youth clubs have been organised in villages with the result that village protection groups, youth welfare centres and other such units work for social education have come into existence.

Women's Committees. In each development centre, women's welfare groups and women's councils should be set up so that women can be given information about and involved in hymn singing, social discussion groups, use of smokeless stoves, knitting, stitching, nutrition and balanced diet, domestic skills, general health care, domestic economics, home decoration, literacy, etc.

The following means or instruments are employed in social education- (a) the common audio-visual aids, (b) black-boards and chalks, (c) charts and flash cards, (d) flannel and other materials, (e) other audio-visual materials, (f) films, (g) radio, (h) television.

The Education Commission has expressed the views that every possible effort should be made to overcome these obstacles, even though 20 years may pass in the process. It has suggested that- (1) For the 6-11 year age group, universal education must be achieved in 5 years. (2) Arrangements must be made for part time education. (3) Arrangements must be made for vocational education.

Various Views

The Commission has suggested that the following two methods should be adopted for this purpose-

Selective Approach. In this context, those groups are included which can be controlled easily, it also includes vocational training, in which industrial and commercial enterprise, large industrial enterprises and the government itself can take up budgets against illiteracy. In this method, the following fields can be comprehended-(a) Most workers in industrial establishments are illiterate, and hence such establishments can be required to make arrangements for the education of their own employees. (b) The state should make arrangements for the education of their own employees. (c) The state should make arrangements for the education of all illiterate classes concerned with social and economic growth, since the number of such individuals is very large. (d) Programmes for imparting literacy should be an invariable part of every scheme of social education.

Mass Approach. This is concerned with developing a general method of public or mass education in which advantage will be taken of all educated men and women for eradicating the illiteracy of their brothers and sisters. Voluntary organisations can take effective steps in this direction. Existing schools can be converted into community centres. Regarding this approach, the Kothari Commission has argued that a movement for collective or community literacy depends largely upon the voluntary services of all educated individuals, including governmental as well as non-governmental employees and other sections of society. It has suggested that students of the primary, secondary, under-graduate students and students of vocational schools should be engaged in the teaching of adults as a part of the National Service Scheme.

This Commission has made the following suggestions for accelerating the literacy movement:-

(A) Organising a curriculum for adult women through the central social welfare board, with 'rural sisters' teaching women in the rural areas with the help of the community.

(B) Generating social skills.

(C) Adopting education as a dynamic process.

(D) Running ad hoc courses.

(E) Training through units which should be for teachers and common people. In this, students should be given suitable opportunities, and use should also be made of radio and television.

(F) Generating a suitable atmosphere before initiating the programme.

(G) Preparing the adults psychologically to make them receptive.

(H) Making use of such means as radio, television, films, lectures, etc., so as to make teaching suitable.

(I) Making schemes for literacy in accord with local circumstances.

(J) Making the programmes attractive.

(K) Seeking the full cooperation of universities, industries, etc.

(L) Organising an effective administration.

Past Experience

The field of social education presents vast opportunities for educating the public. Various kinds of efforts have been made for educating people all over the world, and for this purpose various experiments were conducted. The USA and USSR despite the fundamental differences in their political and economic structure, both accept and understand the importance of kind of education. There, the schools, colleges, clubs and institutes and other institutions which work for improving the standards of the fore mentioned have been provided with extensive cultural facilities. In India, too, various experiments have been conducted in the sphere of social education. These are -

Organisation of Tours and Camps. In such schemes, adults are sent to camps for completing a pre-determined course of study which aims at teaching them reading, writing and healthy citizenship. K.G. Saiyadain has laid special emphasis upon the utility of such organisations, because in camps, the atmosphere generated is suitable for the growth of brotherhood as well as leadership. However, it must also be kept in mind that the organisers of tours and camps should have adequate knowledge of mass psychology. These camps can prove to be the nerve-centres of social education, and so they should be managed with sympathy and understanding.

Janata (Public) Colleges. Like the 'folk schools' of Denmark, Janata or public colleges were established in India, too. After observing their work, one observer commented that the most important element was not the quantum of knowledge obtained by the students but the fact that their thoughts and sentiments were stimulated. It is conceivable that they would forget much of what they had learnt, after they left school, but after leaving school, they appear to be completely changed. By that time, they have learnt to listen, observe, think and make the best possible use of their abilities.

According to Pyare Lal Rawat, the foundation stone for a public and cooperative life will be laid in the social centres in rural society. Janata colleges have been set up to produce educated and trained workers for such social centres. Leadership will take birth in these colleges. They will not have the form and structure of the ordinary colleges because their purpose is to train young men and women to perform activities of social, cultural and educational value among the rural people so that they may be able to provide leadership to the rural areas. In other words, their purpose is to generate knowledge and education among the rural people, to teach the rural people better ways of living so that they may lead a better and more contented life. The objective of these colleges will be to make Indian rural people responsible citizens of a democratic society by arousing their civic, social and cultural awareness.

Community Centres. Community centres were set up in rural areas to provide education, sociability, recreation as well as education in good citizenship. These centres were set up in the village squares (chaupals), panchayat houses and schools, and provided with such materials as carpets, furniture, books, radios, newspapers, periodicals, sports goods, etc.

Intensive Libraries. Where community centres have not been established, intensive libraries have been set up. These libraries contain literature suitable for the adults, as well as books on agriculture, cottage industries, cooperative societies, health and other such subjects of utility.

Educational Caravans. Educational caravans were put into use in the rural areas around Delhi. These caravans are equipped with film projectors, health materials, libraries and other teaching materials. This caravan sets up camp at one place, and then its workers spread all round, making arrangements for adult education.

Adult Education Departments in Universities. The Rajasthan university has made adequate efforts towards adult education by setting up a department, which has also initiated a number of schemes for continuing education. Other universities should imitate Rajasthan in this respect. Universities can make their contribution to social education through postal courses, short-term education, extension services, post education contact programmes, etc.

Mass Education Movement. 20 years ago, the 'Parichaya' (acquaintance) trust was set up for the spread of mass education for the Gujarati speaking people. So far, this trust has published as many as three hundred books on various subjects. This movement was strengthened by the activities of Wadilal Dagli (Editor, *Commerce*) and Yashwant Doshi (Editor, 'Parichaya' trust publications). Dagli was inspired in this endeavour by the Chicago University pamphlets; which he saw at Berkeley (California). He thought of spreading mass education in his mother tongue. The work began with only Rs. 500. Each pamphlet was priced at 0.40 paise. In the first year, the organisation enrolled six hundred members. The publication was based on the principle of giving 10% royalty to authors and Commission to the middle men.

This movement brought about a social revolution, and also provided the illiterate people with a ray of hope. So far, the trust has published 300 pamphlets, thus providing the neo-literates with reading material on a variety of subjects. The trust now plans to publish similar literature for neo-literates in other languages also.

Informal Education. In the fifth plan, one important experiment in the sphere of social education was that of informal education. In this context, the Central Education Advisory Council has prepared a scheme for linking social education with national development. The scheme envisages providing further opportunities for education to those who were compelled to abandon their education too early, Correspondence courses, evening classes, etc.; are part of this scheme. It will provide free and informal opportunities of education for everyone.

Village Education Muhim. This experiment was carried out in Maharashtra. Some social workers conducted adult education classes.

In Vidharabha, some enthusiastic workers were given training and the number of adult education centres was thus increased. This movement was based on the declaration of the workers that they would maintain their own literacy, send their children regularly to school, maintain unity in the village and seek to fulfil the goal of integral development of the village.

Now, this programme is being conducted by District Councils. It has three objectives:-

(i) Putting an end to illiteracy among adults (14-50 age group)

(ii) Granting neo-literates opportunities to remain in constant contact with education.

(iii) Bringing about the comprehensive development of villages through social education centres.

Village Vidyapeeth. This experiment was initiated in Mysore. Through it, the spread of education in economics, agricultural education, etc., was achieved. The project received inspiration from the Danish folk high schools. In these institutions, a class has to remain at the school for 5 or 6 months for studies. This helps to develop a harmonious community life.

Punjab Literacy Project. Mrs. Helen Butt developed an intensive literacy method (Hindi) in the Neelokheri block of Karnal. After its initiation by Mrs. Butt, the project continued with the help of 20 teachers, 7 lady teachers (planning and panchayat department), and 4 supervisors. Its success is proved by the fact that 36 classes for men and 11 classes for women were started. 1000 adults attended these classes. Each full time teacher taught two classes on alternate days. Classes were held on three days a week basis over a period of six months. The learners were taught to read and write Hindi. In addition to literacy, a programme of continuing education was also conducted over 3 months. A short nine-day programme for training teachers was also conducted. Besides, literacy was spread through the Immediate Learning Method. When the project was introduced at the state level, the farmers showed exceptional enthusiasm for it, proved by the fact that attendance in the classes was as much as 19.4%. Mrs. Helen Butt has said after her experience of this project that the total expenditure on adult literacy scheme should be borne by the education department and the institutions (panchayats) which stand to benefit from them.

Adult Education Department Rajasthan University Jaipur. In 1965, the Rajasthan University at Jaipur set up a department of adult education in order to explore the possibilities of adult education by spreading continuing education. This department organises conferences and seminars at regular intervals. It also organises a variety of short-term courses for the neo-literates as well as-the semi-literates. This department has done the following kinds of work with the assistance of the government, the university and voluntary organisations- (i) studies in the philosophy and concept of adult education. (ii) education in literacy-social, economic development and literacy, adult literacy and the methods of teaching, teacher training, village education muhim, (iii) portable audio visual materials, library, conferences, discussions, (iv) liberal education, (v) public cooperation, (vi) training in leadership (Mysore Vidyapeeth), (vii) the sphere of continuing education industrial and vocational development, (viii) education of adult women, (ix) agencies and organisation. This department continues to think upon and discuss such issues as the university and social responsibility, the work done in foreign countries on adult education, the educational requirements of community, continuing education,-vocations, agriculture, training, liberal teaching, evening colleges, correspondence courses. adult education and related disciplines, etc.

Report of Education Commission

Adult education is one of those aspects of education on which the Kothari Commission has thought at length. The Education has expanded the scope of adult education, and for its success and spread, it has suggested the following six-point programme-(1) eradication of illiteracy (2) continuing education, (3) correspondence courses, (4) libraries, (5) role of universities in adult education, (6) the organisation and administration of adult education. We will now consider the recommendations of the Commission in the light of its programme.

Campaign against Illiteracy

The Education Commission has pointed out that as compared to the situation in 1951, there were 26 million more illiterate people in 1961.

As compared to 1951, there were 20 million more illiterates, despite the fact that literacy had increased from 16.6% to 28.5%. It also accepted the fact that the nation was paying a heavy price for this illiteracy, because. illiterate persons are not really independent and complete citizens. Besides, illiteracy acts as an obstacle in economic, social and political development, control of population, creation of security, etc.

The Commission has suggested that any programme for the eradication of illiteracy should have the following bases - (i) As far as possible, adult education should be based on work, and it should aim at change of attitude, creation of interests and skill. The information given should bring about an increase in the learner's skill. (ii) Adult education should stimulate the learner's interests in national problems and also make a powerful and effective contribution to the nation's social and political life. (iii) It should make adults capable of reading, writing and calculation. If the learner's wish they can ensure their own improvement through informal knowledge.

It is evident from these three bases that the literacy drive will have three stages - (a) in the initial stage, the adult should be taught reading, writing and calculation, and also given information about citizenship and national problems. Besides, information about his vocation should also be imparted to the learner. (b) In the second stage, the knowledge obtained in the initial stage should be reinforced and the skills developed further. Adults should be enabled to understand and face their personal problems. (c) The third stage should help the adult to participate in continuing education.

A useful programme of adult education depends upon the acceptance of certain basic facts. We must see such programmes in the light of industralisation and modern agricultural progress, as making illiterates useful instrument in the country's general as well as economic development, as turning them into an effective work force. For this, the following facts should be considered:

Targets. The success of adult education depends upon successful planning. There should be a proper time schedule for programmes for the people, preparation of resources, training of workers and provision of other needs. The Commission has recommended that the programme should not be prepared for the whole nation, instead, state-wise planning should be adopted. The progress of adult education depends upon the educational facilities, public co-operation and existing organisation in each region. The Education Commission has expressed the hope that, on the basis of proper planning and implementation, 60% illiteracy can be eradicated by 1971 and 80% by 1976. Consequently, the Commission has recommended that every effort should be made to eradicate illiteracy. It has hoped that within 20 years, no part of the country should remain backward.

Programmes for Eradication of Illiteracy. The Commission has suggested the following programmes-(i) Providing for compulsory education of at least five years for the 6-11 years age-group. (ii) Providing for part-time education of the children in the 11-14 age-group who had to give up their education for some reasons. (iii) Making arrangements for the part-time general as 'well as vocational education for individuals in the 15-30 age group. This group will include individuals who have received education partially.

Strategy of Approach. The Commission has rightly argued that every effort must be made to overcome obstacles to adult education. We must consider the population in our country and determine our strategy accordingly. According to the Census of 1961, there were 1 million illiterates in the 15 + age-group. Literacy in urban areas was 47%, while in rural areas, it was 17%. The distribution of literacy also depends upon the region. While in Delhi it was 52.7%, in NEFA it was as low as 1.8%. Besides, there was considerable differences between the literacy among men and women. Social groupings, caste and class and the nature of the community have always hindered adult education. Besides, the differences in the nature of a region lead to different levels of motivation towards adult learning. The Commission has felt the need for the acceptance and observation of certain general principles, and so it has suggested two approaches for success in this endeavour- (i) Selective approach, and (ii) Mass approach. Programmes based on both approaches should run simultaneously.

Different Attitudes

According to the Commission, the selective approach is suitable for the group which can be identified easily and also kept under control with relative ease. Such a group can be effectively motivated to obtain education. Such a group can be made useful and the literacy programme can achieve success. Even vocational training can be given to such groups. Under this approach, the following programmes can be formulated :

1. Almost 4% illiterate people are employed in industrial and professional organisation. Hence, the Commission has recommended that large firms, trading and industrial organisations and institutions may be legally made responsible for the adult education of their employees. They should be made literate within three years. The owners of such organisations must bear the entire responsibility of making their employees literate. The government should bear all expenses related to education, such as supply of teachers, teaching materials, books and other tools. The Commission is convinced that the owners themselves will, in the long run, benefit from the education of their employees.

2. The Commission has suggested that large organisations managed by the administration must give primacy to the important programme of adult literacy.

3. The humanitarian attitude is necessarily linked with all programmes for social and economic progress. They include a large number of people who have never even seen a school. Hence, it appears logical to argue that provisions must be made for the education and training of all workers in the schemes for industrial, agricultural, and trading development or improvement in health and education.

4. The Indian government has implemented numerous schemes for social welfare and economic development. These include such schemes as the creation of the Khadi and Village Industries Commission, community development schemes, child welfare schemes, etc. The Commission's view is that adult education should be made an integral part of all such programmes.

In order to put an end to illiteracy, it is necessary to mobilize all literate people in society. This approach is unorthodox, and it has not yet been adopted in practice in India. Russia has achieved spectacular successes in adult education through this approach. In India, Maharashtra has achieved notable success through its Village Education Muhim. In this approach, the workers seek the cooperation of the community and make schemes for mass education. The only difficulty in this approach is the laxity in follow-up, but this can be taken care of. Such a programme possesses the following characteristics:

1. This approach depends more upon political and social institutions rather than administrative educational institutions.

2. Adult education, by its very nature, is voluntary, and the drive behind it is the individual's own motivation. Hence, national unity and security, health and social welfare should be implicit in adult education, a fact which must never be lost sight of by educational planners, administrators or workers.

3. This approach depends upon the voluntary services contributed by such educated individuals in society as doctors, lawyers, teachers, students, engineers and other individuals, though, of course, the brunt of the responsibility falls upon the teachers and students. It is for this reason that the Commission has recommended that adult education should be propagated, through compulsory national service at every level of education.

4. In connection with adult education, a new responsibility should fall upon the schools. This will also help to modify the attitude of the school. This approach comprehends not only the student in the school, but the entire community. It provides an important sphere for extension service.

A programme of adult education cannot be run successfully as long as a proper plan is not formulated. For the success of such a programme, the following points must be considered:-

1. Before the implementation of the programme, the government, and all social and political leaders should arouse the interest of the community and bring about mobilisation.

2. The individual adults taken into the scheme should be psychologically motivated in a suitable manner. They should become aware of the importance of literacy.

3. All means of mass communication, such as radio, television, films, slides, drama and literary organisations should be made use of in such programmes.

4. Whenever the programme is to be implemented, the necessary teaching aids such as books, charts, graphs, guide-books, etc., must be prepared before-hand.

5. In planning for literacy local, needs and conditions should be kept in mind.

6. The literacy programme should also have provision for the continuing education of neo-literates. Follow-up programmes should also be organised.

7. The adult education programme cannot be left entirely and exclusively to the teachers. They must be offered the cooperation and assistance of the following- (i) extension services, agricultural and industrial departments, (ii) the use of mass media instruments, such as the All India Radio.

8. Libraries should also extend their cooperation to this programme.

9. Training in leadership should also be part of this programme.

10. Students, teachers and others interested in the spread of adult literacy should be given suitable training.

11. A powerful administrative and supervisory mechanism must be evolved.

12. In this progamme, schemes should be devised for bringing people into contact with each other through study groups, committees, clubs, recreation groups etc.

13. The public, too, should recognise and appreciate such programmes.

14. The percentage of illiteracy among women is greater than among men. In the urban areas, 34.5% women are literate while in the rural areas this percentage is 8.9, a situation similar to that found existing in the whole world. Hence, as many lady

teachers as possible should be appointed to speed up the education of women.

15. The success of any activity depends upon the follow-up action given to it. Hence, for adult literacy also, properly planned programmes of follow-up action should be devised.

Continuing Education

Adult education occupies the most important place in our country's educational set-up. In the rapidly changing circumstances of today, life as a whole should be conceived of as a continuing process of learning. It is now being generally accepted that the modern method of education does not provide extensive education for one's entire life. Hence, to complement it, full-time, part-time or in-service educational programmes are devised for those who have left school and reached adulthood: Generally, the system of continuing education is devised for two classes:-

(i) Those people who participate in part-time education along with other individuals. Individuals of this class increase their qualifications by receiving part-time education in schools and colleges.

(ii) Those persons who can study only at home, but who need some assistance in getting official recognition for their study.

Continuing education is meant for persons who want to complete the education left incomplete by their leaving school. Individuals working in institutions also need opportunities for improving their qualifications and abilities. There are also some individuals who wish to study literature, language or some special subject merely for the pleasure of it. Adult education seeks to bring education within the grasp of every kind of person by catering to his special needs.

Hence, the Education Commission has suggested the following steps for developing continuing education- (1) For part-time education, a parallel system must be developed within the educational structure. Just as degrees, diplomas and certificates are granted to full time students, similar recognition should be available for part-time curricula and courses also. (2) Education institutions should provide the necessary leadership in this process ; they should understand the individual's problems, solve them and help them in obtaining knowledge as well as the necessary help. (3) Through special part-time courses and mixed programmes, efforts should be made to improve the mental horizon of workers and employees ; their knowledge and skills should be improved and a sense of responsibility engendered in them. (4) Specialised institutions should be established, for example, the Central Women's Welfare Council, Vidyapiths, etc.

Correspondence Courses

For millions of those people who have to stand upon their own feet very early in life and struggle for livelihood and survival, correspondence courses provide a means by which they can satisfy their ambition for education, which would otherwise remain unfulfilled. Such courses are very much in use in foreign countries, such as the USA, Sweden, Japan, the USSR, Australia, etc. In India, too, experiments have been conducted in this form of education by the Delhi, Meerut and Himachal Universities. Although this method does not provide any immediate and direct contact between the students and the teachers, the relations between the two can become quite intimate through exchange of correspondence. Besides, it is also to be noted that there has generally been a dearth of teachers who can inspire students through direct contact.

Correspondence courses should be designed to encourage an exchange of views, and they should not restrict themselves merely to the exchange of written information. Individuals who wish to study science through the correspondence courses should be allowed to make use of laboratories during vacations. Even in education as a subject, there should be arrangements for correspondence curricula through Programmed Learning, a method which has been productive of good results.

The correspondence system of education should also get the assistance of radio and television, which can be used for the expression of fundamental and emotional ideas. Courses of this kind should be designed not only to enable students to obtain degrees, but also to give information and knowledge to individuals engaged in agriculture, industry and other productive activities. These courses should be organised through the extension departments.

The following are the recommendations of the Education Commission for the development of correspondence courses:

1. Those individuals who can take part in courses or curricula should receive education through correspondence courses. For this, extensive correspondence courses should be organised.
2. Students studying through the correspondence system should be given opportunities to meet the teachers at regular intervals. As far as possible, they should also be allowed to avail of library facilities existing in schools and colleges.
3. Correspondence courses should be assisted by the radio and television network.
4. Correspondence courses should also be organised for those individuals who wish to develop their literacy or aesthetic values.
5. Correspondence courses should not limit themselves to helping students merely to obtain university degrees. Instead, they should also contain courses which may lead to increased production in agriculture and industry.
6. Through correspondence courses, school teachers should come into contact with fresh knowledge, new methods of teaching, etc.
7. The education ministry, with the assistance of other ministries, should set up a National Council of Home Studies. Its functions would be to evaluate the correspondence courses, the agencies involved in such education, and the identification of spheres in which correspondence courses can be introduced.
8. Those individuals who wish to appear at examinations conducted by Boards or universities, on the basis of self-study, should be allowed to do so.

Importance of Libraries

Libraries have always played a leading role in the growth of knowledge. In their absence, the possibilities of developing the habit of reading are very few, especially in rural areas. The Commission has suggested that, for the spread of mass education, school libraries should be utilised as public libraries. It has suggested that:

1. The suggestions of the advisory committee on libraries should be accepted, and on its basis, a network of libraries should be spread over the entire country.
2. School libraries should be organised and structured as public libraries.
3. Libraries should be dynamic; they should attract adults towards themselves.

The importance of libraries is reflected in the following statement from UNESCO. It says that in the whole world, and especially in developing countries, there is great need for the expansion of free libraries as a part of the educational programme. Libraries satisfy the needs of the prevailing educational system and help the teachers in their work. In the absence of public libraries, many adults and young men gradually sink towards illiteracy on leaving the school.

Significance of Universities

Commenting upon the importance of universities, the Education Commission has declared that the image of a university is that of an intellectual, 'closed' community which gives rise to knowledge, spreads and preserves it, but this is the traditional image. The walls which divide 'town and town' no longer exist. There has come about a revolution in the life of the university, with the revolutionary idea that the community can be linked to the university for the mutual benefit of both.

The Delhi University introduced the correspondence courses and soon found that the demand for them was growing rapidly. In the same manner, the Rajasthan University set up a department of adult education, which was widely applauded. The idea was widely appreciated in Meerut University also.

The function of the university is to bring about a growth and improvement in the social, economic, educational and cultural spheres, and through special agencies it can have a profound impact upon these spheres. Universities should organise effective and powerful programmes for various vocations. It is their duty to ensure that their teachers are constantly in touch with the latest editions to knowledge. In the context of adult education, the Education Commission has made the following recommendations regarding the role of universities:-

1. Indian universities should shoulder a heavier burden in educating the adults in the country. This can be done in the following ways- (a) departments similar to the Rajasthan University's department of adult education should be set up in other universities. (b) Universities must contribute to social and economic growth. (c) They must nourish community life and cultural values.

2. A Board of Adult Education should be constituted by taking representatives from the various departments involved in making the adult literacy programme a success.
3. Universities should be given financial aid for the proper implementation of the adult education programme.

Infrastructure

The Commission has clearly felt that the basic weakness in the efforts being made by governmental, non-governmental and voluntary agencies towards the spread of adult education lies in the absence of proper planning and cooperation. Hence, it has suggested the establishment of a National Board of Adult Education to overcome this shortcoming. The council should have representatives from all related ministries. It should have the folllowing functions:-

1. Advising the central and state governments on informal adult education, offering for consideration blueprints for teaching and training.

2. Wherever necessary, setting up institutions, helping in the preparation of literature, teaching materials and necessary teaching programmes.

3. Creating harmony between the efforts of various departments and governmental as well as non-governmental agencies.

4. Evaluating the achievements from time to time and making suggestions for future improvements.

5. Encouraging research, evaluation and survey activities.

Similar organisations should be established at the state level also. At the district level committees should be set up to function as integral parts of the district councils. They should be assisted by village and block committees. They should also be in intimate contact with extension programmes in the spheres of agriculture, cooperatives, health, community development, etc.,

On the question of administration, the Commission's view is that a separate department within the ministry of education should organise this work. The government must accept full responsibility, and every department of the government should be cognizant of the importance of adult education. In addition, every department should help in implementing this programme. Undoubtedly, adult education is the concern of the department of education, but it is also true that, in order to achieve success, it will be necessary to depend upon some particular mode of action.

As far as the question of voluntary agencies is concerned, they should be given financial and technical assistance. Adult education is a sphere in which such agencies can work freely. Besides, the nature of the work is such that its progress and mobility provides a necessary background for the success of all our planning for national development.

7

Environmental Education

Bharat H. Desai rightly points out in an article "We are in the midst of a deepening environmental crisis triggered off by unprecedented growth and development of the human race. The unbroken history of rapacious exploitation of natural resources and the continued neglect of the need for regeneration and conservation have begun to boomerang", observes a High Powered Commission in its report submitted to the Government of Gujarat recently.

The twelve-member High Powered Commission (HPC) headed by R. Parthasarathy, Chairman of Vadodara Urban Development Authority (VUDA), was constituted "to study the problems of people affected by large undertakings in Gujarat". However, the findings reached and the recommendations made by the Parathsarathy Commission have wider ramifications, meriting attention for environmental protection in India as a whole especially its recommendation to set up a statutory environment protection agency.

In the post-independence era, urbanisation in the wake of large-scale industrialisation has brought about widespread environmental degradation. Industries sprang up all over Gujarat in the sixties in an unplanned fashion which uprooted hundreds of small and marginal farmers following land acquisition. "The plight of the land losers", according to the HPC, "has been aggravated partly by inadequate negligible compensation and partly by the failure of existing policies and programmes to rehabilitate them adequately, economically and socially." Apart from this, most of the villages affected by land acquisition are suffering from inadequate or near absence of basic minimum needs. The rapid felling of trees, disappearance of greenary, destruction of village forests, indiscriminate disposal of solid and semi-solid wastes by industries in and around affected villages are leading to serious health hazards for the people. "There has been nearly no rehabilitation worth the name of the land losers' families", laments the HPC.

The world is facing or rather passing through many crises but the most dangerous crisis is that of gross and constantly increasing pollution of the environment. Needless to say that if immediate attention is not paid, ways are not rooted out; plans are not implemented in their right direction to put a check on the growing hazards of pollution, the entire humanity may be in the grip of destruction, devastation and it maybe a sign of doom and loom for all of us. For this, proper environmental education is inevitable if we are to attack the problem, not only at the roots but also with a view to have a final solution to our growing gigantic problems of the devilish pollution.

Let us, first of all, see as to what is meant by Environment. In an article-Crisis of Environment-Environment is explained as under:-

Environment refers to surroundings - those natural things around us, from the essentials which sustain human life, such as the earth's atmosphere or healthy air or drinkable water, to the non-essentials that nevertheless make life sustainable, such as wild animals, clean places or human living space.

Thus, the environment is not just pretty trees and tigers, threatened species of birds, animals and plants and the eco-systems. It includes the entire entity on which we live and on which our agricultural and industrial development depends. Saving or preservation of the essential ingredients of life and of the rich natural diversity of the planet is consequently necessary for healthy existence.

The compulsions and complexities of life sometimes require us to make a dent into natural wealth; but everyone now agrees that the fewer such dents human beings make, the better for them and for the coming generations. Certain actions become inevitable, but several others are advisable for man. Continuous destruction of the vital environment certainly robs us, and also the succeeding generations, of variety and beauty in nature.

Undeniably, the environment has become the world's common problem. The environmental health of a country is in fact an indicator of the quality of life of the people. The need for an environmental ethic is now universally accepted. The environment is in grave danger, but it can certainly be saved. Conservation has necessarily to be adopted as a long-term strategy : it must be made a mode of life.

We need air, water and adequate land of sufficient quality to sustain life. Continuous research and monitoring have to be done to ensure that these precious resources are preserved. The importance of their preservation is apparent from the fact that air, water and land are finite, limited sources, and can be exhausted. To use a Term of economics, air, water and land must be regarded as capital, not as income. Even the Vatican and the Holy Sect, representing the Pope, said: "Stewardship of the resources of the physical world has always been a key concern of religion."

Besides this, it will be worthwhile to note that broadly speaking atmosphere that implies both-natural as well as social-in natural atmosphere generally, air, water, trees, vegetables are included. Again it is divided in two parts-biological and non-biological. There may be further sub division-such roots of bio-atmosphere in the forms of generator, consumer and destroyer. Under natural atmosphere all the living beings fall under the head of consumer. The second atmosphere takes into its compass —social, economic, political and family relations.

Definition and Meaning

Balanced use of Natural Resources. There has been a prevalent misconceived notion that more use we make of available natural resources, more the progress of the world. Actually there becomes an imbalance in the nature if there is an unrestricted exploitation of available natural resources. Y. Nondumma is right when she points out that this mis-conceived notion of the exploitation of the natural resources under the pretext that they are meant only for exploitation by and for human being, will take the entire humanity to a point of destruction. As it will lead to the entire change in the environment.

Control over the Waste Material. In every industry there is left enough material which is nothing but waste. This waste is either thrown into the water or somewhere on the ground. In both the cases the atmosphere becomes polluted either through water or through air. To have a control over such a waste material is inevitable if we want to preserve the environment or face pollution.

Check on Industrial Development. Industrial development brings with it environmental degradation and may be a menace for the humanity if no check in the right direction is made on this. Industrial development adversely affects the community and surrounding atmosphere all around.

Proper Utilization of Natural Resources. Nature has given us coal, gas, oil and many other minerals, etc. As there is no limit to the greedy nature of the human being, he has started extracting every thing mercilessly and putting the same at his disposal without caring for its proper utility and the limit to which the same should be exploited, according to need and limit. The result is explicitly clear. At certain places there is drought while at other place there are heavy rains and floods. It brings untold miseries but man has still not learnt a lesson to make a balanced use of natural resources.

Pollution a Worldwide Problem. The United Nations has repeatedly expressed deep anxiety over the ceaseless pollution all over the world and the innumerable problems it creates. In the initial discussions on environment there were wide differences on the issue. The UN Conference on Environment, held in Stockholm in 1972, became known for controversial approach. Two leading US environmentalists openly contradicted each other over whether too many people or too few resources were responsible for the world's deepening ecological crisis.

The Eastern bloc, led by the Soviet Union kept aloof because the UN had not fully recognised the German Democratic Republic. The Third World accused the industralised nations of using the "pollution problems" as an excuse to keep it underdeveloped ; and well-known anthropologist Margaret Mead warned of the need for a "Copernican Revolution" in thinking if we were not to irreversibly damage the natural world.

Since the Stockholm session there have been the UN Habitat Conference on Human Settlements in Vancouver in 1975 and the UN Desertification Conference in Nairobi in 1977. In 1972 only 10 nations had environment programmes ; today the number is nearly 100. Third World attitudes have changed dramatically. As the concern has mounted, so has the Doomsday syndrome.

Scientific agencies issue urgent warnings to emphasise the gravity of the population crisis-four births and two deaths every second; 10,000 new chemicals a year are being introduced into the world some deserts are encroaching at the rate of 30 kilometres annually; a century ago 96 per cent of all energy used was either human or animal and now the figure is 1 per cent ; the oceans are dying and the earth's protective ozone layer is being broken up by aerosols and supersonic aeroplanes. The list of disastrous deeds is endless.

The need to teach people about the environment has become increasingly obvious. In October, 1977, nearly 400 delegates from 74 countries gathered in Soviet Georgia for a major intergovernmental conference on environmental education organised by UNESCO in collaboration with the UN Environment Programme (UNEP). They heard UNEP Executive Directors' blunt warning: "Environmental education is now a matter of life and death." Dr. Amadou Mahtar M'Bow, UNESCO's Director-General, cautioned that the problems of the environment were "jeopardising the development of mankind."

There is a growing number of hopeful examples : 15 out of 18 nations surrounding the Mediterranean signed a "Save the Mediterranean" agreement ; Tanzania had invited international environmental experts to advise on the design of the country's new capital; the USA and Canada were co-operating to revive the Great

Lakes. The Chinese have been conserving energy by the widespread use of bio-gas collectors, which produce gas for cooking and generators, and the Soviet Union is minimising the effluence from the pulp plants around Lake Baikal, which contains one-tenth of the world's entire fresh water supply.

An international conference to consider the question of saving trees and forests was held in Paris in January, 1986. The meeting was convened by President Mitterand and brought together for the first time Heads of States and senior government leaders from 36 nations to discuss forestry issues.

Because the pollution envelops the entire world and as such no country- remains aloof from its evil effects, there is an awakening throughout the world to save it from the fatal clutches, of the fearful dragon of pollution.

Problem of Pollution

Y. Naidumna has rightly stated that the unlimited exploitation of the natural resources has lead to dangerous consequences and now there are only two ways left before the entire human race for its existence-one is to make the environment useful keeping the needs of life while the other is to put a check on waste material along with the use of natural resources. Following are causes of pollution:

Rapid Rate of Development. The editor of *Competition Master* rightly says :-

"The irony of the situation is that the more the economic and industrial development in the world, the more the danger to the environment". At many places, "development" has acquired a sinister dimension—pollution. It threatens forests and farms, human health and aquatic life. Disposal of hazardous wastes is another allied problem.

The United Nations Economic and Social Commission for Asia and the Pacific (ESCAP) warned early in February, 1985, that the Asian environment, already in a critical state, is likely to be burdened with additional load resulting from development activities. Statistical data compiled by this U.N. agency indicated that from 1970 to 2000, the volume of-solid wastes will increase five times- dissolved solids, pesticides, bio-chemical oxygen demand, and particulates.

These statistics mean that every environment has what is termed "carrying capacity", or the amount of pollution or damage an environment can sustain or "carry" without further degradation. A lake that is ten times larger than another one can carry roughly ten times the pollution load. If the loads are not minimised or the environment upgraded to an extent that it will be able to carry them, the environmental degradation will inevitably worsen. As for the size of the expected future loads, solid wastes refer mostly to garbage, there is hardly any Asian city where garbage collection is efficient enough to avoid piles of refuse on the streets.

Bio-chemical oxygen demand (BOD) is a measure of the quality of oxygen required in the natural decomposition and recycling process. BOD is expected to increase four times by 2000, but there are no more sets of clean rivers, lakes and seas to accommodate the additional waste. Many Asian water resources are already at, or past, their carrying capacities.

Chemical Pollution. The editor again throws light on the evil effects of chemical pollution- "There are even more dangerous chemicals in use in India than MIC which caused havoc in Bhopal in the world's worst disaster of this kind. The plastic industry uses a chemical closely related to MIC known as toluene di-isocynate (TDI) to make polyurethane foam. TDI is used more extensively than MIC and is far more dangerous to human beings.

"A group of chemicals called polychlorinated biphenyis (PCBs) are highly toxic. These are widely used in the electronics industry and there is no control on PCB use in India. But only when these chemicals are discharged into water can the Water Pollution Act apply to them.

"There are other equally hazardous chemicals which are being manufactured, sold and used in India, and about which there is no information at all.

"Oddly enough, there is no law in India authorising the Government to collect information on the number of chemicals imported or produced in the country. In terms of tonnage at least 70 per cent of the pesticides used in the country have been classified as highly toxic or hazardous by WHO. Protection and improvement of the environment became a priority issue only in the Fifth Five Year Plan (1974-79)".

Acid Rains. Out of the smoke and other waste material a by product of mills and factories, there is a lot of acid rain which not only damages the outer surface of earth but gives birth to many fatal diseases -amongst human beings and life on this earth.

"Acid rain", which contains 65 per cent sulphuric acid, 30 per cent nitric acid and 5 per cent hydrochloric acid, is caused by pollutants which fossil fuel-based industries emit. It has destroyed considerable vegetation. Sweden and Canada are the worst victims of acid rain which is no respector of national boundaries.

Disturbing the Nature. The pollution caused by machines, motor vehicles, mills, factories, petroleum products, etc., the felling of trees, the digging of the hills and such other fearful devices have given birth to a lot of problems such as soil erosion, the presence of dangerous gases and compounds the layers of smoke and dust prevalent all around are some of the major problems we are facing under its impact.

Population Pressure. In 2000 A.D. there will be 3.4 billion people to feed instead only of 2.6 billion in the early eighties. It is clear, therefore, that if current tends are allowed to persist, Asians will face a grim future-not just zero development, but regression. Undeniably, population pressure is the root cause of virtually all pollution and environmental damage. A realistic national timetable for population stabilisation is clearly indicated.

As discussed in an article in *Competition Master*

"Surveys have revealed that India has suffered greater havoc by destruction of natural wealth and pollution of the environment than other countries. India as a whole is adding about 4 million tonnes of sulphur dioxide, 7 million. tonnes of particulates, one million tonnes of carbon monoxide, besides nitrogen oxide, hydrocarbons and several other toxic substances. Bombay illustrates the catastrophic dimensions of air pollution in the country: With all its industries, it emits daily 1000 to 1700 tonnes of pollutants. In Calcutta about 1300 tonnes of pollutants are discharged every day.

Because of the three thermal power stations and massive burning of domestic fuel, Delhi has suspended particulate matter as high as 640-1000 micro-gram per cubic metre one of the highest in the world. Delhi is a topper in respiratory diseases. The other badly affected towns are Kanpur, Ahmedabad and Coimbatore.

Dr. S. Dillon Riply, an eminent environmentalist from Smithsonian Institute, said at a seminar in Delhi last year that in India "massive exposure of land, the soil and water and the air to the fruits of technological advance and development without regard for essential biological precepts can only hasten the degradation of what has been a fair land and a marvellous one for all manner of life."

Grim evidence of this came through the well-documented World Conservation Strategy prepared by the International Union for Conservation of Nature and Natural Resources in co-operation with the United Nations, Environment Programme and the World Wildlife Fund. This revealed that more than half of India suffers some form of soil degradation.

A recent study of the Doon Valley indicates that the once beautiful area is fast becoming an ecological disaster. The region's 2000 mm rainfall has percolated into its limestone belt-a vital cog in the ecological cycle of hills. Thoughtless limestone mining over the past 20 years has resulted in a 50 per cent drop in agriculture productivity and the drying up of several perennial streams which once watered the land. Very few commercial concerns have benefitted from the "rape of the land", but thousands of residents continue to suffer.

Life and Death Issue. An even more ominous warning was given in November, 1985, through the Second Citizens, Report on the State of India's Environment (1984-85) released by the New Delhi based Centre for Science and Environment (C.S.E.). The C.S.E. has a high reputation. Its first report in 1982 was hailed by the United Nations Environment Programme as "a model for other countries to follow."

The rapid pace of environmental destruction in India through soil erosion, deforestation, pollution and urban decay is already affecting the lives of millions of poor people ; the country faces social, economic and ecological disaster if its environment is not properly managed. The report seeks to establish a link between environmental destruction in rural areas and urban decay. Many slum and pavement dwellers in India's cities are 'ecological refugees'.

A five-year study of air pollution in Bangalore city has shown that pollution due to automobile emissions and domestic firewood consumption (cars and kitchens) pose a greater danger than industries.

The construction of dams and power stations, the growth of the mining industry and the destruction of forests and grazing land have displaced large numbers of people. The World Bank financed Narmada Valley Project involving the construction of 329 large dams at a cost of 3.5 billion will displace a million people.

The report is not merely a catalogue of catastrophes. It points out that, proper environmental management can provide India with opportunities to tackle poverty. Government-controlled waste-land, which covers between one-third and half of the country, has enormous agricultural potential. But where wasteland development is taking place, few attempts are being made to involve the landless. Most afforestation schemes, for example, are designed solely to meet the industrial requirements of paper mills and fibre manufacturers.

In a signed statement at the end of the report, the authors call for a new 'social order' for resource management. Government policies have served to create' a strong sense of alienation' among village communities which should be left to manage forests, grazing lands, rivers and lakes themselves.

'Environmental activism' has increased dramatically in India. The building of two dams has already been stopped as a result of public protests-the Silent Valley Project in Kerala and the Bedthi project in Karnataka. The Munda people of Chhotanagpur are fighting against a third project-the massive Koel Karo Scheme in Bihar. A co-ordination committee and the participation of local leaders of various political parties from probably the strongest popular anti-dam movement in India."

Many dangerous chemicals are used in India. The Plastic Industry uses chemicals Toluene-diiso-Cynate which is closely related to MIC which caused havoc in Bhopal Gas tragedy in 1984. Needless to say that this (TDI) is more fatal for life. Similarly a group of chemicals called Polychlorinated biphenyis (PCB) which are highly toxic are widely used in electronic industry. Besides this there are other hazardous chemicals which are being manufactured sold and used in India. In terms of tonnage at least 70 percent of the pesticides used in the country have been classified as highly toxic or hazardous by WHO.

Work of Education

Before we discuss the role of education in the eradication of pollution let us keep in mind a few things like its impact on health, the radio active waves, rise in respiratory and eye diseases, the growth in diseases caused by virus, the gastroenteritis diseases, various diseases relating to noise resulting in deafness, and other diseases of lungs and heart. The growing adverse effect on all types of vegetation cannot be ignored.

Now it shall be worthwhile to discuss the role of education in the eradication of pollution. Following are the measures if adopted in letter and spirit in the right carnest, may bear fruitful results.

1. New ways of looking at the environment so that its value can be reflected in the national accounts, better planning and legislation, more careful and wider use of existing and new environmental technologies, including the all-important environmental impact assessment-a way of appraising the effect of any proposed project on the environment before it is launched.

2. The new Environment (Protection) Act, 1986, is far better in approach than the earlier laws. The Water (Prevention and Control of Pollution) Act, 1974, and the Air (Prevention and Control of Pollution) Act, 1981, were weak and merely regulatory in character.

3. The aim of the new measure is stated to be: 'To provide for the protection and improvement of environment and for matters connected therewith.' The Act contains provisions for tackling the inter-relationship between nature and human beings and the diverse kinds of pollutants. Section 6 (b) empowers the Central Government to make rules for 'the maximum allowable limits of concentration of various environmental pollutants (including noise) for different areas'.

4. There is a section on hazardous industries and environmental disasters. Thus, hazardous industrial pollution is also covered. A hazardous substance is defined as "any substance or preparation which, by reason of its chemical or physio-chemical properties or handling, is liable to cause harm to human beings, other living creatures, plants, micro-organisms, property or the environment: (Section 2 (e).

5. There are stringent measures to check hazardous pollution. Section 8 of the Act states clearly: 'No person shall handle or cause to be handled any hazardous substance except in accordance with such procedure and after complying with such safeguards as may be prescribed.' Section 6 (f) empowers the Central Government to make rules for 'the procedures and safeguards for the prevention of accidents which may cause environmental pollution and for providing remedial measures for such accidents.' Moreover, it is now mandatory for a person responsible for the discharge of any hazardous substance in excess of the prescribed norms to immediately inform the concerned authorities and to render all possible assistance. Earlier there was no such responsibility.

6. Vigilant citizens can initiate proceedings against an establishment that is polluting the water supply or otherwise ruining the environment. The penalties for defaulters have been made more stringent. The Water Act provided for a maximum imprisonment of six years and/or a fine upto a total of Rs. 5000 ; in the Air Act the limits were a maximum imprisonment upto three months and/or fine upto a total of Rs. 5000. The new Act provides for

imprisonment of defaulters for upto a total of seven years and/ or a fine which may extend upto Rs. 1 lakh.

7. However, there are some flaws even in the new Act. One, all power and authority is vested in the hands of the Central Government.

8. (i) There is no provision relating to forests, even though it is open knowledge that in India about 50 per cent of the energy consumed is non-commercial or collected from fields, trees and bushes.

   (ii) Secondly, supplementary legislation in respect of enhanced penalties and for tightening the enforcement of the provisions has yet to be brought up. Nor is it clear whether the new Act supersedes or supplants the two earlier laws. The enhanced punishments may or may not be deemed applicable to cases which fall under the purview of the other Acts. The areas of jurisdiction have not been clearly demarcated.

   (iii) Thirdly, there is no clear provision for public participation which is vital for preserving the environment. The relevant issues are left to official bodies (Air and Pollution Control Boards) and other regulatory agencies. Any individual can file a complaint with the Government against a factory management, but it requires the complainant to give 60 days' notice, which permits the offending management to bring its emissions within control. The role of the public, especially voluntary bodies, needs to be enhanced considerably under the Act.

9. Section 6 (e) of the Act empowers the Government to make rules for "the prohibition, restrictions on the location of industries and the carrying on of processes and operations in different areas". But there is no mandatory provision for the industry to prepare and submit to the concerned authorities a suitable environmental impact assessment report before the location is approved. The US National Environmental Policy Act, 1969, requires that an environmental impact assessment

must be prepared prior to any federally financed project. In India all that a government-financed industrial unit needs is a simple "no objection" certificate from the concerned Pollution Control Board.

10. Addressing the first meeting of the National Land Use and Wastelands Development Council on February 6, 1986, Prime Minister Rajiv Gandhi called for a nationwide "people movement" to protect the country's ecological balance. He suggested a time bound land reclamation and afforestation programme. The approach to this problem could not be departmentalised or compartmentalised but had to "respond to the differing needs of every section."

    An integrated approach, not hemmed in by internal contradictions, would ensure sufficient food, maintain nutrition levels, meet fuel and fodder needs and raw material requirements of industry and help preserve natural habits. 'We will have to mobilise not just the Government, but we will have to mobilise absolutely everyone. Stressing the need for decentralisation of nurseries, tree growers' co-operatives, he called for the involvement of farmers, youth and women in the programme. The landless and the marginal and small farmers should be the key elements in the programme.

11. Having experienced the ill effects of industrial development, it is high time a long-term strategy for environmental protection is evolved. In this respect, the Parthasarathy Commission has strongly pleaded for a Regional Development Strategy and a National Urban Development Policy with a view to contain metropolitan chaos, for developing secondary cities and to ensure development of existing small and medium towns as well as establishing new ones, as part of a regional strategy generating employment and promoting decentralised urbanisation. In addition, a clear industrial location policy will ensure setting up of specific large industries at specific locations with a predetermined time-frame. It will ensure not only systematic industrial growth but also facilitate in taking

measures for environmental protection economically and in a coherent manner.

12. All State governments, semi-government bodies and municipalities as well as social organisations have been propagating "grow more trees" campaign. To boost the idea of growing more and more trees, the government has taken up the project of "social forestry" on a large scale. The project aims at planting trees singly or in groups wherever they can be grown.

13. Apart from increasing the forest wealth, the programme generates additional earnings to the Panchayats, more employment to labour, and it provides cheap fuel to the village poor. In Dhanoli, a village in Valsad district of Gujarat, social forestry has achieved remarkable progress. By adopting the scheme of raising village forests in only four hectares of land a net income of over Rs. 43000 was generated.

14. Social forestry not only prevents felling of trees but also tries to distribute the produce of the project directly to the people of the area. The scheme also aims at growing more trees and forests on unused land and promotes research in the science of trees and their varieties.

15. Community lands in villages are wasted and used only for grazing village cattle. This unproductive use of land yields the village panchayats hardly Rs. 4000 to Rs. 5000. But the same land, if utilised for a cluster of trees for which the Government provides free seedlings, can fetch a much higher income to the Panchayats. The Gujarat Government has decided to give 50 per cent of the net profit realised from the sale of village wood-lot to the Panchayat. Crores of trees are required to strengthen and support agricultural and animal husbandry, to combat pollution and to attract adequate rains and also to stop erosion of fertile soil.

16. But social forestry, especially the growing plantations of eucalyptus, has been criticised by several ecologists,

sociologists and economists. The environmentalists claim that social forestry is encouraging monoculture, and in particular the plantation of eucalyptus, which makes up 80 to 90 per cent of all the trees planted so far under these programmes: Eucalyptus, it is contended, degrades the soil and permits nothing to grow beneath it. It is a heavy consumer of water and lowers the water table.

17. The Government of India has launched a Rs. 292-crore project to clean up the mighty Ganga, which has been greatly polluted as a result of the inflow of effluents and dirt from various sources. There are about 100 cities situated along the banks of the river, in the States of U.P, Bihar and Bengal. Nearly 4200 small and medium units are responsible for polluting the holy river. The Ganga Project is the largest and most ambitious of all the environmental protection plans launched in the country.

18. The cleaning up work began at Rishikesh and Hardwar in September, 1985. Cleaning the Ganga is also in progress at Varanasi waterfront, which is heavily polluted. A Central Ganga Authority had been constituted under the chairmanship of the Prime Minister himself.

19. The wanton destruction of natural wealth, including forests, and the indiscriminate setting up of chemical industries endangers the lives of both human beings and animals. The greed for personal gain, the general decline in values, the knowledge that one can flout the laws with a vengeance and get away with it, or at worst to pay a small fine, have cumulatively rendered ineffective the agencies entrusted with the duty of protecting the environment. There are poachers galore, but it is only rare that legal action is taken against such offenders.

20. Besides, there are wide variations between official data and the actual position. For instance, the Forest Departments in the States have been spending crores of rupees during the past 30 years and claiming that a large area has been brought under forest cover. The Union Minister of State for Environment and

Forests Mr. Z.R. Ansari, said in the Lok Sabha that only 13 per cent of the country's geographical area is under "forest cover" according to satellite pictures, whereas the revenue records show the area to be 22.7 per cent.

21. In February, 1986 the Supreme Court directed the Union Government to examine the possibility of setting up environment courts. The court judgement in the Shriram Foods and Fertiliser Industries case may well provide a basis for action by the Government to safeguard the environment in areas where potentially hazardous industries are located. The court has in fact set out a framework for appropriate governmental action. It has also set up a monitoring committee to ensure that the expert bodies recommendations are implemented. Even more significant is the suggestion that measures should be taken to educate the workers and provide early warning systems for the public.

Review

While the increasing awareness and rethinking about the importance of preserving all aspects of the environment, including forests, clean air, and wild life is welcome, there is an urgent need for earnest implementation of declared policies. So far, the implementation has been poor and, consequently, the environment has been deteriorating; forests, in particular, are disappearing at a disconcerting pace. It is time to recall the farsighted Chanakya's observation in the 4th century B.C. that "the stability of an empire depends on the stability of its environment:" Strong and committed machinery is needed and it must have sufficient resources.

Ecology also has some effect on poverty. Undeniably, an ecologically and scientifically sound afforestation programme can provide a solution to the problem of India's poverty, if it is not based on the profit motive alone. More research is undoubtedly needed to evaluate the costs of monoculture based social forestry. Unless afforestation programmes are linked with the basic needs of the rural poor, they will prove economically counter-productive and ecologically disastrous.

Obviously, the plunder of what nature has built over billions of years has to be stopped. We need a new life-style with environmental ethics as an integral part of it, not only for this generation but also for the future generations to live and enjoy the freedom of this planet and beyond. It is important in this regard to reduce the rate of population growth to one per cent from the present 2.2 per cent, as China has done. Industries generating high pollution should be moved out of the perimeters of cities. Environmental education should be made compulsory at every level of learning.

For the rapid protection of environment the following measures should be adopted:-

1. Aesthetic sense among the citizens be developed.
2. Attitude towards cleanliness be evolved.
3. Civic sense must be prevailed.
4. Social forestry be adopted.
5. Religious attitudes towards trees be scientifically developed.
6. Eco club be established.
7. Research in Environmental Studies in every subject be promoted.

PART TWO

STAGES OF EDUCATION

8

Higher Stage

Evolution and Development

Higher education is not new for India. In the ancient times, students lived with their teachers in gurukuls and ashrams, and received higher education in particular subjects. The curriculum of higher education, at this time, was dominated by the teaching of the Vedas and Vedangas. Three kinds of educational institutions- called *shaakha, charana* and *kshetra* existed. Councils also existed for the purpose of directing higher education. Later on, during the Buddhist period, higher education was imparted in Viharas and Sangharamas. Such universities as those of Nalanda and Taxila had won international renown, and students from many countries came there to receive education. Nalanda provided free education to all students, including students coming from as far away as China, Korea, Java, Sumatra, Borneo, Cambodia, etc. The following subjects were taught in these universities:

(1) Religious rituals, (2) Preparation of manuscripts, (3) Grammar, (4) Astrology, (5) Medicine, (6) Logic, (7) Various branches of philosophy. In addition, there were provisions for education in the curing of diseases (snake bite, blood-testing, orthopaedics, etc.), veterinary science, military science, the fine arts and handicrafts, etc.

Medieval Times

The Muslim system of education developed because of the policies and work of Muslim rulers. Higher education was imparted in Madarasas. Iltutmish was the first to establish such institutions. Badayun, Multan, Bijapur, Golkunda, Ahmednagar, Mand and Gaur were famous as centres of Muslim education. The subjects taught included philosophy, religion, logic, mathematics, grammar, law, history, geography, literature, agriculture, medicine, etc. Aurangzeb laid emphasis upon using the mother tongue as the medium of education instead of Arabic.

Madarasas were established for imparting higher education and they imparted both religious and utilitarian or materialistic instruction. Mathematics, history, geography, philosophy, diplomacy, logic, economics and astrology were taught.

Modern Times-1

The introduction of a systematic higher education was the contribution of the British period. During the administration of the East India Company, it came to be felt that administration could not be carried on without education. Hence, some colleges were established. The importance of this period can be gauged from the fact that on the 18th page of the Hunter Commission's report, this period is referred to as the age of colleges. According to this report, most of these colleges evolved from schools which used to teach the English alphabet. At the same place, under the same roof, Shakespeare's *'Calculus'*, Smith's '*The Wealth* of Nations' and '*Ramayana*' used to be taught.

The following are the names of some of the famous institutions of the British period :

(1) Calcutta Madarasa, (2) Banaras Sanskrit College, (3) Hindu College, Calcutta, (4) Scottish Church College, Calcutta, (5) Serampur College, Christian College, Madras, (6) Agra College, Agra, etc. The names of vocational institution of that period are as follows-(1) Calcutta Medical College, (2) Bombay Medical College, and (3) Roorkee Engineering College.

Keeping in view the expansion of higher education, efforts were made between 1845 and 1852, to establish a university at Calcutta, but these were in vain. In 1852, the Madras Presidency College was converted into a university. In 1854, the Wood Despatch brought about a revolution in the educational world, and as a consequence of its declaration, the universities of Calcutta, Bombay and Madras came into existence. These universities were structured on the pattern of the London University. In 1882, the Punjab University was created and in 1887, the Allahabad University came into existence. The offices of these universities began to function in rented buildings, but the number of colleges affiliated to them soon began to grow. In 1902, the Indian University Commission was appointed and it presented its report in 1904. It recommended that these universities should conduct classes themselves, and for this facilities should be provided to them. It suggested that, for a period of 5 years, between 50 and 100 members should be taken into the Senate, which should also provide place to representatives of teachers. The Commission also framed rules for the affiliation of colleges to universities.

In 1913, the position of these universities was re-evaluated, and as a result, the Banaras University and the S N D T University in 1916, the Patna University in 1917, the Hyderabad and Mysore Universities in 1918 were set up. In 1916, a decision was taken to set up a post-graduate department in Calcutta University.

Modern Times-2

The Calcutta University Commission was appointed in 1917. It made the following recommendations :

1. The new universities should be of a residential kind, residential facilities should also be created in the universities already existing.
2. Two kinds of courses should be conducted- (1) Honours course, (b) Pass course.
3. A director of physical education should be appointed and a student welfare council should be organised.
4. Technical and Technological institutions should initiate courses which are relevant to local needs.

5. In universities, Chairs should be established in the names of famous persons and posts of readers should be created.

6. Informal meetings of representatives of different universities should be encouraged so as to initiate discussion on administration, curriculum, etc.

On the strength of these recommendations, new universities were set up.

During the British period, the number of colleges and students was as follows :

	1920.22	1931.32	1946.47
Colleges	231	417	933
Students	59,591	99,493	1,99,253

In Free India

After independence, in this field, the first problem was the administration and running of the existing universities, and the second was that of creating new universities. For these reasons, the University Commission was set up under the chairmanship of Dr. Radhakrishnan in 1948. The Commission considered ways and means conducive to the growth of higher education.

In 1968 the Rural Higher Education Committee stressed the importance of setting up some rural institutes. These institutes formulate their own curriculum and conduct examinations. The universities to which they are affiliated only issue certificates or degrees. Among such institutions are -

1.	Shri Niketan	West Bengal
2.	Gandhigram	Madras
3.	Jamia Milia	Delhi
4.	Udaipur	Rajasthan
5.	Barauni	Bihar

6.	Bichpuri	UttarPradesh
7.	Sansaura	Gujarat
8.	Coimbatore	Madras
9.	Garameti	Maharashtra
10.	Amaravati	Maharashtra
11.	Rajpura	Punjab
12.	Vardha	Maharashtra
13.	Hanuman Mathai	Mysore

In these institutions, the following curricula are taught:-

1. Three year rural service course
2. Three year civil and rural engineering course
3. Health inspector's course of one year
4. One year's introductory course

Education in Universities

The prefactory note of the Radhakrishnan Commission declares universities to be an essential part of culture. Universities must carry on the task of nation-building and this is conceivable only when a country's civilisation and culture are enriched. The building of a modern India depends upon the structure and pattern of its universities. The term 'pattern' includes two elements- organisation and method of working of the universities. There are two organs of universities- (1) administrative, (2) academic. Both are intimately related to each other. Educational administration, as compared, for example to civic administration, is more academic than civic.

Three kinds of universities exist in India-

Centrally Administered Universities. Among these are the Kashi Hindu University, the Aligarh Muslim University, Delhi University, Vishwa Bharati University, the Jawaharlal Nehru University, North East Frontier University which are administered by the Central government.

State Administered Universities. All universities other than the ones mentioned above are administered by the state-governments.

Both centrally administered as well as state administered universities are classified again as follows:

Affiliating Universities. The function of such universities is to hold examinations in the colleges affiliated to them. The task of teaching is performed by the affiliated colleges. The university exercises administrative and academic control.

Unitary Universities. Such universities exercise complete control over the colleges located at their own centres. Teaching is done either by teachers appointed or by the university itself or by teachers working under the supervision of the staff of the university.

Federal Universities. Universities of this kind have the following features- (1) The colleges linked to them are near the university. (2) Each college functions at the university level. (3) The colleges are themselves autonomous. (4) Teaching is carried on under the guidance of the university.

In addition, some institutions have been recognised as universities of a third kind. They are deemed to be universities. The pattern of universities, depends to a large extent, upon their activities and achievements. The situation with regard to this is determined in the following manner :

1. Higher education comes into existence with the creation of universities. Their nature is clearly distinct from the education department of the government, groups of non-government officials, and affiliated' colleges. The university places its stamp of approval, or otherwise, upon the working and standard of the colleges.

2. The existence of universities is determined by an act of parliament or legislature, which also sets out the basic principles or facts and the educational programme of the universities.

3. In universities, the standard takes the form of symbol. But, unfortunately in democratic countries, it has become a matter

of leisure, and a situation exists in which the future of universities is being formulated over cups of tea.

4. Universities are not coming into existence due to the wishes of the people. Neither do they fulfil the needs or aspirations of the people. Many of the universities created in recent years have actually only fulfilled political needs. Wherever a university is established, it should have a perceptible and desirable impact upon the community.

5. The working of a university is also influenced by the academic approach and the administrative method.

Recently a new university has been started having a unique idea, this university is Indira Gandhi National Open University meant for those who want to cope with the time. Various types of modern courses are being taught through correspondence courses and contact programmes.

Some states have also started open universities on the pattern of Indira Gandhi University.

Speaking about the pattern of universities, the Kothari Commission has spoken of the setting up of leading universities in which each department would work on the lines suggested by the advisory committee. According to it a university exists for humanity, patience, tolerance, rational thought, courage and the search for truth. It exists to bring about progress of the human race, in fact, for even higher purposes. If a university really fulfils its obligations, it will bring about the welfare both of the nation and of the people. Thus, it is obvious that the clearer the pattern of universities; the higher will be the standard of education.

Objectives and Purposes

The Radhakrishnan Commission proposed the following objectives and purposes of higher education:-

1. In the changing political, social and economic conditions, providing healthy representation in politics, administration, professions, industry and commerce.

2. In the universities, developing an intellectual attitude towards things and encouraging growth of knowledge among the youth.
3. Emphasizing social reform through the creation of foresighted, intelligent and courageous leadership.
4. Encouraging universities to play their part as organs of culture and the intellectual leaders on civilisation.
5. Making an endeavour for the success of democracy.
6. Discovering the innate qualities of individuals and developing them through suitable training.
7. Promoting social emancipation.
8. Creating the sentiments of national discipline, international awareness, intellectual development, justice, freedom, equality and brotherhood.

The Kothari Commission has expressed its view of the objectives or ideals of higher education in the following terms :

1. Seeking knowledge within the framework of truth, using traditional knowledge,in new circumstances.
2. Developing leadership in every sphere of life.
3. Giving educated and trained people to society in the spheres of arts, science, agriculture medicines and industry.
4. Encouraging social justice.
5. Nourishing the right values among students and teachers.
6. Reducing social and cultural disparities.
7. Working for the development of a national consciousness..
8. Developing the programmes for adult education.

The Kothari Commission's conception of these ideals is inspired by the desire to translate the dream of building a new India into a concrete reality. And, it is undoubtedly true that our objectives cannot be high in the absence of glorious and laudable ideals. The objectives of higher education have a universal validity, because it is through higher education that intellect of nations can be used in the international sphere for the betterment of the whole human race. In consonance with this, in India too, the same objectives have been prescribed for the development of higher education. These objectives are as follows:-

1. Obtaining new knowledge and nurturing it, searching for truth with courage and complete dedication, elaborating traditional knowledge and beliefs in the light of new needs and discoveries.

2. Providing the right kind of leadership in every sphere of life recognising the talents of young men and women, developing their potential abilities, training them in physical and mental health and inculcating in them the desired attitudes and healthy interests, and the right moral and intellectual values.

3. Giving to society educated individuals who have received training in agriculture, arts, medicine, science and technology and various other techniques, and who are also infused with social responsibility; in other words, giving society truly cultured individuals.

4. Encouraging equality and social justice through the spread of education and seeking to reduce social and cultural differences.

5. Generating and nurturing in students and teachers, and through them in the whole of society, the values and attitudes which are required for the 'true life' both by society and the individual.

For the fulfilment of these universal objectives, the Commission has formulated an outline of various programmes, based on the following foundations- (i) Total reform in higher education and research, from the viewpoints of quality and standards. (ii) Development of higher education for the purpose of fulfilling the aspirations and ambitions of the people, to some extent, so as to meet thereby the manpower needs of national development. (iii) Reform in the organisation of universities.

These objectives and programmes offer a strong challenge for higher education in India today. So far, it has failed to achieve its objectives in a satisfactory manner, and consequently, a condition of anarchy has come to exist. Contemporary politics has entered India's universities in the form of communalism (casteism) and regionalism. The consequences are painfully obvious to everyone. If the Commission had shed some light on this aspect, its work would have been even more valuable.

When the question of survival faces us, many beliefs assume the shape of question marks and stare us in the face. What the Kothari Commission attempted was to find an answer to the question which Jawaharlal Nehru had expressed in the following term a university exists for humanism, intellectual courage and the search for truth. Its aim is that the human race should strive for ever higher goals. The happiness of both the nation and the people lies in the fact that the universities should continue to fulfil their obligations with success.

Latest Facilities

Unlimited opportunities for expansion exist in the world of university education. The curriculum and the nature of education are both undergoing changes in keeping with the various needs of man. In the world of today there are, not one but many aspects in the sphere of education in which we feel the need for expansion. The number of colleges, teachers, part time education, etc., are among the many aspects which constantly influence the individual. Extravagance, too, is an obstacle in the spread of education.

The twin problem of stagnation and wastage exist not only at the primary and secondary levels, they are equally noticeable in higher education. Scholars declare that more people are studying today. We have become despondent and pessimistic about the process of education. The problem of education has further aggravated this stagnation. The country's youth fails to contribute to the nation's development because, despite his excellent talent in science and mathematics, in the absence of knowledge of English, he does receive the licence to exhibit his talent. The result is that students feel compelled to resort to cheating and other unfair means in examination.

The Kothari Commission considered the admissions to higher education as well as other factors. It is planned to give higher education to between 1 and 4 crore individuals by 1986. The Commission has made special provisions for agriculture, engineering and medicine in higher learning.

For the extension of the facilities, the Commission has made the following suggestions:

Hard Selection

1. Admissions should be in proportion to the number of teachers, the places available in the departments and in the college.
2. The university should lay down the qualifications for admission.
3. Only capable students should be admitted, though in this, apart from the results of examinations, attention must also be paid to the socially and economically backward sections of society. Competitive examination should be used for admissions, as long as other suitable means are not discovered.
4. A Council should be set up in each university for examining the question of admissions and giving suggestions thereon.
5. The UGC should set up a Central Testing Organisation for developing instruments or means which can be used in selecting students for admission.

Parallel Education

Postal education or correspondence courses and evening colleges must be established. In such courses, education in science and industry should also be amalgamated. Meerut, Himachal and Delhi Universities are already conducting experiments in education through correspondence courses, and they are proving very useful in the spread of public education.

College System

As a general rule, facilities for higher education should be provided only in financially viable and reputed educational institutions. The UGC should also consider the location of small colleges. Each college should have not less than 500 students, and not more than 1000. Instead of opening new colleges, the existing colleges should be developed and improved.

Study at Post-graduate Level

Post-graduate study and research should be conducted in the university itself. For these studies, admission tests should be administered before granting scholarships. Loan scholarships should also be given.

Education of Women

1. In higher education, the proportion of women's education is 1:4. This should be brought down to 1:3. For this, women's colleges should be set up though at the post-graduate level, there can be co-education.
2. Free education should be provided.
3. Research into the sphere of women's education is desirable.
4. If there is a local requirement, special colleges for girls and women should be set up at the undergraduate level.
5. There should be progress in domestic science, nursing, social service, etc. Women should also be given training in business organisation and management.

New Varsities

New universities should be set up, but they should be located where there is potential for higher education and research. No new university should be established without the advice and concurrence of the UGC. In good universities, no more than 30 colleges should be affiliated.

New Streams

1. For the first degree, there should be flexibility in the combination of subjects which students can choose.
2. Courses at the master's level should be renovated.

3. A period of 2 or 3 years should be allowed for research. Those aspiring for the Ph.D. degree should be required to know one other language of the world.

At the under-graduate level in all universities, there should be Pass, Special and Honours courses. Affiliated colleges should be given permission to run either one of the two (Pass or Honours) or both kinds of courses.

Social sciences should get adequate importance in the curriculum. Teaching in the humanities should be such as to encourage creative activity.

Academic Research

1. Educational research should be conducted and its findings applied.
2. It should be conducted through groups.
3. A national academy of education should be created.
4. An educational research council should be set up.
5. One per cent of the state's budget for education should be invested in educational research.

We have observed that the Commission has not neglected even a single aspect of education. It has expressed its views regarding every aspect. It has organised the educational system and the entire curriculum in such a manner as to ensure that it achieves the national objectives. It has declared that the development of education should be of such a kind that it leads to increase in production, social and emotional unity, strengthening of democracy, acceleration in the rate of modernization, generation of social, ethical and spiritual values. Dr. Sampurnananda said that these recommendations would not lead to a revolution in education and the development of men would not be in harmony with Indian culture and style of life.

Five-Year Plans

It is impossible to hope for systematic progress in education without a plan. In Indian society, the universities are subject to government control, and it is only through the government's plans and help that the universities can hope for progress. In the Five Year Plans over the years, the following provisions were made for higher education:-

Higher Education in the First Five Year Plan. Higher education has developed systematically after independence. In 1950-51, 74% colleges were being managed by private management committees, but now their number has become 80%. In the same proportion, the expenditure has risen five-fold. In the same way, the setting up of the inter-university board is another step towards the development of higher education. The University Grants Commission is assisting this process of development in higher education.

Second Five Year Plan and Education. Concerning university education, it has been said in the second five year plan that the standards of education have been gravely affected, in recent years, by the increase in the number of universities, colleges and students. Five years earlier, the number of students was 4,20,000. By the end of the first plan period, this figure rose to 7,20,000. Students passing the degree and higher examinations in the arts and sciences rose from 41,000 to 58,000 annually, during this interval. The University Grants Commission is making numerous steps to improve university and college education and also to reduce the hindrance of students who fail to pass examinations. Some of these steps, for example, are introduction of the three year degree course, organisation of lectures and seminars, improvements in libraries and laboratories, provision of facilities in hostels, provision of facilities for outstanding students, provision of scholarships for research, and increase in the salaries of university teachers. Many complex problems and factors influence university education. Introduction of a multi-faceted curriculum at the secondary level may lead to a reduction in the rush for admissions to arts colleges. A committee appointed by the Central government considered this question. There was provision of Rs. 57 crores for university education, of which Rs. 22 crores 50 lakhs were earmarked for the State schemes and Rs. 34 crores 40 lakhs for the Central government's schemes. The latter figure was inclusive of the Rs. 27 crores meant for the University Grants Commission. Rs. 4 crores 60 lakhs were set aside for agricultural education and Rs.10 crores for health education.

Higher Education in the Third Five Year Plan. By the conclusion of the Second Five-Year Plan, the number of universities and colleges had risen to 41 and 1050 respectively. The number of students in the arts, sciences and commerce groups had increased from 4,36,000 in 1955-56 to 9 lakhs in 1960-61. During the same period, the number of science students had risen only from 2,09000, to 2 lakh 2,70,000, from which it is evident that the proportion 0of science education in this period was very low. In the third plan it was proposed that facilities for teaching of science should be increased so that this figure should rise by 4% so that the requirements of various spheres - teachers of science, engineering, technological institutions and industries-should be met. This target is possible if the problems of laboratories and the number of teachers is solved. The University Grants Commission was making special efforts in this direction.

In the third plan, a sum of Rs. 75 crores was allocated to higher education. The money was meant for such programmes as teaching of science, improvements in the pay-scales of teachers, scientific laboratories, libraries, post-graduate studies, research, scholarships, three-year degree course, residential facilities for employees, hostel facilities, etc.

The nation's progress depends upon the growth of higher or university education. The nation will progress only when, at the university level, the creative talents of our youth are developed.

Enrolment. There has been rapid expansion in university education. By the end of the fourth plan, the enrolment in arts, sciences and commerce institutions reached 3.5 millions, which is 3,70,000 more. In the first three years of this plan period, 8 new universities were established, their number thus reaching 89. Of these, 10 are agricultural universities. The number of colleges also increased in number, while correspondence courses were introduced in 9 universities. For every 1 million of population, the enrolment in Andhra, Assam, Bihar, Madhya Pradesh, Orissa, Rajasthan and Tamil Nadu is below the average national rate of enrolment of 5197. The second fact is the difference in the number of students in institutions. In the arts, science and commerce, 43% of the institutions had less than 500 students while 30% of them have more than 1000 students. Thus, on the one hand we have uneconomical units, while on the other, there are the overcrowded ones. A similar situation exists in many universities also. After reveiwing the enrolment and location, it is also evident that most institutions are located in urban areas.

A survey of the expansion has also brought to light the fact that most students end their education after completing their graduation. Secondly, the expansion in arts and commerce has been more than the growth in science.

Qualitative Development. Many programmes for qualitative improvement have been introduced at the level of higher education with the help of the University Grants Commission. Among such programmes are development of Advance Study centres, specialised development of postgraduate central universities, professional and intellectual development of teachers, organisation of summer schools.. seminars, refresher courses, orientation for new teachers, research assistance, teacher exchange programmes, national professorships, travel allowances, arrangement for retired teachers, housing facilities, etc. In order to increase the attachment of students for their institutions, provisions have been made for introducing recreational facilities, health services, vocational guidance centres and study centres. But, it has also been observed that, at the graduate level, only 50% students get success. The number of students with third divisions is increasing, a fact which is hinted at by the declarations of the Education Commission and the Public Service Commission.

Graduate Unemployment. The situation of employment, both at the graduate and postgraduate levels, is deteriorating rapidly. Attractive programmes should be adopted for fighting this situation. Vocational guidance centres and information cells in universities and colleges can be very productive in this situation. Varied and professional oriented courses in science, arts and commerce, have achieved a high degree of success in this direction. Delhi and Rajasthan universities have done commendable work in this field. The University Grants Commission has made provisions for Rs. 3 crores to be spent on workshops, laboratories and short courses in practical science.

The more important of the many problem of higher education are : expansion in inverse proportion to the existing physical facilities, indifference in community towards higher education, falling standards and increasing unemployment among graduates. Hence, it is essential that education should be related to social demands and needs, that it should satisfy the needs of the newly evolving socio-economic groups in the country. Otherwise, university education must necessarily suffer from stagnation. Besides, there is also the corresponding need for the restructuring of courses so that students may be enabled to become productive members of society. For the fulfilment of these objectives, the following programmes will be adopted :

Admission Policy. Because of the excessive expansion in general education, colleges are suffering from extreme over crowding, which then becomes the cause of declining standards as well as increasing unemployment. Hence, caution must be adopted. At present, the Indian economy is not strong enough to shoulder the burden of providing higher education to every individual who seeks it.

The utility of any procedure for selection is often doubted because there is a lack of a desirable objective evaluation. The middle and upper classes in the urban areas will also be adversely affected by such a policy because the opportunities for employment will also not be generated in the same proportion. Hence, there is every need for the greatest care in framing a policy on selection and admission. Hence, the following policy should be adopted for admission :

1. At the graduate level, in order to stop the flood and to turn it into various streams, it is desirable that students be given admission to specific colleges, correspondence courses, etc. In addition, students should be admitted to examinations as private candidates. These streams should be 50,20,20,10 respectively. Later on, this should convert itself into short-term or self-education.

2. The standard and recognition of self education and short-term education should be the same as in the formal education.

3. Since self education and part-time education differ in their nature from formal education, some central institution should be established to organise it.

4. Institutions granting self education and part-time education should also keep in view the languages of the state and the country.

In implementing these policies, it is essential to pay attention to the student's intellectual prowess as well as his other activities, while granting admission to a college. At the post-graduate level, admission should be granted only after considering the question of employability. A system of hostel facilities and scholarships is an inalienable part of this policy.

Institutional Expansion: Colleges. The rapidly growing student population compels the authorities to set up new colleges, but for this, it is essential to have a national policy. If we have such a policy, we can control the uneconomic institutions. It is necessary both to have specific rules regarding admissions in colleges and also to implement them, though it is difficult to create suitable norms. Only the concerned universities can give any sensible advice on this subject. However, the following points should be kept in mind in creating new colleges-

1. New institutions should be established only after a survey so that the existing institutions are not adversely affected.
2. The ideal size of a college should first be determined so that the new college does not become an uneconomic entity.

New Universities. New universities, too, should be opened only with the utmost caution because the setting up of a new university, of the existing pattern and size, involves an expenditure of Rs. 4 to 5 crores, apart from an annual expenditure of Rs. 1 crore. Hence; before making financial provisions, due consideration must be given to the academic, material and economic aspect of any new university. But, the truth of the matter is, that it is the political aspect which actually dominates and guides the establishment of universities. However, the following policy should be adopted in this regard.

1. A new university should be based upon the academic needs of the community.
2. New universities should not bring about a shuffling of academic eminence, administrative ability and money.

3. Arrangements for post-graduate education should be made at post-graduate centres which are suitably equipped with libraries, laboratories, etc. Gradually, these centres can themselves assume the form of a university.

4. It is essential to set up new universities which differ from the traditional ones. Such experiments have been conducted in foreign countries. In India, too, Open Universities should completely open their doors for everyone.

5. Graduate teaching, post-graduate education and research should be separated from each other. Arrangements for postgraduate education should be in keeping with needs of the community and the facilities available at the centre. It is graduate education alone which is a separate entity, and which in reality, is called a university. Besides, the per capita expenditure in it is also very high.

Autonomous Colleges. There is one school of thought which opines that some good colleges should be converted into autonomous colleges which will have the freedom to make their own rules, curriculum, and to conduct their own examinations. These colleges will make use of modern techniques of teaching. As these colleges gain in experience, more such colleges will be created.

The Process of Evaluation. The need for an improvement in the system of examination has been felt for a long time. In 1949, the Radha krishnan Commission had pointed out that if no improvements were made in the existing system of examination, it would mean that university education was only being played with. The University Grants Commission has made some important recommendations on this issue, the more important among them being :

1. The evaluation should be done by the teacher who teaches.

2. The result of continuous and semester evaluation should be separately displayed in the result card or mark sheet.

3. There should be generalisation in the standard of each institution.

4. Each course and subject should be separately evaluated. If a student fails in one subject, he should be required to re-appear only in that subject, not in all.

5. The ability of students should be evaluated at regular intervals, instead of waiting only for the final examination.

6. The evaluation should be expressed in terms of A,B,C,D, etc., grades, instead of marks.

7. The basis of evaluation of the student should be a test of aptitude taken at the time of admission. Admission tests have also proved of use in this direction.

8. Examinations of the graduate level should be conducted by a Central Authority. This authority should formulate question papers which make it possible to evaluate creative thinking, awareness, etc.

9. Students who fail in the examination should study through the correspondence courses, Open universities, etc.

10. The University Grants Commission should call for the examination papers of colleges and universities and determine their standards.

Development of Courses or Curriculum. At the university level, the curricula are rigid and narrow. For instance, if a student wishes to take an M.Sc., degree in Physics, he must necessarily start studying Physics from class 9. The combinations of subjects which a student may select are inflexible. Most universities do not allow an arts graduate to study science. Hence, in universities, the courses of study need to be reorganised on the lines of the Interdisciplinary. Approach apart from the introduction of vocational courses at this level.

Student Unrest. The very noticeable degree of student unrest prevailing today is evidence of the shortcomings of the educational system. This tendency is almost universal, and it has emerged as a result of such varied factors as generation gap, socio-economic factors, the inattention of parents towards their children, gradual erosion of traditional values, the conflict arising from social change, ambition, frustration, injustice, inequality, etc. The present situation is Three

Dimensional- (1) improvement in the general atmosphere, hard work, social justice, clean conduct, and service, (2) superior educational opportunities leading to development of creative power, (3) a challenge for youth. Youth is a period of ideals and idealism, and hence the power of youth must be turned towards social and economic development.

Higher Education and Finance. For the last 32 years, universities have been receiving grants and economic assistance from the Central and State governments. In addition, they enjoy an income from fees and endowments. In order to increase their financial resources, it is necessary to consider the use of private resources. In the existing system of fees, there is a need for greater aid. If the fees are increased, the poorer sections will be denied higher education. Hence, it is suggested that while fees at the post-graduate and vocational levels may be raised, the scholarship programme should be accelerated.

Development of Libraries. The development of libraries in the country should be based on the recommendations of the Sinha Committee (1957). In addition to the National Library, Calcutta, regional and district level central libraries should also be created. Emphasis should also be laid upon the continuous and regular use of these libraries.

Production of Books. At the university level, there is a shortage of good books, in requisite number, in the mother tongue of the students and the regional language. In the fifth five-year plan, provisions have been made to overcome this deficit. Arrangements have been made for the production of original text-books as well as the translation of good books. The National Book Trust is giving grants for good books.

Technical Education. High-level technical education is the foundation for the progress of the country. Hence, technical institutions should also work towards (1) counselling, and (2) solution of problems. This will strengthen the country's industrial development. It is necessary to maintain a continuous liaison between the economic sector of the country and technical education. It should also keep in touch with small-scale industry. The fifth plan should prove the pivot of this programme.

Reorientation of Courses. The introduction of new courses, such as organisation and management, research, design development, production, surveying, examination, evaluation, repair and maintenance, assembling, etc., and the re-structuring of the educational programme should be such that these have a direct relationship with the country's manpower. In technical education, the degree should be directly linked with production, planning and organisation, while at the diploma level, it should be related to inspection, workshop, etc.

In addition, there is also the need for a programme for the extension and expansion of technical education, and through such a programme, technical education acquires greater responsibility in numerous spheres such as regional planning, design development, quality control, town planning, water supply, sewerage system, electrification of villages, etc.

Continuing Education. In this concept, education has been defined as a continuously flowing, never-ending stream, and accordingly, it has been thought that every individual should get opportunities for education on a full-time, part-time or self-education basis.

In view of the new socio-economic conditions, which have come to exist in the country, it has become necessary to bring about changes in the existing pattern of higher education to make it viable in the new situation. The following points have been taken into consideration in the fifth plan:-

Consolidation and Improvement. The following programmes have been formulated for the growth of higher education in the fifth plan- (i) Providing grants and aid in other forms to university department and selected colleges for the development of post-graduate and research education, development of computer techniques, etc. (ii) Establishing Pace-setting Centres to act as centres of continuing education. (iii) Granting scholarships and research assistance liberally. (iv) Developing innovative courses, seminars, conferences, housing facilities attractive scales of pay, etc. (v) Giving help to the concerned universities on the basis of their achievement. (vi) Establishing new universities of the affiliating type.

Employment Orientation. Provisions have been made for linking education with employment, introducing vocational courses, research and practical schemes in higher education, and setting up employment and advisory bureau in universities and colleges.

Student Service. In view of the student unrest that keeps on erupting from time to time, arrangements have been made for initiating a student service in the fifth plan. In this connection, hostel facilities, play grounds, equipment, guest house, etc, are being created.

Additional Enrolment. It was estimated that by 1973-74, the enrolment would be 35.47 lakhs, and by 1978-79 54.51 lakhs, which implies that additional enrolment should be approximately 19.04 lakhs.

At present, facilities for part-time education and self-education are available on a limited scale. Some universities have set up correspondence courses, while a few universities allow candidates of specific categories to participate in their examinations as private candidates. In the fifth plan, the facilities for part-time education and self-education are expected to be of the order indicated on next page.

In the fifth plan, the per student and per unit teacher expenses for the P.U.C., Inter, Graduate and Post-graduate levels will be 353.80, 90.95, and 200.75 Rs. per annum. In this, the ratio (in the above order) will be 1: 251: 20, and 1:12. In addition, the expenditure upon other programmes such as improvement in existing facilities, development of research, setting up of computers, correspondence course institute, setting up of new universities, advanced study centres, autonomous colleges, education and productivity, aid to special colleges, adult education, student service, housing for teachers, hostels, etc., will be Rs. 526.09 crores. As a whole, provisions for Rs. 310 crores have been made on an inter-sectoral basis. This provision has been made out of the fund of Rs. 2200 crores set apart for education.

New Approach

It is quite self-evident that our existing system of education is almost completely alienated from real life. In it, there is a vast gulf between subjects and the objectives. It is, therefore, completely incapable of achieving the objective of national development. For examples :

1. Our education does not attach due significance to agriculture, neither does it attract talent and capable individuals towards agriculture in our universities.
2. The major goal before the country is the goal of economic development. In order to achieve it, it is essential to link education with production.
3. Schools and colleges are almost completely indifferent towards the task of nation-building.
4. Instead of fostering the spirit of national and social unity, the educational institutions today are encouraging divisive tendencies, casteism and political strife. The difference between the rich and the poor is palpable in our educational institutions.
5. Almost no importance is given to the generation of ethical, religious and spiritual values.

The Education Commission has suggested the adoption of an interdisciplinary approach only to overcome the defects pointed out above. According to Commission, there is no bigger or more efficacious instrument than a change in the nature of education. It should be linked with education. It should be made to fulfil the ambitions and satisfy the needs of the people. It should become a means for the achievement of national ideals through social, economic and cultural change. This can be done, if :

1. Education is linked with production.
2. It develops social and national unity, strengthens democracy and becomes acceptable to the people as the right mode of life.
3. Contributes to the process of modernization.
4. Forms the character of the people through growth of social ethical and spiritual values.

All these facts are profoundly interrelated. None of them can be achieved in the absence of the others.

According to Brubacker, "The contemporary spirit favours interdisciplinary study by actual terms of scholars from diverse fields of study."

According to Dr. G. Chaurasia, "It is universally accepted that there can be not better plan for improving the quality of teacher education than by integrating content and methods, i.e., through the interdisciplinary approach."

These two definitions together clarify the nature of interdisciplinary approach.

New Courses

At present, our universities suffer from the lack of a suitable curriculum. According to Sridhar Nath Mukerji, the most serious problem in our universities is that of providing a balanced curriculum. It should be so organised that each student can receive training according to his own interest and aptitude. It must provide suitable opportunities for the adaptation and adjustments of the Misfits and the Unfits, so that their personality may undergo complete development.

At the university level, the problem of curriculum arises because of the subjects taught at the secondary level. There should be as great an expansion of the subjects of study as possible. Arts, science, agriculture, technology, fine arts, domestic science, engineering and many other subjects should be recognised and build up into components. 'But this kind of restructuring can be done only, if :

1. The ideal is transformed into practice.
2. The student is given subjects to study which accord with his ability, interest and aptitude.
3. Maximum opportunities are made available for the misfits and the unfits.

In view of all these circumstances, it can be said that the solution to this problem lies in adopting the interdisciplinary approach. Life, today, has become very complex. Complexity is never due to one single factor. Numerous factors react together to create complexity, and the result is that the individual's problem is viewed from a single, biased viewpoint. Therefore, in order to bring in a liberal and electric approach, the curriculum of schools can be looked at in the light of such subjects as educational psychology, sociology, humanism, anthropology, comparative religious study, etc. In the opinion of the Education Commission, special efforts are necessary for encouraging interdisciplinary students in those universities in which there are sufficient teachers in related disciplines. For this, new combinations of subjects, new methods of co-operation between various institutions, and a new class of teachers will be required.

In this connection, the Education Commission had said that in order to study the problems of education in all their complexity, interdisciplinary study between the departments of education, sociology, psychology, comparative religion, economics, public administration and law, is essential. Every department for a particular subject in a university for example physics, chemistry, or history, studies the problems of school curricula and methods of teaching in its own field. At the pre-graduate and post-graduate levels, the various curricula of education can be brought into close relationship with curricula of other subjects.

The objective of the interdisciplinary approach is to give practical shape to the knowledge of various subjects. The Education Commission has clarified the idea by giving the example of education as a subject. Universities should make special effort towards developing this approach.

The interdisciplinary approach has various forms. Some scholars believe that the introduction of many subjects into a single subject constitutes an interdisciplinary approach. For them studying the concepts of economics, sociology, politics and philosophy under the, general heading of knowledge constitutes the interdisciplinary approach. But, I do not agree with the interpretation. If a student studies drawing and Hindi in addition to education at the graduate level. Education can teach him the right methods of teaching Hindi and drawing. In this way, the subjects he studies will become more dynamic and useful.

Some thought has been given to interdisciplinary studies in other subjects also. For example, in such subjects as physics, chemistry, geophysics and physics, mathematics and économics, interrelated or articulated courses can be useful and suitable.

Reflecting upon the interdisciplinary approach, the Kothari Commission came to the conclusion that special efforts should be made in universities to adopt the interdisciplinary approach. In particular, such efforts should be made in those departments which are closely related to each other. For this, it will be necessary to offer a new combination of subjects, and also to seek the assistance and co-operation of various institutions and the teachers of new subjects. For example, one may take education. For a soluuion of its problems and complexities, an interdisciplinary approach which brings into close relationships such subjects as education and psychology, sociology, comparative religions, economics, public administration and law, can be employed. Every department of a university, such as physics, chemistry, or history can work on school curricula. The curriculum of education can be linked with the courses in other subjects, irrespective of whether these subjects are being taught at the degree, or post-graduate levels. It is for this reason that the Education Commission insisted upon the setting up of an education faculty in four, or five universities.

In order to make the interdisciplinary approach a success, the Education Commission sought to establish Education Departments in four or five universities through the assistance of the UGC. These departments will perform the following functions :

1. Making arrangements for the study of degree and post-graduate subjects in education.
2. Initiating training courses in vocational education at various levels, such as pre-secondary, primary and secondary levels.
3. Introducing extension services in some of the training institutions at every level.
4. Organising summer institutes and in-service courses in various subjects.
5. Exploring the possibilities of research into the syllabus and other spheres of education, after establishing contact with schools at various levels.
6. Ensuring the development of research in education.

Dr. Kothari clarified the concept of interdisciplinary approach in one of his speeches. He said that in our country there had been lack of contact between university teachers and school teachers at the primary and secondary level. But, now this contact was being created through summer schools. In this view, education is a single structure with three storeys-primary, secondary and higher education. The weight of higher education rests on the foundation of primary education, but if the lower storey is weak, the structure cannot remain standing for long. If we want to raise this structure even higher, we must strengthen the foundation. In other words, the primary education level. In our country, we must reiterate the fact that these three storeys constitute a single structure, that it should, therefore, be possible for the teachers to communicate from one storey to another. The primary teacher should have facilities for going to the university, but if he finds that he does not enjoy working in the university, it should be possible for him to return to the primary level. It is wrong to assume that those in the highest storey, the university level, are superior or those in the lowest storey, the primary level. Who ever does his work efficiently and devotedly is good, and whoever does his own work well should be regarded as progressive.

We can say that the interdisciplinary approach is an excellent means of creating harmony between various levels and faculties, and also for giving the individual an opportunity to study with complete freedom as well as act with freedom in life. It helps in relating education to production, bringing about the comprehensive development of personality, and it also obviates any need to formulate a long-term plan for any specific study. The truth of the matter is that knowledge is a unity, and in order to maintain its unitary nature, it is essential to adopt the interdisciplinary approach.

Academic Liberty

Indian universities are gifts of the state; they come into existence by an Act of Parliament or a state legislative assembly. These bodies formulate the nature and functions of a university in elaborate detail. It is constituted as an institution with a clear jurisdiction. Although the state government assures that the university's activities will be in keeping with the Act, this is not inevitable. In recent years, many examples have come to light in which the government has not stopped itself from amending the relevant acts in order to destroy the autonomy of universities. According to Dr. Sridharnath Mukerjee, in recent years there was a considerable debate on the autonomy of universities. Government had developed a tendency to interfere in educational or academic matters. There was evidence to show that political pressures were being employed.

The autonomy of universities applies to three areas : (1) selection of students, (2) progress and promotion of teachers, (3) selection of a curriculum for study, the methods of teaching, problems of .research, etc.

In thinking about the autonomy of universities, the following points should be kept in mind : (1) There should be an interrelationship between various departments of university, the teachers of colleges and the students. (2) One university should be in touch with another through the University Grants Commission and ultimately through the Inter-university Bureau. (3) There must be relationship between the Central and State Governments.

A second kind of autonomy is inherent in the nature of a university. The fundamental principle of autonomy in this sphere is that there should be academic achievements, liberal administration and organisational discipline. There should be a balance among the academic workers.

Radhakrishnan Commission Report

The university commission became aware of the numerous defects in the organisation of universities, and felt that the main cause was the lack of autonomy in universities. It therefore, put forward the following suggestions-

1. Universities should be put in the Concurrent List.
2. The Central Government should maintain contact with the universities for the following things— (i) finances, (ii) harmony in facilities for special studies, (iii) national policies, (iv) able administration, (v) creating a link between universities and national research laboratories, scientific surveys, etc.

3. A central grants commission should be appointed for giving grants to universities.
4. Government colleges should be converted into representative colleges of the university.
5. Each university should have the following officials :

Visitor. The President of India

Chancellor. The Governor of the State (Central universities are not subject to this provision).

Vice-chancellor. He should be a paid officer working on a full-time basis. He will be appointed on the recommendation of the Management.

Senators. This should have maximum number of 120, consisting of 40 teachers, 40 teachers from affiliated college, 40 external members.

Executive Council. It should have a maximum of 25 members.

Academic Council. It should have not more than 25 members. In addition there should be faculty, study council, finance council, selection committee.

Kothari Commission Report

Kothari Commission believes teaching, research and propagation to be the main tasks of universities. In general, autonomy is taken to mean a chain of responsibilities, acceptance of functions, and creation of economic and performative efficiency. Universities should create modes of working suited to their structure and organisation. In addition, the UGC. should take steps for proper administration and organisation of universities.

The Kothari Commission has made the following recommendations regarding the autonomy of universities :

1. The autonomy of the university is inherent in its power to appoint, and promote teachers, choose its method of teaching, select students for admission, determine the curriculum and take the examination.

2. The non-academic individuals in the university exist only to give suitable representation to every class and interest, not to allow them to dominate the university's activities. Encouragement should be given for the formation of study groups to look into the problem of organisation, management or administration.

3. The position and autonomy of colleges should be given a place at the university level.

4. In every department, there should be a joint committee of students and teachers. Above this, at the institutional level, there should be another committee to consider problems.

5. The university should grant autonomy to its departments. Economic matters should be handed over to a committee, headed by the head of department.

6. The UGC and the Inter-university Board should constitute a committee for taking decisions about the number of students, the curriculum, etc., and it should arouse public awareness so as to impart strength and firmness to the autonomy of the university.

7. The universities should maintain their autonomy by giving rise to a superior academic class in society.

Bertrand Russell once opined that, in reality, as soon as free thought comes to an end, irrespective of whether the cause is lack of courage or absence of discipline, unfair propaganda and authoritarianism begins to flourish. Hence, the stifling of criticism is a far more serious matter than many people imagine. Instead, of giving rise to unity, the process of social purpose thrusts a kind of dull monotonous unity on the whole of society. It is a matter of great sorrow that people occupying positions of authority and responsibility fail to experience this vital truth.

What is seen in India today is that the police frequently invades the university campuses, and fearsome pressures are exerted to ensure that governmental directives are obeyed. In such a situation, can autonomy continue to exist at all?

In order to maintain autonomy, it is essential to get rid of the following shortcomings:

1. In Indian universities, there is a lack of mobility. Students, too, generally lack any inner inspiration or drive. The stink of officialdom pervades the whole atmosphere. Students resort to repressing their juniors and make no attempt to develop their own talents. These are major drawbacks.
2. Members of the senate of the university do not fulfill their responsibility and the syndicate often takes advantage of this situation.
3. Even the academic councils are subjected to pressure in the determination of the curriculum.
4. Universities are also found to be suffering from structural defects.
5. Undesirable pressure also comes into play in matters of admission.

Dr. Lakshmiswami Mudaliar did not want the kind of autonomy often spoken of by people. If the truth be said, it is only the wearer who knows where the shoe pinches. The existing autonomy is no autonomy at all. The education ministry sends numerous directives, and one secretary after another instructs the university in what should be implemented and what should not. The directives issued are such that if they are obeyed, the officials of the university become similar to the characters of the ass, the child and the man portrayed in *Aesop's Fables*.

Stressing partial autonomy, Dr. C.A Deshmukh said that autonomy often becomes responsible for disorder and a defective administration. This happens only in the absence of control. Some universities have become transformed into centres of internal jealousy and politics. But universities should not take the nature of some of the additional departments of the education ministry. At the same time, the Central, and State Governments should seets it that they maintain sufficient authority with themselves to ensure that the grants given to universities are utilised efficiently. What is needed today is to win the co-operation of the community in maintaining the autonomy of universities. The degrees they grant should prepare the individuals for academic leadership and creative activities. Our universities should face the challenge of the time in order to satisfy the needs of a changing society. Only then can their autonomy be maintained intact.

Issue of Autonomy

In recent years, the pressure of government influence upon the autonomy of universities has been increasing, and one Act of the Government of Uttar Pradesh has practically put an end to it. By virtue of this Act, it has been decided that the Chancellor and the Finance Officer will be government officials. The government claims that it gives grants for higher education, and hence, it must keep its check upon it. The appointment of Vice-chancellors of Universities has also given rise to shameful situations. The Inter-University Board has expressed the view that the State and Central Governments give some grants to universities only on this condition. Changes which bring about a complete modification in the organisation, method of working and efficiency of a university can not be justified, particularly if they lower the dignity of the concerned university in the eyes of the academic world. The situation of a legally established university is similar to that of a legally established political administration and so the mere fact that the legislatures of such a government have the right to make laws should not be converted into a power which can be used to undermine the dignity of Indian universities or to make impossible their proper administration :

The committee of autonomy of the Inter-University Board has declared that on the basis of universally accepted principle that universities provide the intellectual leadership of the community, universities are the capital for social and economic progress. It is of the utmost importance that universities should be assisted in developing and improving their personality, without being subjected to external pressures. The maximum possible autonomy is essential for universities in their functioning and development, in view of the nation's vested interest in progress. It is equally essential that attention should be drawn towards tendencies which hinder this objective. These tendencies should be countered through effective policies. In view of these ideas, the committee put forth the following recommendations-

1. The President of India should be the Visitor of each university.
2. The tradition of appointing Governors as the Chancellors of the universities in the state may, in general be accepted as good but only in so far as the Governors, in their individual capacity, perform this function. They should take the advice of the state government only when they consider it unavoidable.
3. Legislators may discuss the educational policy but they should avoid subjects which fall within the jurisdiction of the university itself.
4. No minister should be allowed to occupy any salaried post in the university.
5. The practice of issuing ordinances and directives to universities is not appropriate, because they are violative of the autonomy of a university. The officer issuing the directives is in no position to make a useful contribution in the educational context.
6. The conditions of service of the Chancellor should not be unattractive and insulting.
7. The judiciary should accept universities as an area of autonomous public life.
8. Finance Commissions should distribute money to the universities in an equitable manner.
9. Ideal ordinances must be prepared.

Keeping in mind all these factors, any external control which destroys autonomy should be vigorously opposed. If this is not done, then higher education will undoubtedly become subservient to external forces, and lose its peace for ever.

Past Experience

The Kothari Commission has suggested the introduction of work experience at every level of education. Its aim is that the nature of education should be transformed in order to bring about social, economic and cultural transformation of Indian society. The utility of work experience was evaluated at the general and vocational levels of education. According to the Commission, "We define work experience as. participation in productive work in school, in the home, in a workshop, on a farm, in a factory, or in any other productive situation."

Work experience has been accepted as an integral part of education. The question we now face is: why the need for such educational programmes was felt, soon after independence? The reason is that the system of education prevailing in the country has produced a class of educated persons who are not dependent upon themselves, who have no faith in hard work. A nation's progress becomes impossible if the people become indifferent towards work. In view of this, the idea of work experience was developed so as to take the nation to the peak of progress and development.

The Education Commission has analysed the country's problems, in the educational context, in the following terms- (1) our education is not oriented (2) Our education is too bookish and inclined to take the student far away from the realities of life. (3) our students have made a negligible contribution to national development. The Commission has sought remedy to these defects through the concept of work experience.

1. "As another programme to relate education to life and productivity we recommend that work-experience should be introduced as an integral part of all education — general or vocational."

2. "Work experience which involves participation in some form of productive work under conditions approximating to those found in real life situations should be introduced as an integral part of education at all stages."

The Commission has stressed the fact that the productive work should take place in conditions similar to those obtaining in real life.

Later Experience

An important fact regarding work experience is that it is based on self-determination. Some important assumptions basic to it are the following:-

1. In every kind of work experience, physical labour is inherent necessarily. Hence, such activities as book-keeping or working in an office do not fall within its sphere.

2. Work experience is itself inspiring, i.e., the work should itself possess some motivating elements so that the students may willingly become involved in it. Work experience should not be thrust forcibly upon the student.

3. Work experience is essential for the proper education of the child. It helps him in understanding and solving problems, and at the same time makes him aware of the productive process contributing to national development.

4. Work experience is forward looking, i.e., it should be intimately related to the scientific industrial and technological methods of production. Work experience should give the student not only the experience of working with his hands but also an acquaintance with the progressive techniques of production employed in the country. This principle also implies that the method of working should progress and improve continuously.

5. The work experience should be in accord with the actual working conditions in real life, i.e., the student's activity should take place in exactly the same conditions as those obtaining in real life. In other words, the student should work in the same manner in which India's farmers and workers perform their functions.

6. Work experience is inalienably related to production, and so, as far as possible, work experience should also give rise to income.

7. Work experience should be in accordance with the student's age and his physical and mental capacities.

8. Work experience should also be in consonance with local conditions. For example, at places where bamboos are available, the work experience should centre on industries producing goods from bamboos.

9. For the next few years, work experience must be accepted as an extra-curricular activity, and not a necessary part of the curriculum. Hence, it cannot be evaluated in terms of marks, and thus, it should also not influence a student's passage from one class to the next.

Utility of Experience

1. The most important objective of work experience is to accustom the child to physical labour, to develop in him the ability to do physical work for some time continuously, and to make him a participant in the country's economic production through physical labour.
2. Another objective of work experience should be that the child should be able to earn something by his own labour so that he may share the burden of his education, which his parents have to bear.
3. A third objective of work experience is to acquaint the student with the world of employment, agriculture, industry and other pecuniary activities. The student should become conscious of the fact that, in the years ahead, science and technology will play a very important part in every kind of activity taking the form of employment.
4. The purpose of work experience is not to prepare the child for a particular profession. Instead, the purpose is to develop in him those abilities which may facilitate his choice of a profession.
5. Its aim is to make the child conscious of the fact that whatever work an individual does at his own level contributes to the productive effort of the whole nation.
6. Finally, we must. also ever keep before us a long-term. objective. Through work experience we have to eradicate the differences between the educated and the uneducated and thereby make steady progress towards our cherished goal of a ciassless society, a society in which differences of high and low will be unknown.

Guidelines

1. In preparing a programme of work experience, it must be remembered that a scheme involving vast expenditure is not to be considered. Instead, the programme must envisage only the maximum utilisation of the facilities commonly available in schools.

2. Every activity indulged in must have a vocational basis. The income or production obtained from work experience, must, in every case, be more the expenditure incurred on it, whether it be agricultural or industrial activity.

3. The profit from work experience should flow to those who have worked for it. In other words, the cost of the raw materials involved should be deducted from the income, and the profit handed over to the students.

4. Any scheme of work experience should not be made compulsory for any school.

5. Work experience will not be a part of the curriculum. Hence, arrangements will have to be made in the time-table to ensure that the regular teaching time-table is not disturbed or reduced.

6. The division of time in work experience will be in accordance with the nature of the activity. For example, in agricultural activity, it will be necessary to devote 2 or 3 days continuously at the time of sowing or harvesting whereas in wood-working for instance, two periods of 90 minutes duration in the week may prove adequate.

7. In places where industrial training institutes or polytechnic institutions are available, the retired teachers from such institutions can be made use of. With the help of these institutions, some general tool kits can be prepared for use in work experience.

8. Wherever opportunity is available, the use of technological means should be taught in work experience.

9. In rural areas, where schools do not have their own land, students can obtain work experience by working on the farms

of private individuals at a time when there is additional demand for labour, for instance, during the sowing and harvesting seasons.

10. Children who enjoy facilities for obtaining work experience at home should be encouraged to learn the family occupation. If the school, college or university can assist the student in improving this occupation, it should extend its help.

11. From the educational viewpoint, it is desirable that the child should be made aware of every activity concerned with a particular mode of production so that he may develop the capacity to produce the complete product through his own effort.

12. Work experience should be job-oriented. The term 'job', in this context, should be taken to refer to one complete unit of work in any occupation, for instance, varnishing of furniture, joining together various parts to produce a complete chair, carpentry, weaving, etc.

Work Experience in the Fifth Plan. In its report, the Steering Group of the Planning Commission has said that work experience should be a part of the educational programme at every stage. Student should have knowledge of the work-a-day world. This programme can be effective by introducing students to the real conditions of work, putting them in touch with public and private producers, etc. In order to take this process a step further conditions favouring work experience should be created by creating contact with factories, farms, laboratories, workshops, etc.

Finances for Universities

An activity can be performed efficiently only if the money invested in it is adequate. In education, we find that standards have declined owing to lack of funds. Money has necessarily to be spent upon the salaries of teachers, student welfare, libraries, curriculum and other educational activities.

The Radhakrishnan Commission has offered the following suggestions for strengthening the economy of universities :

1. The state must accept its responsibility of providing financial aid to higher education.
2. Individual colleges should be given aid for constructing buildings and other activities.
3. The income-tax laws should be reformed so that the money invested in education should be free from taxation.
4. The government should provide additional grants where ever necessary.
5. A Wants Commission should be appointed for determining the grants to be given to educational institutions.

The Kothari Commission has offered the following suggestions for putting the finances of universities on a sound footing-

1. State governments should conduct themselves, with reference to universities, in such a manner that necessary financial resources should be available to universities for performing their necessary functions. If the state governments take the advice of the UGC, it will prove beneficial for both.
2. Whenever the need for caution in financial matter is felt, or whenever there is a need for suitable economy, it is necessary to ensure that rules are simplified so that progress and efficiency are not hindered. The commission admitted that it is difficult to make a valid and accurate projection of the expenditure in higher education, but it suggested that Rs. 42,22,021 should be spent on it by 1985-86.

For this, we must consider many angles.

1. Central universities should obtain money from the University Grants Commission.
2. The UGC should be authorised to give grants to universities in the states. If the state governments fail to give adequate grants, the UGC should compensate the difference. The UGC provides complete grants for some activities and matching grants for

others, but the matching grants from the state governments are often not available on time.

3. State governments finance the state universities in the following manner :

    (1) Matching grants for the funds provided by the UGC for development activities in the sphere of student welfare.
    (2) Non-plan grants for the development of the university.
    (3) Grants for the authorised expenditure.

4. The Commission has suggested the following improvements in the practice of giving grants :

    (1) State governments should give adequate financial aid to universities. and also give them freedom to spend this money.
    (2) The UGC should provide the necessary facilities for development to the state universities.
    (3) The UGC and the state governments should share equally all developmental expenditure.
    (4) Universities should be given a block grant as a collective whole.
    (5) Universities should be set free from governmental audit and interference.

Many interesting facts have come to light after surveys into the financial affairs of many universities. In recent years, the central government has played a very important role in the development of higher education, and, as a result, the amount realised from fees, securities and other sources has declined. Hence, it is necessary to think seriously and extensively on donations, fees and other sources of revenue. In the existing system of fees, a subsidy is inherent in the fee. The subsidy is made available to every student, irrespective of his financial position. If, on the other hand, the fee is raised, it will mean shutting the doors of education for the poorer classes. This will lead to student unrest and indiscipline. Hence, it will be better to increase the fees at the post-graduate and vocational levels and thereby facilitate an increase in the number of scholarships. In addition a development fee should also be charged.

Further Promotion

Our country is a nation of diversities and unity. Though education is a state subject, the central administration extends its co-operation to ensure the development of education. Hence, it is necessary to harmonise various interests in defining the nature, standards, curriculum, etc., of education. The following institutions are responsible for the development of higher education :

1. The Inter-University Board.
2. The University Grants Commission.
3. State university grants commissions, National Council of Educational Research and Training. The organisation and mode of working of these three institutions is described in the following paragraphs.

The Inter-University Board came into existence as the result of a decision taken at the first Conference of Vice-Chancellors in Simla in May 1924. At that time, India, Ceylon and Burma were its members. Today, its membership consists of 47 Indian universities, universities of Ceylon and five Indian Institutes of Technology. In addition some institutions of the stature of a university are also its associate members. This institution has now been renamed the Association of Indian Universities.

Functions of the I.U.B. The prime function of this board is to bring about harmony at various levels of higher education. For this, it performs the following functions:

1. It provides the vice-chancellor's a suitable stage for the discussion of common problems.
2. It lays emphasis upon the determination of standards and the framing of rules for their implementation.
3. It provides the government as well as the UGC with a valuable source of information concerning the problems of higher education.
4. In the capacity of a representative it brings about to the government and the public at large the views of universities.

The United Kingdom Committee of Vice-Chancellors defined the functions in the following ways. It said that, despite, this board offers recommendations to universities for formulating general policies. It acquaints the education ministries and University Grants Committees with the reactions of universities and also with the suggestions and ideas being considered by the universities. In addition, the committee of vice-chancellors itself establishes contact with the UGC or other institutions concerned with universities.

In addition to these activities, the IUB also performs the following functions :

1. Functions as a department of information for the International University Organisation.
2. Arranging the exchange of professors.
3. Providing for communication and collation in order to give a boost to the activities of universities.
4. Giving recognition to the curricula, degrees and diplomas of Indian universities in foreign countries.
5. Sending representatives to the Imperial conference on higher education.
6. Solving disputes regarding the recognition of degrees.

The Kothari Commission's view on the I.U.B. are as follows:

1. The work of the IUB should be organised and its membership should be made more effective. Every university falling within the purview of IUB UGC Act must be made a member of the board.
2. At present, the membership of this institution depends upon the institution itself, i.e., it may allow a university to become a member, or refuse membership. Similarly, the universities are also free to seek or avoid its membership. This is the main weakness of the IUB Each university should automatically get membership of this Board.

3. Today, it is general practice for every university to grant recognition to the certificates of every other university. The Board should make it a duty to ensure that the degrees, certificates and diplomas of Indian universities are accepted by foreign universities. This is an important task because many of our talented and brilliant students face difficulties in getting admission in foreign universities because the degree of their university is not recognised by the foreign university, to which they are seeking admission.

4. The Council also functions as a clearing house of information for the universities. However, the Board should also set up committees for providing guidance and advice on research, examinations, etc.

It is undoubtedly true that this Board does play a significant role in establishing harmony between the various aspects of higher education.

Central UGC

The University Grants Commission was created by an act of Parliament in 1956, on the basis of the recommendations of the Radhakrishnan Commission, which defined its functions in the following terms :

1. Creating the interest of the central government in the problems of higher education.
2. Examining the financial position of universities and making necessary arrangements with the help of the central government.
3. Making arrangements for the distribution of grants to universities.
4. If and when necessary, giving advice regarding the setting up of new universities.
5. Finding out the curiosities being harboured by the universities as well as the government.

6. Advising a university on such matters as the recognition of a degree.

7. Guiding the university with regard to development and spread of higher education.

8. Performing all other tasks contributing to the spread and improvement of higher education.

Today, higher education is divided into numerous sections and departments, but between them there is little contact. The UGC has to maintain contact with almost 130 universities and to provide them financial aid from the funds of the central government.

The Kothari Commission has come to feel that every activity concerned with higher education should fall within the purview of the UGC Agriculture, Medicine, etc., are directed by their respective ministries, though they are integral parts of higher education. It is for this reason that the Commission has accepted the recommendations of a committee on higher education, composed of Members of Parliament. According to it, the whole stream of education should be regarded as a single composite unit, for example, vocational education cannot be separated from general education. Hence, it is necessary that the jurisdiction of the UGC should extend over agriculture, medicine, engineering, etc., also.

The Kothari Commission has suggested the setting up of similar commissions at the state level also. Other institutions of a similar nature should be set up to create harmony between agriculture, medicine, engineering, etc., to create harmony between them and general education.

The Kothari Commission visualises the functions of the UGC in the following terms-

1. Higher education in its entirety should be regarded as a unit and the UGC should direct it.

2. Institutions similar to should UGC be created for education in agriculture, medicine, engineering, etc.

3. The membership of the UGC should be between 12 and 15, one third of whom should be high officials of the government.
4. The UGC should set up permanent committees to perform its various functions.
5. The UGC should be given adequate financial resources.
6. University grants commissions should be set up in the states also.

Mechanisms of this kind contribute to the development of higher education. They also bring about the growth of a proper material outlook which lays the right stress on freedom of thought, liberality and reality.

State UGCs

State governments have also set up University Grant Commissions for the development of higher education. Uttar Pradesh, Bihar and some other states have already done this. Their functions are :

1. Making arrangements for the necessary grants to colleges and universities.
2. Informing the government of the new expenditure in higher education.
3. Considering the development and reorganisation of universities and colleges.
4. Advising the state government about the setting up of new universities.
5. Synthesizing teaching and research.
6. Keeping an account of the property or assets of universities and colleges.
7. Advising the state government on academic legal and administrative problems of higher education.

NCERT

The National Council of Education Research and Training came into existence as an autonomous body in 1961. In the same year, it took under its wing the Institute of Education (1947), Central Bureau of Text-Book Research (1954). All India Council for Secondary Education (1955, 1959), National Institute of Basic Education (1959), National Fundamental Centre (1956) and the National Institute of Audio-Visual Education (1959). All these various institutions had been created for the development and improvement of school education.

The entire expenditure of the Council is borne by the government. It functions as the academic wing of the education ministry.

Functions of the Council. The functions of the Council are- (1) Organising studies, surveys and research connected with school education, (2) Defining pre-service, in service and continuous training, (3) organising extension services. (4) introducing improved and developed techniques in schools, (5) functioning as a clearing house for all information regarding school education.

Mode of Working. The Council works with the cooperation of education departments of the states and the universities. It remains in touch with all institutions of national and international importance. It publishes books. It has set up many organisations for performing its functions. Its main office is in Delhi.

The Departments of the Council. the NCERT has the following departments :

National Institute of Education. (1) Pre-primary and Primary Education Department. (2) Text-book Department. (3) Teacher Education Department. (4) Social Science and Humanities Department. (5) Department of Educational Psychology and the Bases of Education. (6) Educational Material Department. (7) Department of Analysis of Statistics, and Educational-Survey, (8) Library (9) Information Service Unit. (10) Publication Unit.

Central Institute of Education. (Now under Delhi University) 3, Regional Colleges of Education (Ajmer, Bhopal, Bhuvaneshwar, Mysore).

Organisation. The chief of the management committee of the council is the Education Minister. All state Ministers of Education and the Chief Executive Councillor of Delhi are its ex-officio members. The chairman of the UGC , 4 Vice-chancellors of universities, 14 persons nominated by the government, together form the Council. The secretary, Ministry of Education, Government of India, too is an ex-officio member. Because of this organisation, it is easy for the council to formulate its policies. The administration of the council is in the hands of its Director. The working committee of the council is comprised of its director, chairman, deputy director, the chairman of the UGC, representatives of the education and finance ministries, two teachers, two educationists and three representatives of the various organs of the council. In addition there is a committee, headed by a vice chancellor of a university, for the regional colleges.

Activities of the Council. During the few years of its existence, the council has done commendable work in the sphere of teacher training and school education. It has published text-books of a superior quality. It has also developed teaching aids for science teaching with the co-operation of UNESCO and UNICEF. Among its major achievements are providing facilities for research, part-time B.Ed. courses, and organising summer institutes

Educational research is in its infancy in India; its quantity is small enough and quality even less. Most of the research is limited to training institutions. Even if the quantum of research activity is considered sufficient, the work is being done mainly by M.Ed. and Ph.D. students, and even among the research articles of the former can hardly be classified as research work. And, at the Ph.D. level, the research programme is weak from the viewpoint of methodology. The shortcoming here is that research for Ph.D. is permitted only to those who have obtained their B.Ed. and M.Ed. degrees. Besides, the scholarships available for educational research are very few. Some work has been done on intelligence testing, but not much attention has been paid to it. Besides, facilities for computation, consultation and documentation are not available. There is not even a single research journal in the country which can be of used in the publication of research. In addition to all this, there is considerable repetition in many spheres of work. Even where work has been done the research documents are merely the showpieces of archives, because the administration has not even tried to make use of them in formulating its policies. What is truly astonishing is that the total amount spent on educational research is only Rs. half a million per year.

The Commission, laying stress on the need for educational research, has made the following recommendations-

1. The NCERT should establish document collection centres and clearing house. (The NCERT, in collaboration with the central government, has made arrangements for the publication of a research journal).

2. Educational research should be conducted by teams working in interdisciplinary spheres. In training colleges, encouragement should be given to advanced research.

3. Schools of education should be established in at least three or four universities.

4. A national academy of education should be established with the help of eminent educationists. For this purpose, the Central Government should extend all necessary assistance.

5. The NCERT should not function merely as an agency for distributing grants. A strong Education Research Council should be established.

6. Training should be imparted in statistical analysis in order to make educational research more comprehensive as well as profound.

7. At the central level the NCERT and at the state level the State Institutes of Education should assume the responsibility for educational research.

The Education Commission has pointed out that there are numerous problems in the educational sphere which should be made the subject of research. In the humanities, much research has been done on the subjects but very little concerning teaching. This research has been done by candidates for M.Ed. and Ph.D. degrees. The provisions for scholarships are also inadequate. Much repetitive work has also been done. The Commission has therefore said that if we really want to change the picture, steps must immediately be taken for developing educational research, and this research must then be effectively linked with educational policy and reform. In this context, the following steps will have to be taken:

1. A national information distribution centre and one archieve concerned with educational research should be developed in the NCERT.
2. Research into education should be conducted by teams working in the interdisciplinary sphere.
3. A national education council should be established.
4. NCERT should organise programmes for educational research with the help of state educational councils.
5. More money must be invested on educational research.
6. Officials of education departments also should be given opportunities for gaining research experience.
7. An educational research council should be organised.
8. The question of giving priority to a particular subject in educational research is a complex one. There are many problems clamouring for priority. In this regard, it has been suggested that research should be initiated at the advice of education planners and administrators.

The amount spent upon educational research should also be increased. In the fifth plan, there was a provision for only Rs. 15 crores for this research. Instead, at least one per cent of the total expenditure on education should be earmarked for research.

Functions. Universities should impart knowledge in the context of national consciousness, and so they should encourage the development of individual differences and manners within the limits of tolerance.

1. Spreading the programme of adult education over a large area.
2. Helping schools for qualitative self-development.
3. Universities should set up their centres in various parts of the world so that India may be able to secure a place for itself in the world.

The following programmes should be given priority so that the foregoing objectives may be achieved :

1. Making revolutionizing efforts to improve the standard and quality of higher education and research.
2. Spreading higher education for satisfying the need for manpower and thus making possible national development.
3. Improving the organisation and administration of the university.

For implementing the foregoing programme, the Kothari Commission has offered the following suggestions :

1. The UGC should adopt one IIM, one agricultural university and any four of the existing universities for development as the leading or main universities.
2. The teachers in the leading universities and colleges should be the best available.
3. Affiliated colleges should be classified and given aid according to their respective standard. While one or a number of colleges have attained a higher standard, they should be given the status of autonomous colleges.
4. The work-load of classroom teaching, laboratory or workshop on the teacher should be reduced and the remaining time should be utilised in guidance, self-study, authorship or carrying research projects.
5. In degree colleges, the medium of education should be the regional language, although at the post-graduate level, English may be used.
6. Student service should be developed and organised as an integral part of education. Such services should include health services, residential facilities, guidance and counselling, helping in finding employment, student welfare, aid, etc.
7. Each university should decide how its student union should work and conduct itself. Experiments should be conducted in this field. The UGC should make arrangements for annual conferences of student representatives.

8. Education should be capable of encouraging young men and women to behave in a cultured manner and generate special values. The life of the whole university should be a unit, and there should be no distinctions between teachers, students and officials of the administration.

System of Admission

National needs must be kept in view while thinking of the expansion of higher education. Admissions to higher education will keep on rising till 1985-86. Hence vocational courses should be expanded. The view of the Education Commission is that :

1. The selection method should be employed in granting admission. It can have the following three criteria:
   (a) In institutions, admissions should be in proportion to the teachers and facilities available so that the standards are maintained.
   (b) Admission should be according to the qualifications specified by the university.
   (c) Institutions should choose the best students only.
2. Provisions should be made for part-time (evening colleges, correspondence courses, etc) education in science and technical education. By 1986, one third of all higher education should be through the part-time programmes.
3. Arrangements for post-graduate education and research should be available in universities or centres established by the university.
4. At present, the ratio of girl students is 1: 4 which should be raised to 1: 3. Economic hostel arrangements and scholarships should be introduced in a planned way.
5. New universities should be set up only where they are needed. For this, the permission of the UGC should be set up.
6. Universities should implement their programmes on the basis of cooperation.

7. The combination of subjects should be more flexible.
8. Social sciences should be given more importance.
9. Area studies should be initiated at least in some universities.
10. Human science should be organised.
11. Stress should be laid on educational research. For this purpose the NCERT should develop documentation centres and clearing house. A National Academy of Education should be set up. The total expenditure upon education should be increased.

Whether universities should be independent in themselves and whether their organisation should be subject to governmental control or not has been a debatable question. The suggestions of the Commission are the following:

1. The autonomy of a university is inherent in its selection of students, selection and promotion of teachers, its determination of a curriculum, its choice of teaching methods and spheres of research. In India, the tradition of autonomy in universities has been a strong one. Despite this, the responsibility for universities rests with the governments, the IUB and the UGC. Hence, some mechanism should be evolved for exchange of views between the IUB., the UGC and the universities themselves. The two institutions mentioned above should generate public opinion in favour of university autonomy, but the universities should evolve it through their own responsible activities.
2. Universities should grant similar autonomy to their own departments and faculties.
3. There should be committees for the selection of students and appointment of teachers. Besides, student representatives should participate in academic councils and university courts.
4. State governments should extend financial aid to the universities as far as their means allow, and rules pertaining to the use of these finances should be simple. The UGC should provide developmental and maintenance grants to the state universities.

- The policy of granting block grants should be implemented. Universities should be secured against governmental and public interference.

Procedure for Appointments

1. Vice-chancellors should be appointed according to the pattern of Delhi.
2. They should be appointed either by the Visitor or the Chancellor.
3. They should be educationists or scholars of renown.
4. Their period of office should be five years, which may be extended by two years.
5. They should have extensive powers so that they can help raise the standard and efficiency of the university.

Relevant Acts

1. There should be a university court, responsible for framing laws and policy. It should not have more than 100 members.
2. The executive council should consist of 15 to 20 members with the Vice-Chancellor as its chief executive.
3. The academic council should be the body which determines the curriculum and prescribes the standard. The standing committee should look after special matters.
4. The IUB should constitute a committee for looking into the ways of holding convocations or other common activities of universities.
5. A suitable mechanism should be evolved, between the IUB., the Education Ministry and the university for university law and rules.
6. The Government of India should request the Supreme Court to frame a policy for establishing the autonomy of university.
7. In each affiliating university, there should be a council of the affiliated colleges. Affiliation should not be a matter of right,

instead it should be based on the standard achieved by the college.

8. Rules relating to grants to colleges should be simple.

9. An organisation of the type of UGC should be created for engineering, agriculture and medicine.

10. The UGC should not have more than 12 or 15 members.

It is evident, thus, that the Education Commission has given its best thought to every aspect of higher education, and its meditations reflect its foresight. If the recommendations of the commission are put into practice, we will undoubtedly succeed in achieving our objectives.

Major Issues

The progress of higher education in India is established by the fact that the country now has 123 universities. But, these universities are facing certain problems and obstacles. The following are the main problems :

New Universities. Today, India has 123 universities, but despite this, frequent demands are raised for the establishment of new universities. The obvious question is: Do we really need more universities? In India, only 1 out of every 40 individuals receives higher education, while in the USA this ratio is 1: 3 and in England 1: 12. A committee appointed in 1961 to consider the potential for new universities found that Unitary or Federal types of organisations fulfil the potential as well as the sphere of higher education. In each state there should be one federal university, and the upper limit of enrolment of students for one university should be 10,000.

In India, there is a need for new types of universities. There is also greater potential for single faculty universities, examples of which are the universities at Jamshedpur (mining and metallurgy), Sevagram (basic education), Kanpur and Ahmedabad (textile engineering), Roorkee and Khairagarh (engineering).

In addition to the establishment of new universities, there is great need for proper planning. Almost 90 universities have come to be established since independence. In some cases, the background was fully planned, but in most cases, their development even today indicates a complete lack of direction, because of which their standards have also declined.

Government and Universities. According to our Constitution, education is a state subject, and the body which framed the Constitution laid great stress on the states making provisions for higher education in their territories. Same people were of the view that higher education should be a central subject while the states should be entrusted with secondary education.

The University Commission (1948) was not in favour of putting higher education in the hands of the centre. Its reasons were two- (1) the existence of stereotyped education, (2) the fact that primary and secondary education was in the hands of the state governments. It was felt that this would lead to grave imbalance between the centre and the states. In order to obviate this possibility it was felt that the two governments should share the burden of higher education.

According to M.V. Pillai, universities should generate a certain minimum standard. Local and parochial politics should be eradicated since it is ruining the atmosphere of universities today. Academic isolation should also be ended, so should the prevailing despair. Emotional and intellectual unity should be protected.

State Governments and Universities. Indian universities are dependent upon state governments in two ways :

1. They came into existence through the laws of the state, and they depend upon the state government both for the constitution and organisation.

2. They receive recurring and non-recurring aid from the state, the quantum of which depends upon the sweet will of the legislators.

Autonomy of Universities. The events of the last few years have brought to the fore the question of autonomy of universities. Governments interfere in the working, organisation and policies of universities, because of which the importance of the university is eroded. The Vice-Chancellor has to obey the dictates not only of the Chancellor (Governor) but also of the state's ministers. Dr. John Mathai declared that reaching from the Chancellor to the Minister and then returning to the Chancellor sets up a current of a kind in which the influx of the political current is quite natural. For this reason, the Kothari Commission strongly recommended that universities be given adequate authority and freedom of action.

Financial Arrangements. One major problem facing the universities is that of finance. The state's administrative organisation and its policies have a profound impact upon the university's economy. It has been seen that the expenses of a university are met (1) 50% from the state treasury, (2) fees, and (3) local councils. The colleges affiliated to a university do not receive their grants directly from the university, instead, it is the State Department of Education which provides them with grants and other financial help. The Radhakrishnan Commission concluded that grants should be given for the fulfilment of the following objectives- (1) grants for constructing buildings in universities and colleges, (2) means grants, (3) library grants, (4) hostel grants, (5) salaries, provident fund, pension, etc., (6) scholarships and fellowships, (7) study leave and travel grants, (8) post-graduate work and research grants, industrial and vocational education.

State governments generally give blockgrants which only compensate for the losses, and because of these grants, the budget of the university remains unbalanced. Endowments are enough only to meet about 3% of the expenditure of a university.

Private Colleges. Two thirds of the colleges have been set up by private initiative. Regarding the constitution of the working committees of colleges, the Commission has recommended the following posts :

1. Representatives who give endowments:
2. Principal and representatives of teachers.
3. Representatives of the college.
4. Representatives of the university.

5. Representatives of the government (if the colleges receive direct aid from the government).

6. A leading and renowned representative of the community.

This body should consist of 12 to 15 members.

A university performs the following four functions-

Instruction. Universities provide instruction through institutions, classes and colleges. The problem of unemployment has led to grave overcrowding in universities. It was because of the increasing number of students that evening colleges and morning colleges were increased, and experiments were made on the utility of postal instruction. K.R.S. Aiyangar said that our standards, whether in scholarship or in teaching, never remained high or stable, and now it is declining rapidly.

The percentage of passes at the university level have remained low, thus encouraging wastage and extravagance. In this context, the University Commission opined that the public fund has been wasted continuously from year to year. On the one hand, there is wastage of public money, the student's money, time and effort while on the other their guardians are thrust into despondency and despair.

The problem of admission throws light on two facts : (1) What should be done with those students who have obtained higher education but have not found employment in any institution? What should be done with those students who are not considered fit for higher education at all? The solution to the first problem lies in the establishment of new colleges while to the second, the solution lies in the introduction of a variety of new programmes. The UGC's views on the qualitative improvement and development of education are that higher education has already undergone rapid expansion which has led to deterioration all round, affecting the staff as well as the material resources of the universities. If increasing numbers continue to get admission in our universities and the facilities do not expand in the same proportion, there is grave danger of a fall in academic standards in the near future. Because of the pitiable conditions of private colleges, the standard of instruction is falling even more rapidly.

Research. In general, there has been a dearth of academic research in our country. The standard education depends upon research. The need for higher education and research in our country is as follows:

1. Many universities and colleges try to introduce postgraduate courses, but they have neither adequate resources nor teachers. Only those students take admission in such institutions who cannot find a place elsewhere. But this leads to a decline in standards.
2. Before setting up a post-graduate department, a university should reflect upon the possibilities many times. According to S.N. Basu, it will be found in every university that young teachers want to work, and they often express their resentment at the lack of space, lack of research material, and even more, at the absence of people to whom they can voice their problems and their grievances.
3. The standard of post-graduate instruction and research should be equivalent to international standards.
4. Research centres should be set up for facilitating research.

Affiliation. Almost 40 of the Indian universities affiliate colleges. Because of this, the UGC is considering ways to raise the standard of instruction in colleges.

Expansion. According to James Rowland Angels, universities are biological organisms which are governed by the principles of evolution. They cannot remain stagnant, and if forced to do so, they perish. Two programmes should be taken up for the spread of education-

Adult Education. For this programme, education should be given the prevailing form. Students should be present regularly in classes. Specialists should introduce programmes for training and leadership in their own areas.

Community Service. In order to arouse the desire for education in the community, universities should set up community centres.

In addition to this, student welfare services are part of the university's function. The reality is that the functions which the universities had in days gone by have now changed radically. We conclude this issue with a quotation from a lecture by Cardinal Newman, delivered a hundred years ago, "A university training ... aims at raising the intellectual tone of society, at cultivating the public mind, at purifying the national taste, at supplying true principles to popular enthusiasm and fixed aim to popular aspiration, at giving enlargement and sobriety to the idea of the age, at facilitating the exercise of political power and refining the intercourse of private life."

9

Secondary Stage

Background

The present secondary education has behind it the growth and traditions of the last one hundred years. Alongwith the East India Company and other trading companies came the missionaries for the propagation of their religion, and they made provisions for the education of the native children. In 1830, the Directors of the Company decided to impart education of English to these children. Their purpose was, as N.N. Basu puts it, "to raise a body of native qualified by their habits and acquirements to take a large share and to occupy high positions in the civil administration of their country than as hitherto been the practice under our Indian Government." On March 7,1835, Lord William Bentick affixed his signature to the educational policy evolved by Lord Macaulay, and in 1844, Lord Hardinge opened the doors of employment for educated Indians. The outcome was that western education began to grow and spread at a rapid pace in India. By 1862, 32 approved schools had come to exist in the country.

From 1854 to 1904. In the growth and development of secondary education, the Wood Despatch played a very significant role, since it provided the foundation for secondary education. The Wood Despatch was framed and declared in the following words- "That the people of

India should be made familiar with the works of European authors with the results of the thought and labour of Europeans on the subjects of every description and to extend the means of imparting this knowledge must be the object of any general system of education."

"On the basis of this approach, universities were set up at Bombay and Calcutta in 1857. These universities began to control and administer secondary schools on the basis of the matriculation examination, and thus it became the function of these schools to create a foundation for the colleges."

In 1882, the Hunter Commission suggested various syllabi for secondary schools. It suggested that the higher classes of the secondary schools should be divided into two parts - one should prepare students for the matriculation examination, and the other should prepare youth for commercial and non-literary activities. By 1904, the number of secondary schools rose from 3916 to 5124, but this unplanned expansion soon manifested a number of shortcomings. The Department of Education had no control over the schools which did not receive government aid. The universities, too, granted recognition to schools with reluctance. In 1904, rules for the matriculation examination were framed in accord with the Indian Universities Act; and as a consequence, the secondary schools passed even more firmly into the hands of the universities.

1905 to 1917. Three notable characteristics mark this period-

Emergence of Nationalistic Tendencies. A national consciousness arose as a reaction to the educational policy of Lord Curzon. A National Council of Education was established in Bengal, and national colleges, technical institutes, etc., came to be set up.

Medium of Instruction. It came to be felt in this period that the medium of education should be the mother tongue, and not English. Shri Rayaninagar placed this question before the Council, but the proposal was objected to on the following grounds- (i) The students knowledge of English will decline. (ii) There was a dearth of text books in Indian languages. (iii) There will be numerous difficulties in places where many language are spoken. (iv) English is a language of international importance.

Control Over Secondary Schools. In this period, the schools were subjected to control by the universities for granting recognition as well as by the education department for granting aid to them. Later on, it was decided that the education department alone will exercise control over the secondary schools.

1917 to 1947. During this period, secondary education was evaluated from time to time by various commissions.

Calcutta University Commission. This Commission (the Sadlar Commission) put forward the view that "No satisfactory reorganisation of the university system will be possible unless and until a radical reorganisation of the system of secondary education, upon which university work depends, is carried into effect."

This Commission put forward a suggestion for the introduction of two examinations-matriculation and intermediate. In the same way, different inter-colleges for the arts, sciences, medicine and engineering, were established.

Hertog Report. The Hertog Report, too expressed the view that the matriculation examination had influenced the whole syllabus. It also suggested that, in the middle schools, the vernacular syllabus should aim at the fulfilment of various needs. Professional or vocational curricula should also be introduced.

Sargent Report. The Sargent Committee was set up in the context of the post-war conditions which came to exist in 1944. The suggestions of this committee were that - the secondary course should extend over 6 years, the age of admission after primary education should be 11 years, only brilliant students should be selected for the high schools, and the selection should be unbiased and effective. Besides, there should be two types of courses in the high school- (1) intellectual (2) vocational.

After Independence. After independence, the path for the progress of secondary education was charted by four important committees and commissions.

Tarachand Committee (1948). This committee suggested that multipurpose secondary schools should be established. It felt the need for the appointment of a commission.

University Commission (1948). The University Commission opined that secondary education is the basis or foundation of university education, and therefore improvements in it were essential.

Secondary Education Commission (1952.53). This commission was appointed to study the organisation of secondary education. It put forward a blue-print for the reorganisation of secondary education along the following lines-

1. An eight year syllabus for the 6 to 14 years age group.
2. Various 3 year courses for children in the 15-17 age group.
3. A 3 year degree course after the higher secondary examination.

Education Commission (1964-66). This Commission, set up under the chairmanship of Dr. Daulat Singh Kothari, recommended the introduction of uniformity in secondary education throughout the country. It also suggested that provisions be made for various syllabi, subjects and correspondence courses.

On the whole, then, it is clear that from 1830 to 1953, secondary education passed through numerous ups and downs. As time passed, the objectives, organisation, the programmes of secondary schools underwent changes. It is hoped that, since the country has now accepted national development as its objective, secondary education will change in accordance with this objective.

Previous Sctup

In India, secondary education does not have a uniform nature throughout the country. The Secondary Education Commission, in its survey, discovered the following forms of it in the country-

Higher Elementary or Middle School. In some states, the middle schools are known as Higher Elementary, Vernacular middle schools, etc. These schools provide education for classes six, seven and eight, subsequent to primary education.

Secondary Schools. At the secondary level, education is generally split into two parts(1) Junior level, (2) Higher level. In some states, the senior basic schools also come within the ambit of the secondary schools. These schools provide education for 3 to 4 years. The high schools represent the higher level of secondary education. In some regions, the working period for this stage is more than three years. ,

Higher Secondary Schools. The higher secondaıy schools are the most modern institutions. These have provisions for education for three or four years. They have been established by taking away one year from the intermediate level.

Higher Education. In some states, the pre-university level and the first year of the degree course together fall within the sphere of secondary education.

Intermediate Colleges. As a result of the Sadler Commission's recommendations, intermediate colleges and boards of secondary and intermediate education came to be established. These institutions have a two-year syllabus, which is divided into the two classes; eleventh and twelveth.

Vocational Colleges. There are many vocational colleges at the secondary level, which provide education in engineering, technology, medicine, veterinary sciences, agriculture and commerce. Admission to them is possible, at some places, after high school, while at others, after intermediate.

Technical Institutes. At this level, there are many technical institutions, including professional colleges as well as polytechnics, many of which have arrangements for the education and training of children of 12 years of age.

Polytechnics. In many states, arrangements have been made for the setting up of polytechnic institutes which provide training in various trades and professions. Admission to such institutions is available to students possessing qualifications equivalent to high school or middle school. Such institutions provide training in technology, arts and crafts, secretarial practice, domestic science, home-craft, and general knowledge.

Modern Setup

When the issue of restructuring secondary education was being considered, the Secondary Education Commission was confronted with the following three questions-

1. To which age-group should secondary education cater?
2. What changes should be made in the existing system?
3. How should skills be developed in schools left untouched by the new changes?

It must be remembered that the Kothari Commission regards education as a life-long process, while the Secondary Education Commission regards the various levels of education as independent units. According to this Commission, "We bave to bear in mind the principle already noted that Secondary Education is a complete unit by itself and not merely a preparatory stage; to that at the end of this period the student should be in a position, if he wishes to enter on the responsibilities of life and take up some useful vocation.

The new structure of secondary education suggested by the Commission took the following shape. Keeping in mind the comprehensive blue-print, the new structure of secondary education should become functional after four or five years of education in a primary or junior basic school.

In this, there should be a three year syllabus at the middle school, junior high school or senior basic level.

There should be a 4 year syllabus at the higher secondary level. The Commission suggested changing the existing intermediate system into the higher secondary level, comprising 4 years of education, inclusive of one year of the intermediate level.

In the same way, the degree course should be of three years' duration. Thus, the entire secondary level is broken up into two parts-(1) junior secondary level, (2) from class 9 to class 11.

The Commission clearly found the intermediate system of examination defective. It argued that the intermediate examination destroyed the continuity of college education and creates difficulties in the planning of the syllabus for the degree course. This is worst defect. Adding one year to the secondary level will bring about an increase in skill and efficiency while an additional one year with the degree course will generate educational skill. In this way, uninterrupted progress continues to take place over a three year period.

At places where the higher secondary syllabus cannot be taught, and in the colleges which have a four year syllabus- i.e., a two year syllabus for the intermediate and a two-year syllabus for the degree course, provisions should be made for introducing a one-year pre-university course before granting admission to the university. This syllabus should be implemented in colleges.

The Commission suggested the abandonment of the intermediate level, in line with the suggestion put forward by the University Education Commission (1948). Its view was that, by putting an end to intermediate classes, the standard of secondary as well as higher education can be improved. It felt, on occasion, that intermediate education has failed to achieve the desired objectives.

Kothari Commission Report

Although many states had accepted the proposals of the Secondary Education Commission, various types of institutions- middle schools, junior high schools, senior basic, higher elementary, high school, higher secondary, intermediate, etc. continued to function. In some states, pre-professional, pre-university, pre-medical, pre-engineering, and other such institutions have functioned within the sphere of secondary education. The Kothari Commission laid special emphasis upon bringing uniformity into secondary education for the whole country, at the time of implementing its new form. It divided the secondary level into two parts- (1) lower secondary level, consisting of classes 8 and 9 or 9 and 10; (2) higher secondary level, for classes 11 and 12.

Welcoming this suggestion of the Kothari Commission, National Solidarity (July 7, 1966) declared that the commission had put forth a practical curriculum for continuous education by virtue of which education would become uniform and undergo progress.

However, what actually happened was, since the Secondary Commission had declared the abandonment of the intermediate method, some states replaced it with the higher secondary system, but other states, which continued with the intermediate system fared better because the very structure of the Secondary Education Commission soon collapsed. Of course, the little that was achieved was the change in nomenclature -Kothari Commission substituted the name higher secondary for the earlier terms intermediate.

In brief, the prevalent and the suggested forms of secondary education can be represented thus through the following table -

	Existing Form		*Proposed Form*
1.	High School	1.	Secondary class 8 to 12 or 11-12
1.	Class 11 or P.U.C.	(a)	Lower Secondary Education Class 8-10
2.	Junior College (Kerala)		or class 1-10
3.	Intermediate College (U.P., Bombay)	(b)	Higher Secondary Education class 9-11
4.	Pre-professional, Pre-medical, Pre-engineering.		

The reality underlying this whole issue is that uniformity must be imparted to the whole educational organisation in the country so that national unity and social unity can be awakened. Education should include programmes for social service and national service. These should possess infinite potential for the comprehensive and positive development of the child.

Keeping in mind the growth and tradition outlined above, it is necessary to pay attention to the fact that the very concept of secondary education has suffered a profound transformation in past years. For this reason, an eleven-year national structure was developed, comprising of five years for the primary level, three years for the secondary level and three years for the higher secondary level. As education is a state subject, some states accepted this structure while others did not. It remains to be seen how the structure proposed by the Kothari Commission is accepted.

New System

The fundamental fact accepted by the Education Commission (1964-66) in its comprehensive analysis of education is that -there must be a uniform system of education for the whole country. In this country of varieties, education flows as a part of the variegated stream, with the result that it is difficult, if not impossible, to say with certainty which State has a higher standard of education than any other. The general assumption is that the standard of education is higher in states in which the medium of instruction is English. This is the reason why, in every competitive examination, success goes to those who have grown up and have been nourished in the shadow of this adopted mother tongue, while those who have suckled at their own mother's breast are compelled to mingle their existence with the mainstream of communality. They remain silent, unknown and unsung.

There is widespread discussion on the new educational structure, the much talked of 10 + 2 + 3 system. Central universities accepted it as the basis and conducted some experiments. Criteria of success were determined. But it came to be observed that these central universities, which began to search for a common educational system for the whole country, are unable to discover a suitable path to their goal. Mr. Rajni Kumar who was concerned with the formulation of this new system, asked whether we could not organise or implement a syllabus of a local philosophy for understanding the dynamic forces in society, if we could successfully implement hundreds of summer schools to orient teachers in the teaching of modern mathematics and science. This alone was the basis of a transformation in the social and economic structure. It was not possible to neglect this huge base of education.

The seeds of the 10+2+3 system are to be found in the proposals of the Hunter Commission in 1882, which has said that after the determined level of secondary education, the educational process should divide into two streams—one, that which is the threshold for university education, and two, that which is more closely oriented towards more practical, vocational or non-literary education for the masses. It was our country's misfortune that neither the government nor the people could digest this valuable peace of advice.

Subsequently, in 1929, the contemporary government appointed the Hertog Committee to assess the prevailing system of examination. The committee laid stress upon the need for vocational, technical and industrial syllabi. However, the government failed to create such a programme at the secondary level, and this suggestion continued to collect dust in official files for a very long time.

In 1935, analysing the effects of economic depression, the Central Educational Advisory Committee once again proposed the introduction of vocational courses at the secondary level. The Abbot and Wood committee was asked to give its opinion of this suggestion. The Committee offered its report in two parts in 1936. In the first part, they reflected upon the complexities of vocational education in India. In the seccond, they suggested the creation of two kinds of schools for vocational education : (i) Junior, (ii) Senior. The junior vocational schools were to be of the secondary standard. The proposal envisaged that various kinds of vocational courses would be taught in these schools. The senior schools were expected to provide specialised training. In this proposal, the continuous process of general education was adopted as the basis, as a result of the proposal, polytechnic schools came into existence in the country.

The second world war started and ended. The structure of the country began to undergo profound changes. At this juncture, another Commission was appointed under the chairmanship of Sir John Sargent to propose a restructuring of education in the country. The committee suggested the setting up of two kinds of high schools : (1) Vocational and Technical; (2) Academic. Provisions were made for imparting education of practical science and industry in the first kind, and theoretical education in the latter. In consequence, the All India Council for Technical Education was set up in 1945, and the Delhi Polytechnic for Commerce Education was born. The plan was enthusiastically received but the cry of paucity of funds prevented the dream from being translated into reality.

In the same decade, India became independent, and, focussing attention on some basic questions and the need for an educational system for independent India, the Central Advisory Board of Secondary Education emphasized the setting up of a commission. The product of his suggestion was the Mudaliar Commission. For secondary education, this commission proposed two kinds of syllabi which, along with general education, provided for certain vocational courses, such as technology, agriculture, commerce and the fine arts. The outcome of this was that there was a rapid increase, in every stage, in the number of polytechnics and multi-purpose schools. In 1950, the Central Advisory Board felt the need for the establishment of four regional colleges to fulfil the demand for teachers in these schools. In 1963, these colleges also came into existence.

In this variable host of commissions and committees, the one to achieve the maximum publicity was the Kothari Commission which, completing its horrendous task in 1964-66, put fourth a massive scheme for a uniform educational structure for the whole country. The Commission planned that by 1986, 50% of all children at the higher secondary level should be studying under a vocational syllabus. The Commission said that its main proposal was that of the registrations at 20% of the lower second level and 30 per cent of all registrations after class 10 should become involved in part-time or full-time vocational courses. Students between the ages of 14 and 18, boys as well as girls, must be encouraged, as far as possible, to adopt vocational and technical courses.

Many years have passed since India became independent. This means that one generation has now grown to adulthood. And yet, the plant of imported education has continued to flourish and prosper. The education provided by it never had any links with either national character or the task of national reconstruction. From time to time, the Emotional and National Integration Committee (1962) has pointed towards this fact. It has said that, keeping in view the interests of the student community, it felt that the nature of education throughout the whole country should be the same so that disunity may be rooted out, harmony between various parts may be encouraged and standards may be maintained. The atmosphere that has existed in the country in the last decade can be improved only if a single system of education is implemented throughout the country.

The Kothari Commission has divided education into three levels. The first level comprises all schools and primary education, the second, high school and higher secondary education, and the third, graduate, post-graduate education and research.

From this viewpoint, the form of 10+2+3 system was determined thus-

1. Completely school arrangement for one to three years,

2. The primary stage for seven to eight years, which should consist of two sub-divisions-first, lower stage of four to five years, second, higher primary stage for the next three years;

3. Lower secondary or higher school stage in which there should be 2 or 3 years of general education or 1 to 3 years of vocational education.

4. Higher secondary stage in which there should be 2 years of general education or 1 to 3 years of vocational education.

5. The stage of higher education, in which there should be a first degree course of 3 years or more, after which there should be a second degree course or courses for less than one degree, with varying periods of time designated for each.

The foundation of the 10 + 2 + 3 system is vocational education. A voice often rises in our country, and it vehemently asks-why does the existing system of education not provide jobs for the students? Why does it fail to arouse love to work, labour and duty in them? Perhaps, the Kothari Commission accepted this challenge, and that is why it fixed national development as the objective of education. It has identified self-reliance in foodgrains, economic development, universal employment, social and national unity, and political development as the most significant aspects of national development.

The new structure of education and its implementation by the central schools poses a question before the other schools in the country- will they be able to adjust harmoniously to this new structure, and will they be able to achieve the desired standards? The answer to these questions is filled with doubt. The reason is also quite obvious. These schools run by the centre have ample resources; besides admissions to them are not open to the common public. Thus, they have been created for a special, privileged class. Admission to them is controlled by competition, and hence, once the cream has been extracted from milk, it can be utilised for making either butter or ghee. The separated milk thus left is handed over to the regional schools, which may churn it as much as they like.

Setting up the aims of education in the context of the new educational structure, the Education Commission has said that the most important and essential reform in education lies in the need for changing its form, for relating it to the ambitions and needs of the people, and thus making it a powerful medium for the social, economic and cultural changes necessary for the achievement of national objectives. For this purpose, the development of education should be so designed as to bring about a large-scale social and national unity, as acceleration of the process of modernization, and the development of moral and spiritual values.

For these objectives, and for the desired social change, it has been determined to relate the 10 + 2 + 3 system to production. It has been said that the education of science and technology, industrialization and vocationalization should be brought into intimate relationship with work experience. Stress has been laid upon similar schools, social and national service, a proper policy on language, encouragement to a national consciousness, etc., for bringing about social and national unity. In order to mould education according to the mainstream of modernization and also to provide education in social, moral and spiritual values, arrangements have been made for providing religious education.

The declaration of emergency has brought about a revolution in every sphere of national life, and possibly it is because of this that every state is echoing the call to adopt the 10 + 2 system, based on the syllabus prepared by the NCERT, without giving a thought to local conditions and environments. Probably they did not consider the fact that Uttar Pradesh, too, is a part of the country, and it is a state -in which the 10 + 2 system already prevails. As far as the question of class 8 adopting the new mainstream, the syllabus upto class 4, which means the syllabus for the first eight years is general, while specialisation is to be introduced from class 9. It is at this point that the syllabi oriented to work experience are also to be introduced. By adopting them, the child can move towards vocationalization. The notion that a child-can become skilled in 16 subjects by the time he reaches class 10 has been framed by educationists and psychologists, but it is a patently unpsychological concept. Thrusting this on the child only means increasing the educational load to an unbearable extent. In fact, in the 10 + 2 system, we actually need a plan or scheme which is suitable to the soil of our own country. We cannot hope to succeed if we keep on picking up the crumbs of educational research in Russia or the USA.

In the 10 + 2 scheme, the three-language formula has been adopted in a most willful manner. It has been assumed that it is impossible for us to achieve anything without English. The Secretary of NCERT stated at one place that English could be introduced at any stage between classes 3 and 9, but he did not make any provisions ensuring that the national language Hindi should be taught in every state from class 3. Neither did he ensure that the learning of at least one of the regional languages be made compulsory. There is a grave doubt whether such a language policy in education will be able to maintain our national unity.

Our national leaders are ignorant of the fact that our bureaucrats do not want that leaders from among the masses may enter the services or the administration. What they want is that their own generations only should have access to these avenues.

In the country in which higher, education was inaugurated, the period of higher education was fixed at 4 years, the 4 years that come after the child has gone through a curriculum of study stretching over 12 years. The Mudaliar Commission recommended the abolition of intermediate, and instead proposed a higher secondary syllabus of 11 years. Most of the states accepted this proposal, but now most of them are returning to the old path. This is mere extravagance and waste, from which national welfare can never be expected to flow. Even today, it is impossible for us to switch over to the new system in the whole country. We are faced with numerous managerial, administrative, organisational and educational problems. Hence, the conjunction of the + 3 syllabus to the 10 + 2 syllabus is in itself a big question mark. The problem cannot be solved merely by increasing the time period of the syllabus to three years.

After this long deliberation, the question is; how can this powerful programme for national reconstruction be implemented? This author's suggestions are the following: -

1. The study of 16 subjects in the first 10 years is unpsychological. The uniform teaching of literature, science, mathematics and other subjects, without any attention to individual differences, is only an unwarranted assault upon the child's potential for development. Hence, the secondary school syllabus prevalent

in Uttar Pradesh should be accepted as the norm. Intensive teaching in five subjects should be the aim. Among them, there are many sub-classes in which the compulsory subjects (Hindi, Mathematics) should not be combined with the optional group. Upto class 8, education of a general nature should prevail everywhere.

2. The national language should be the medium of education, and the mother tongue should be taught at a certain fixed level. It is obvious that while English does link us closely with the world, it also alienates us from our own country.

3. By preparing its text-books in English NCERT has clearly published its innate tendency and inclination. It would have been much better had these books been prepared either in the national language or the mother tongue.

4. Tying work experience to the bounds of the classroom means, implicitly, putting an end to the basic intention of linking education with production. It would have been much better if work experience could have been provided in realistic situation, where the student could be in touch with society and the community.

5. In our opinion, the new system of education should be structured in the following way-

   1- 8 = General education flow.

   9-10 = General tendency towards specialization; in this field language and mathematics should be compulsory, and the student should choose three other subjects, according to his taste, from a number of alternatives.

   11- 12 = Specialization, in which the various branches can be literary, technical, vocational, fine arts, education, etc.

6. The + 3 level should be obtained at the + 2 level, but there should be intensive study during this period.

7. In the + 2 level, that is, at the post-graduate level, primacy should be given to specialization.

The foregoing suggestions will not entail any excessive financial burden on any state government, and through slight modifications in the existing circumstances, the challenge of the 10 + 2 + 3 could then be faced.

Mudaliar Commission Report

Secondary education gives desired direction to the nation's power, an idea of which the government has always been conscious. Consequently, from time to time, commissions and committees have been set up to study secondary education. In the following paragraphs, there is a consideration of the Mudaliar Commission, the Acharya Narendra Dev Committee (1953), and the Kothari Commission, and their impact upon secondary education.

Secondary education is the backbone of the country's entire educational programme, and the importance that the backbone has for human physiology is shared by secondary education in the country's economy. After independence, the need for a revaluation of secondary education in the country was urgently felt, and hence a commission was appointed in 1952, and it submitted its report in 1953.

Appointment and Membership. The establishment of the Secondary Education Commission took place in compliance with the government's proposal number F: 9.5\52-BI, dated September 23, 1952. The members of this commission were the following :

1. Dr. A. Lakshmanswami Mudaliar-Chairman.
2. John Christ-Member.
3. Dr. Kenneth Rost Williams -Member.
4. Mrs. Hansa Mehta-Member.
5. Mr. J.A. Taraporewala-Member.
6. Dr. K.L. Shrimali-Member.
7. Mr. M.T Vyas-Member.
8. Mr. K.G. Saiyyadain-Member.
9. Mr. K.N. Basu-Member.

Dr. M.M. Chari performed the function of assistant secretary to the commission.

Terms of Reference. The terms of reference of the Commission were :

1. Conducting a study into the existing state of secondary education in India.
2. For the reorganisation and development of secondary education- (i) clarification and statement of the objectives, organisation and syllabus of secondary education, (ii) a study of secondary education in the context of primary, basic and higher education, (iii) a study of the correlation between various secondary schools, (iv) a study of other related problems so that, according to the country's needs, the uniformity of secondary education for the whole country could be determined.

Objectives of Education. The secondary Education Commission fixed the aims of education in the following terms -

Growth of Democratic Citizenship. In this field, praising and glorifying the social and cultural achievements of our country, removing the weaknesses of our country, arousing the desire to serve the country, according to one's abilities, sacrificing personal interests and preferences for the good of the nation.

Vocational Progress. By the end of education, children should possess sound professional knowledge.

Development of Personality. Considering all possibilities for the development of personality of the child and acting thereon.

Training in Leadership. The Secondary Education Commission has placed training in leadership among the aims of education as a necessary condition for the success of democracy.

Reorganisation of Secondary Education. The following is the scheme put forth by the Mudaliar Commission for reorganising secondary education with a view to putting an end to the alienation between secondary and university education -

Period. The period of secondary education is from 11 years to 17 years of age. There should be no contradiction between the methods of teaching at the basic and secondary levels. This period is inclusive of (1) three year education at the middle, junior, secondary or senior basic levels, and (2) a four year curriculum at the higher secondary level.

Three Year Degree Course. The Commission put an end to the intermediate level and made provisions for 11 years of higher secondary and three years of a degree course.

Varieties of Syllabi. The Commission has harmonised various syllabi so that every student may be able to choose subjects according to his talents and inclination. These syllabi begin from the first year of secondary level.

Internal Evaluation. The Commission has accorded an important place to school records in the process of evaluation. Through this method students will be assessed more accurately, and there will also be an improvement in discipline in schools.

Technical Education. Although the Mudaliar Commission put forward numerous valuable suggestions for the development of technical education at the secondary level, and on the basis of these suggestions, many multipurpose institutions came to be set up, these schools failed to fulfil the needs of the country.

The following are the Commission's suggestions in this regard-

1. Technical schools should be run, in large numbers, as multi-purpose schools, or as a part of such institutions.
2. In large towns, central technical schools should be established so that the needs of local schools can be met.
3. Rules should be prepared for training through apprenticeship.
4. Technical and technological schools should be set up in constitution with educationists.
5. A cess for industrial education should be imposed.

Other Kinds of Schools. The purpose behind the establishment of such schools was the fulfilment of specific objectives. In the context of such schools, it was recommended that these schools should be set up. (1) Public schools should continue. (2) The states as well as the centre should assist brilliant students. (3) Residential schools should be established. (4) There should be more for the education of children.

Co-education. On the subject of women's education and co-education, the Mudaliar Commission said that there is no difference between the education of boys and girls, despite which, there should be provisions for education to girls in domestic science. The major recommendations in this context are - (1) Despite the absence of any difference in the education of boys and girls, the study of domestic science should be given primacy in co-educational schools. (2) Where necessary, separate schools should be set up for girls. (3) Specific conditions should be imposed upon co-educational schools.

Study of Languages. The Mudaliar Commission classified languages into five groups- (1) mother tongue, (2) regional language, if it is not the mother tongue also, (3) the official language of the Centre, (4) classified language, (5) English. It made the following recommendations regarding the study of languages- (1) at the secondary level, either the regional language or the mother tongue should be the medium of education; in this, special facilities should be provided to the linguistic minorities, (2) At the middle level, our children must know two languages. Hindi and English should be introduced at the Junior Basic level. (3) At the High School or the higher secondary level, there must be at least two languages, of which at least one must be either the mother tongue or the regional language.

Syllabus. The Commission suggested a syllabus at two distinct levels-

At the Middle Level. 1. Language, 2. social studies, 3. general science, 4. arithmetic, 5. art and music, 6. industry, 7. physical education.

At the High School and Higher Secondary Level. Complete syllabus for either the mother tongue and the regional language, or the mother tongue and a classical language.

In addition, one of the following languages—

1. Hindi (for those who do not use Hindi as mother tongue)

2. Elementary English (for those who did study English at the Middle level)
3. Higher English (for those who have already studied English)
4. Modern Indian language (in addition to Hindi)
5. Modern Foreign language (in addition to English)
6. Classical language
7. 1 Social studies.
   2 General science for the first two years.
   3 One of the following handicrafts- (i) Weaving, (ii) Wood work, (iii) Metal working, (iv) Gardening, (v) Stitching, (vi) Typing, (vii) Workshop, (viii) Stitching, knitting, etc. (ix) Modelling.

Text-Books. The following are the Commission's suggestions for the improvement of text-books-

1. A high-powered text-book committee should be set up, consisting of one judge of the high court, a member of the service commission, chancellor, headmaster, two educationists and education director, and it should function independently.
2. A fund should be created from the sale of these publications, and it should be utilised for helping students through scholarships and book-aid, etc.
3. This committee should set up at various specific levels.
4. The central government should establish art schools for the technique of text-books.
5. The central and state governments should make a collection of books which can be loaned out to the publishers.
6. One single text-book should not be prescribed for any one subject.
7. Specific text-books should be prescribed for the study of languages.

8. Any text-book hurting religious or social sentiments should not be prescribed for study.

9. The tendency to change text-books frequently should be discouraged.

Dynamic Methods of Teaching. The Commission turned its attention towards the methods of teaching also. Its suggestions in this regard are the following-

1. The method of teaching should aim not only at imparting information, but should be one which helps in the formation of desirable values, attitudes and habits.

2. Activity and Projects methods should be adopted. Students should be assigned work which allows them scope for expression.

3. In every kind of teaching, the stress should be on clear thinking and expression.

4. The tendency to work in a group should be developed.

5. Progressive educational technique, should be employed in experimental and demonstration schools.

Administration. Reflecting upon the problem of administration, the Mudaliar Commission opined that development and reorganisation in education is of no utility as long as indiscipline prevails in schools. It further said that-

1. Education for character building should not be part of the school syllabus.

2. A school government should be set up for the development of discipline.

3. Collective games should be given encouragement.

4. An act should be promulgated by Parliament, forbidding the use of students in elections.

Religious and Moral Education. Moral and religious education should be imparted in schools only on a voluntary basis, and it should

be given to those who profess faith in that religion. The Commission expressed its view that religious or moral education should not be given on the criterion of education in the arts; instead, it should depend upon the influence of the school and the conduct of the teachers. Thus, religious education should be given only on a voluntary basis.

Extra-curricular Activities. Extra-curricular activities are of the utmost importance for the development of the child's personality. Hence-

1. Extra-curricular activities should be regarded as an inseparable part of teaching.
2. The state should extend help to the child movement.
3. The central government should promote the NCC.
4. First aid, Red Cross, etc., should be encouraged in every school.

Guidance and Counselling. The Mudaliar Commission felt the need for a programme of guidance for the students. For this reason, it has included vocational as well as intellectual syllabi in the educational plan. Its views on these aspects are the following-

1. Special attention should be given to educational guidance at the secondary level.
2. Various vocational films should be exhibited in order to increase the knowledge of students.
3. There should be an increase in the number of trained officials, career, masters etc.
4. The central government should assist in the training of guides.

Student Welfare. In the sphere of student welfare, the Commission has recommended that health and physical education should be implemented. Its suggestions are that -

1. A school medical service should be initiated in every state. In every school, students should be given a medical check-up and treated, if necessary.
2. In residential schools, nutritious food should be made available.
3. Schools should keep their environment clean, and encourage respect for work in the students.

4. All teachers below the age of 40 should participate in the physical activities of students, and a record of each student should be maintained.

Evaluation. Examination or evaluation is the very foundation stone of education, and so it is essential for teachers that they should become aware of their students' progress. Hence, the Commission has recommended that :

1. The number of external examinations should be curtailed. Individuality or subjectivity in essay-type examinations should be reduced and objective tests should be taken.
2. In order to determine a child's future, a detailed record on his development in every sphere should be maintained.
3. In the final evaluation, attention should be given to internal evaluation as well as to the school record.
4. Instead of awarding marks, the system of grading should be adopted. At the conclusion of the secondary curriculum, there should be only a single public examination.
5. Subjects should be mentioned in the certificate. Supplementary examination should also be taken.

Development of Training Skill. The Mudaliar Commission was conscious of the importance of development and improvement of teachers. In the course of its survey, the Commission felt that, without any doubt, the levels of teachers and their conditions of work had to be improved in order to overcome their despair and their existing dissatisfaction, and also to generate the requisite atmosphere for education. For this, it suggested that-

1. There should be uniformity in the selection of teachers.
2. In private schools, there should be a selection committee for the appointment of headmasters as well as teachers.
3. The period of probation should be one year.
4. Teachers teaching high school classes should be trained graduates, while those teaching the higher secondary classes

should have qualifications similar or equivalent to those of teachers teaching intermediate or university classes.

5. The three benefit schemes (pension, provident fund, insurance) should be implemented.
6. At the school level, children of teachers should be given free education.
7. Houses for teachers should be constructed on a co-operative basis, and they should also be given travelling allowances for attending seminars, campus, etc.
8. Posts of teachers should be made more attractive.
9. There should be two kinds of training institutions-
   (a) those which train individuals with a high school or higher secondary qualifications.
   (b) those which train graduates.

   The first programme should be for one year, while the latter should be spread over two years.
10. For training in M.Ed., admission should be available only to graduates with three years of teaching experience.

Problem of Administration. The achievement of the objectives of education depends upon an efficient administration, besides which, the cooperation of various ministries is also essential. The Commission made the following recommendations in this context regarding organisation, administration, inspection, recognition and conditions, buildings and resources, hours of work and holidays, entry into public service, etc. -

1. The education director should be responsible for advising the education minister. He should also function as the joint secretary.
2. There should be a committee, comprising the central and the state ministers of education, which should also work for the progress of education.

3. There should be a board consisting of 25 members, with the education director as its chairman. There should also be a teachers' training board.

4. The work of inspectors should be to study problems and suggest solutions. A special panel should be appointed for granting recognition in domestic science, art and music.

5. Inspectors should have high qualifications, Teachers with ten years of experience, headmasters, etc., should be appointed teachers in training colleges.

6. New schools should be granted recognition only if they fulfil all the conditions.

7. The headmaster and representatives of teachers should be part of the management committees of schools. No member of such a committee should interfere in the working of the school. Each committee must formulate specific rules. It must adopt the policy of the education department and submit reports on its working.

8. Schools should be set up in villages. Aid for constructing buildings should be extended to them. In the schools to be set up in the future, attention should be given to introducing varied syllabi.

9. The working of the school should not create problems for the community. The working year should have 200 days. There should be summer vacations for 2 months, and brief vacations lasting 10 to 15 days twice a year.

10. In the governmental sectors, individuals in the age groups of 16 to 18, 19 to 21, and 22 to 24 should be appointed. 50% of the appointments should be made directly.

Arrangement of Finances. The Secondary Commission made a strong recommendation for the provision of adequate finances for the development of education. Its recommendations are-

1. Education should be financed by the centre and the states. A board of vocational education should be set up, for the development of vocational education. Representatives of related ministries should be members of this board.

2. An industrial education cess should be levied.

3. A cess on railways, transport, and postal services should be levied. All donations to educational institutions should be free of income tax, and the wealth of religious institutions and trusts should be invested in educational institutions.

4. Wealth tax should not be applicable to the property and playing grounds belonging to educational institutions.

5. The central and state governments should grant land to schools for buildings and playing grounds.

6. The central government should accept a part of the responsibility for restructuring secondary education.

At that time, these manifold suggestions of the Secondary Education Commission were welcomed. Now, the situation has changed, and in accordance with them, a new commission has been appointed. It has produced its own recommendations. It is to be seen how useful they are.

Acharya Narendra Dev Committee Report-1

Background. The Acharya Narendra Dev Committee (1953) was set up for the reorganisation of secondary education. But, prior to this, before the attainment of independence, in 1938, a committee was set up under the chairmanship of Acharya Narendra Dev to look into the primary and secondary education, and particularly vocational education, in Uttar Pradesh. In 1938, this committee had put forward a comprehensive blue print. Soon after, however, the Congress governments tendered their resignations, and hence the recommendations could not be implemented. No work at all was done in the sphere of secondary education, in particular. The recommendations of the first committee are as follows:-

1. Secondary education work is a complement to college education. Hence, the secondary education system should be complete 'in itself, and hence all secondary schools should be called `colleges'.

2. Less attention should be given to (*shilp kala*), and English should be made compulsory.

3. The syllabus should be made more practical.

4. Extra-curricular activities should be expanded to include debates, study centres, students unions, dance clubs, literary clubs, national history, photography, geography, scouting, guiding, school, bank, co-operative store, youth exchange, and other such institutions.

5. Technical and engineering colleges, with syllabi for four or five years should be opened; their syllabi should be practical and utilitarian.

6. Intensive efforts and useful programmes for the expansion of women's education should be set a foot.

7. Traditional institutions (sanskrit *pathshalas* and urdu *maktabs*) should be so reorganised as to ensure that their students can continue their education in a proper manner.

8. Intelligence testing should be introduced into the examination system. Schools should be subject to administrative inspections from time to time. The Education Council should organise tests in general knowledge.

9. Training schools and colleges should be set up for providing vocational training.

10. Text-books should be improved.

11. Education should be subject to various kinds of control. A central pedagogical institute should be established.

In addition to all these suggestions, the first committee had also expressed its views on the development of existing schools, their administration, civics; control of education, etc.

As a result of the World War II, the system of education was once again destablised, and no steps, could be taken to implement the foregoing suggestions. After independence, circumstances changed to such an extent that the Uttar Pradesh administration felt the need for appointing a new committee to look into secondary education and give recommendations for its restructuring.

Acharya Narendra Dev Committee Report-2

The second committee was set up in pursuance of the government of Uttar Pradesh order no A/550/X-30 30-52, dated May 8, 1953. This committee consisted of 29 members, its chairman was Acharya Narendra Dev, and its secretary Shri Bhagwati Sharan Singh.

The terms of reference of the committee were expressed thus:

1. To reflect upon a new scheme for secondary education.
2. To inspect the groups A, B, C and D of the board of high school and intermediate education.
3. To consider the differences in the syllabi for boys and girls.
4. To reflect upon the utility of a syllabus in a specific field.
5. To inspect the instruments of education, and the teaching staff.
6. To look into the utility of practical and industrial subjects.
7. To harmonize and blend technical education with general education.

Eight sub-committees of this committee were also set up-(1) terms of reference and jurisdiction, A, B, C, D group syllabus, (2) women's education, (complete), (3) the achievements and practicability of groups C and D, (4) vacations and holidays, (5) education of girls, (6) harmonization of general and technical education, (7) text-books, and (8) management committee. These committees conducted their meetings and established contact with the public, from time to time.

This Committee, as a whole, put forward numerous and wide-ranging suggestions on many subjects related to education. Here, these recommendations are being given in brief, so as to bring out the standard or level of thought.

Syllabus. The committee paid particular attention to the recommendations of the earlier committee (1939), and also to the syllabus recommended by Uttar Pradesh (1948). It also considered the increasing needs and changed circumstances. Its suggestions regarding the syllabus were the following-

1. Sanskrit should be compulsory along with Hindi, and so should passing the examination in both languages. In addition to Hindi, another modern Indian language should be studied. General knowledge should be kept outside the prescribed syllabus. In the first two years, study of arithmetic should be compulsory.
2. In higher secondary schools, domestic science or home science should be compulsory for girls.
3. For the first two years, six subjects should be compulsory, while for the last two years this number should be reduced to five.
4. Students should be permitted to take examinations in additional subjects also.
5. Schools providing teaching in commerce, agriculture, aesthetics, pre-technical or creative subjects should be selected with great care. Institutions imparting training in agriculture must have a resourceful laboratory as well as at least 10 acres of land.

Technical Education. The committee's recommendations regarding the spread and improvement of technical education are the following:

1. Technical school should provide general education along with technical education. As far as possible, the education department should itself make arrangements for such schools, and if necessary, their management should be entrusted to other departments as well.
2. A council should be set up to establish harmony or synthesis between industries and the education department.
3. At every level, efficient services should be organised. More schools of the technical and creative type should be established. The Board of Technical Education should issue certificates. The practical syllabus should also be stimulating. In such institutions, education should be provided free.

4. Short term courses of programmes should be conducted for training in psychological services, guidance and advice.
5. A council should be set up for the construction of tests, educational and psychological research, etc.
6. Psychological laboratories should be established at the district level.
7. Change should be made in the syllabi for training colleges and colleges granting degrees in education.

Examination System. On this issue, the following recommendations have been made after considering that; suggestions of the first committee, the Radhakrishnan Commission, etc. -

1. The intermediate examination should continue as at present. In the high school examination, the private candidates should also get benefit. A survey should be conducted for research into the system of public examination. The lowest age for sitting for the intermediate examination should be 16 years.
2. Attendance of 75% classes should be necessary for sitting for the examination, and students from the examination on account of shortage of attendance should have no right to appeal against the decision of the principal of the college.
3. At the high school level, a scholarship examination should be organised. Changes regarding promotion of students should be modified from time to time. In each class (9,10,11) there should be three mid term tests, while in class 12 there should be two such tests. Promotion should be based on the result of the collective examination.

Vacations. The committee suggested a working year of 200 days. This period of work should not exceed 235 days. Schools should open every year on the eighth day of July. There should be 31 holidays. The summer and winter vacations should be about six to seven weeks long. There should be 5 hours of teaching each day. The annual examination should take place in May, and after the declaration of the result, schools should close for the summer vacations.

Moral Education. A moral and humanistic education should be an integral part of the syllabus. Students should be made aware of the basic facts and principles of every religion. Before the start of teaching work every day, a congregation should be assembled every morning for prayers for at least ten minutes. The biographies of great persons should be studied.

Discipline. Groups or unions of students, teachers and parents should be organised for maintaining discipline. The prefect system should be introduced. The headmaster should be the highest authority in matters involving suspension from school, rustication or giving of corporeal punishment. The sentiment of social service should be encouraged. Films should be given distinctive A or U certificates to clarify whether they are suitable for all viewers or only for adults. Radio programmes for schools should be well arranged.

Management Committees. The term management committee refers to the committee of local persons belonging to the community who manage schools in their own respective ways. The committee has put forth the following suggestions in this respect-

(a) Schools which are efficiently managed should be encouraged by the government.

(b) Where the management committees perform their task unsuccessfully, the local administrator should take the management of the school into his own hands, and for this purpose, even two or three persons may be appointed.

(c) The principal and a representative of the teachers should also be members of the management committee.

(d) The practice of issuing the salary of missionary managers from the maintenance fund should be adopted.

(e) If a single trust or institution has a number of schools, the management committee for each school should be a different one. The committee should have a maximum of 12 members, and its period of office should be three years.

(f) Vacancies should be filled only through advertisements in the newspapers. Teachers should be appointed on probation, and the conditions of service should be explicitly stated in the Education Act. In the absence of written agreement, teachers should not be subjected to injustice.

(g) The government should extend the desired aid and help to management committees and schools. A development fund should be charged from the students.

Text-Books. The prevailing method of recommending text-books should be modified. The principal of a school should have the right and authority to select text-books, though the department of education may, to assist him, suggest certain books. Encouragement should be given for the production of suitable text-books, and sufficient time should be granted for their preparation. Their printing should be of a high standard.

It was on the basis of the recommendations of this committee that the monolith of the examination system and system of education in Uttar Pradesh was raised. But, circumstances have once again changed, and demands are being made for a change in the educational structure.

Kothari Commission Report

The Education Commission of 1964-66 held secondary education to be the very backbone of education and its growth. Its main recommendations are-

For the next twenty years, secondary education should have the following form-

(i) Proper planning of the schools to be established in the future.

(ii) Determining admissions after taking note of the facilities available so that standards can be maintained.

(iii) Selection on the basis of self-evaluation at the primary level, but at the secondary level, on the basis of an external examination, coupled with the school record.

Avoid Stagnation Wastage. In setting up new teaching institutions, the national policy should be designed to avoid stagnation and wastage. Efforts should be made to prevent the setting up of small and uneconomical secondary schools. Besides, existing schools of this nature should be restructured. Industrial training institutions should be set up in the proximity of industrial centres.

Balanced Syllabus. The variation in the syllabus at the secondary level should be arranged in such a manner that, in any one group the student should be able to study three subjects intensively. For a balanced development of personality among adolescents, at this stage, half the time should be given over to the study of optional subjects, while a quarter of the time should be reserved for physical education, art, handicrafts, material as well as spiritual education.

Study of Languages. The three language formula should be implemented after suitable modification- (1) mother tongue or regional language, (2) the subsidiary or main language of the Centre, (3) a modern Indian or European language not covered under either of the first two categories. At the secondary level, only two languages should be compulsorily taught.

Science and arithmetic should be taught compulsorily. At the lower secondary level, the teaching of these subjects should aim at making them means of mental discipline.

Social studies and social sciences should be so taught as to bring about an increase in citizenship, emotional unity, national unity and human brotherhood.

Work Experience. From the lower secondary stage, student should get an opportunity to obtain work experience through laboratory or workshop training, and at the secondary level, experience of school, workshops, fields, and, training as well as industrial establishments. This work experience should, from the viewpoint of the new social structure of the country, be a progressive one.

Social Service. Programmes which contribute to community development and which encourage social service should form a part of education at every level. In every district, an organisation should be created for this purpose.

Physical Education. The programme of physical examination needs a revaluation. It should be restructured to bring about the child's proper development.

Moral Development. One or two periods should be allotted in each week for moral and spiritual development.

Creative Activities. A committee should be appointed to study the potential for the teaching of art.

Guidance and Counselling. The work of guidance and counselling should start from the primary stage. Teachers should be acquainted with the problems of individual differences as well as remedial testing. In secondary schools, there should be a guest counseller who can visit ten schools and tender advice to students. Every teacher should have a clear concept of guidance and counselling.

Evaluation. The teachers who set examination papers should adopt new methods. The state board of school education should try to give a correct impression of the student's particular ability in the certificates issued after the external examination. It should not contain any indication whether the student has passed or failed. The student should be permitted to take an examination again in subjects in which he secured unsatisfactory marks, so that he may be able to overcome his deficiency and develop his ability. The internal assessment should be separately shown.

Problems in Development

Jawarharlal Nehru was of the view that the prevailing system of education may have been suitable in past circumstances, but in the modern circumstances, at a time when stratification is taking place, it could cause nothing but harm. The new generation is the country's future hope. The manner in which we developed their innate powers and the direction in which we bent their minds would determine the future of the country. Hence, the highest priority must be given to their education.

Today, the problem which is confronting us is that of growth and expansion. In our country, public education has not grown in the desired manner, though we had decided to secure this expansion through our Five-Year Plans.

Role of Five-Year Plans

In 1951, at the beginning of the plan, the number of students in government schools was 15.7%, in local institutions 12.4%, and in private schools 71.9%. By 1962, these figures stood, respectively, at 21.3%, 11.3% and 67.4%.

Expansion in Second Plan

The directives given by the Secondary Education Commission for the reorganisation of secondary education were implemented in the last two years of the first plan and the succeeding years of the second plan. By 1960-61, the number of multipurpose schools rose from 25 to 1187. In order to bring about development in the agricultural sphere, specially designed syllabus for teaching in agriculture was introduced in 200 secondary schools in rural areas. In order to provide useful employment to students after the completion of their secondary education, 90 low technology schools were set up to absorb them as semi-skilled workers. According to the structure proposed by the commission, 1200 schools were converted into general secondary schools. the number of students rose from 23 lakhs to 31 lakhs.

Third Plan

As in the case of the second plan, the expansion of education in the third plan followed the following lines- (1) additional facilities were given for teaching of science. (2) The multipurpose schools established during the second plan period were improved, and their number increased. (3) New higher secondary schools were established and the maximum possible number of existing secondary schools were converted into higher secondary schools.

In this plan period, 1550 secondary schools were converted into multipurpose schools. The major problem before them was the paucity of trained teachers. Hence, it was suggested that, along with the process of conversion to multipurpose schools, the existing schools should be given adequate facilities so that they could develop suitably. Four regional training colleges were set up to overcome the shortage of trained teachers for these institutions. It was accepted as a principle that all new secondary institutions should be of the higher secondary type. In the second plan, 2250 secondary schools were converted into higher secondary institutions.

By the end of the third plan period, it. was expected that the number of secondary schools would rise to 18 thousand. In the second plan, of 14 thousand secondary schools, 11,500 had facilities for the teaching of science, though the teaching of science faced two major difficulties — lack of adequately equipped laboratories and the shortage of suitably trained and educated teachers. In accordance with the suggestion of the All India Secondary Education Council, special programmes for teachers were implemented and standardised patterns of scientific apparatus were produced. In the third plan, 2000 schools were converted to higher secondary schools, and 4000 new ones established, thus bringing their total number to 9000, i.e., exactly half the number of all secondary institutions.

Junior High Schools

At the end of the second plan period, the total number of admissions to classes 6,7 and 8 (for the age group of 11 to 14 years) was 66.56 lakhs, which meant a percentage of 22.4. In the third plan, the emphasis was upon achieving the target of 11.33 lakh admissions. Among them, the number of admissions of girls rose to 28.35 lakhs.

In the third plan, stress was laid upon improving the standard of education. Admissions rose from 10.6% to 28.87%. Importance was also given to the teaching of science. At this level, the following steps were taken- (1) Post-basic schools were made a part of the secondary education structure. (2) Secondary education made production oriented. (3) Training institutions were strengthened. (4) Educational administrators were given suitable training. (5) Multipurpose schools were improved and strengthened. (6) Suitable arrangements for the training of teachers were made, and minimum standards for them were clearly formulated.

Fourth Plan

One gigantic problem before secondary education is that many students enter active life soon after completing their secondary education, though they are not properly equipped for it. The result of this is an increase in the level of educated unemployment.

The achievements of this plan are as follows —

Registration. Secondary education expanded at a satisfactory rate. The registration of boys went girls rose. There was a fall in the registration of children coming from families completely without facilities and those which received partial aid. Less facilities were made available to children coming from tribes and Scheduled Castes and Tribes.

Institutions. Because of various political factors, the number of uneconomic educational institutions increased. Half of them had a total enrolment of only 140 students. 30% of such schools were situated in towns.

Reorganisation. The Kothari Commission had recommended the restructuring of secondary education, but no efforts were directed towards this. Uttar Pradesh followed the 10 + 2 + 2 pattern, but no thought was given to the introduction of a 3 year degree course.

Quality. Efforts were made to -improve the syllabi, particularly in science and mathematics. Significant work was done in this direction by the NCERT, state educational institutions, the state science educational council, etc.

Vocationalisation. Nothing commendable was done in this direction, and students were still scampering to colleges for further education. In 1972, 19 lakh high school and intermediate students registered their names with the employment exchanges.

Teachers. By the end of the fourth plan period, 85% were expected to have received training, though even at this time, the need for a qualitative programme in this sphere was being felt.

Fifth Plan

Many programmes were devised for the expansion of secondary education during the fifth plan period. The investment on these programmes was as follows -

Secondary Education in the Fifth Plan (Crores)

S.N.	*Programmes*	
1.	Expansion Facilities	191.50
2.	Depressed and Girls' Education	24.65
3.	Teacher Education	4.24
4.	Reorganisation of Secondary Schools	6.25
5.	Qualitative Improvement of Education	64.56
6.	Teacher-Welfare	6.36
7.	Research	1.100
	Total	298.86 or 300.00

Expansion of Facilities. Keeping in the view the pace of increase in registration, provisions were made in the fifth plan for an additional 4 million registrations. It was anticipated that by 1979, 30% of all children in the 14 to 17 age group would have registered for admission to classes 9,10 and 11, while in 1974, this percentage was 23.5. There was no particular problem regarding registration in towns, and hence special attention was needed for rural areas. For this, (1) provisions were made for 250 girls' hostels and one lakh scholarships to ensure a growth in the education of girls, (2) facilities were provided for one lakh scholarships in the rural areas and setting up of hostels. (3) one lakh scholarships were reserved for children belonging to the weaker sections.

In addition to this, Rs. 26.25 crores were allocated for improvement in school buildings and their development, improvement in design. Introduction of the shift system, the load upon the local community and creation of 2500 new school buildings. For the remaining programme 189.15 crores were also allocated.

Education of Teachers. Arrangements were made, at the secondary level, for the qualitative development of teacher education, increase in registration, of setting up a state teacher education council, strengthening training schools and development of regional educational universities. There was also a scheme at the district level in which 300 teachers were to undergo refresher courses.

A Uniform Pattern. The plan also included a scheme for bringing uniformity into the structure of school education. There has been a tendency for the public to favour the opening of a college instead of a school. Hence, an intensive school programme was envisaged. It was projected that the standard of 250 schools would be improved and for this purpose Rs. 6.25 crores were allocated.

Qualitative Development. In this plan, attention was given to the qualitative improvement of education also. Education was linked with skill, efficiency and productivity. Since secondary education makes a profound contribution to national development, the need for qualitative improvement in this sphere was felt acutely. The following programmes were suggested for this purpose-

1. Introduction of work experience at the secondary level.
2. Vocationalization of secondary education.
3. Strengthening of guidance and counselling services.
4. Development of teaching in science and mathematics.
5. Development of selected schools.
6. Opening of Teachers Centres in every tehsil for teacher's welfare and professional development, construction of houses on a cooperative basis, provision of medical and other facilities and encouragement to research.

In view of the above facts, we conclude that secondary education determines the standard of the country, and hence, it must be allowed to expand even further. For expansion in Sixth, Seventh and Eighth Plan, read the respective chapters of this book.

Expansion of secondary education has constantly faced various problems, and these have influenced, in particular, efficient functioning as well as educational policy. The major obstacles to expansion are the following-

1. Lack of clarity in defining objectives in the five-year plans.
2. Absence of facilities for admission.
3. Lack of proper management by management committees.
4. Absence of growth in the number of institutions.
5. Absence of proper wages and other necessary facilities for teachers.
6. Inequality in the sums allocated in the budget for secondary education.
7. Absence of loyalty among the employees.

Extension of Kothari Commission

The suggestions of the Kothari Commission for the expansion of secondary education are the following-

1. For the next 20 years secondary education should expand in the manner outlined below: -
   (a) Schools should be located at suitable places.
   (b) Admissions should be based on available facilities.
   (c) Brilliant students should be selected.
2. Programmes for the spread of secondary education should be implemented in a planned manner at the district level so that existing schools can achieve the desired standards.
3. Students should be chosen for admission to secondary schools on the basis of self-selection. In this, attention must also be paid to the school record.
4. By 1975-76, 20% of the secondary schools should become institution providing vocational training. By 1985-86, there should be a 50% increase in such institutions.
5. Provisions for part-time as well as full-time vocational education should be made from class 7 or 8. The education of girls should emphasise training in domestic activities.
6. Education of girls should spread. At the lower stage, this proportion should be 1 : 2, and at the secondary stage 1: 3.

There should be separate schools, hostels and scholarships for girls.

The chief endeavour of the commission was to ensure a qualitative improvement and development in education so that education may achieve the desired standards, which may also undergo constant upward revision and thus, at least in some spheres, conform to international standards.

System of Assessment

The word examination implies casting a careful look all round. An academic examination can be thought of as a systematic arrangement for the testing and measurement of the students' knowledge, general ability or particular skill by some internal authority or external institution. In fact, teaching and examination are co-extensive processes. In a more comprehensive sense, one may even say that life itself is an examination. Without examination, it is not possible to determine whether teaching is progressing in the desired direction or not.

However, the prevailing system of examination has become the subject of a widespread and bitter criticism. Examinations have come to be regarded as a horror or an evil. The Radhakrishnan University Education Commission declared that till the middle of the present century, the system of examination in India was regarded as the worst form of Indian education. W H. Ryburn expressed the view that, irrespective of context, it could be said that examinations are the enemy of creative work, especially in the form in which they are administered.

The Kothari Commission said that evaluation is a continuous process, an inseparable part of the entire educational process, which is intimately connected with educational objectives. It has a profound influence upon the student's habit of study as well as the teachers mode of teaching, and thus it is of assistance, not merely in measuring the output of education, but also in its improvement and reform.

In evaluation, the maximum importance belongs to reform and improvement in cumulative record (*sanch itvrata patraka*) and external examinations. External reforms consists in improving the ability of the examiner who sets the paper, framing question papers with clearly defined objectives, improving the format of question, scientific evaluation of answers, and using calculative mechanisms, etc. These must be considered from the practical viewpoint.

Generally, people consider examination as a means of passing from one class to the next. Thus, it has become a habit, among teachers as well as students, to think that the student is required only to memorize the given syllabus in such a way that he can pass the examination. But, such habits of thought only alienate the progress of society from the educational process. They have resulted in giving education the sole aim of passing an examination and obtaining a degree, and not the aims of becoming cultured, developing good habits and conduct, improving mental and physical well-being and health or becoming an ideal citizen and working for the nation's welfare.

The Motive

An examination has the purpose of discovering the individual's achievements, abilities, standard and mental power. Its objectives are-

1. Discovering whether the student has the ability necessary for studying the given text and sustaining the role entrusted to him, or not.
2. Finding out whether the student is absorbing the material taught to him or not.
3. Determining whether the student is fit for an award or a scholarship or not.
4. Evaluating the ability and skill of the teachers.
5. Evaluating the extent to which the student possesses such qualities of character as patience, determination, ability to work industriously, etc.

The Importance

Upon the importance of examinations, the Mudaliar Commission pointed out that examination and evaluation have an important place in the educational sphere. The evaluation of the degree to which the student has progressed during his period of study is of value both for the teacher and the parents. Examinations have always existed in one form or the other. In the ancient past, education was imparted in ashramas, and examinations had a form different from their present one. In India, according to the Wood Plan and declaration, London University was assumed to be the ideal, and accordingly, universities came to be established here after 1850. With them, the modern system of examination came to India. Since then, examinations have remained, in one or the other forms.

Examinations are of two kinds. (1) External, and (2) Internal.

External Examination. These examinations are conducted, by the secondary board and the university.

Internal Examinations. If the teachers of the schools themselves seek to assess how much the students have learnt in various subjects, it is called an internal examination. Among this type are such tests as admission tests, monthly, quarterly, half-yearly or annual tests or examinations.

These examinations stimulate the student as well as the teacher, and also provide the following advantages-

1. The teacher is inspired to make greater efforts for achieving his goal.
2. The teacher develops awareness of the general standard.
3. It is only because of examinations that goals are clearly defined.
4. The student is realistically evaluated.
5. Having passed the examination, the student wins social recognition.

Drawbacks of Present System

The prevailing system of examination is defective. In it, passing from one class to the next is treated as the sole objective. Some of its major defects are: -

1. The prevailing system is defective because the student considers passing the examination as his objective. Neither the student nor the teacher pays any attention to knowledge or standards.

2. Examinations have become so important that, instead of being directed towards knowledge, they are directed towards wealth. It is felt that the sole aim is passing the examination and obtaining employment.

3. The student depends upon help-books or 'keys'. He has to display his skill only in learning by rote and providing subjective, essay-type answers.

4. The teacher, too, aims only at helping the student to pass, instead of seeking to develop the requisite qualities of character in the student.

5. The teacher's worth is measured in terms of the number of his students who pass from his class.

6. The parents, too, are interested solely in their children passing the examination and obtaining a job. Even those offering employment base their judgement upon the applicant's certificates and degrees.

7. The prevailing system does not measure the child's abilities effectively. Examinations have become a 'chance', and hence they are not a complete standard of measurement.

8. Students learn the subject by rote and succeed, but this is no measure of their intellectual prowess.

9. Education, today, has come to be dominated by examinations, and thus, the means have become an end in itself. The system of examination has become a barrier which prevents a clear perception of the purpose of education. It appears that the future of this educational system must be dark, since its sole objective is to prepare the student for an examination.

10. This system of examination has also encouraged the tendency to copy or cheat, since the students want to pass the examination, by fair means or foul. In this connection, R.C. Wren has remarked that the examination system is a suitable servant, but it is also bad. It depends upon the headmaster whether he treats the examination system as a slave or a master.

11. At present, passing the examination is an art. Those skilled in it get success with very little study while those who study in detail but lack the necessary skill of preparing for an examination are condemned to despair.

12. The examination is taken after a year, at a fixed time. If the child unfortunately falls ill, he cannot participate in the examination, though he may have worked hard throughout the year. In contrast, one who has studied even for a few days may pass the examination.

13. In a written examination of three hours, it is not possible to test the student's knowledge of the whole syllabus. Even theoretically, this kind of testing is unsatisfactory and unjustified.

Despite all these grievous defects, the system continues to prevail for the following reasons:-

1. It is because of this system of examination that students pay attention to what is taught.
2. Millions of examinees can be evaluated within a few days, and at comparatively little expense. From this viewpoint, the prevailing system is good.
3. The modern system of examination generates the feeling of competition among children.
4. In the written examinations, the student has the opportunity to express his own views.
5. It provides insight into the teacher's depth of knowledge and his efforts.
6. This prevailing system is considered suitable for a system of collective education because it provides a single criterion for all the students. In any individualized system of testing, it becomes extremely difficult to pick out the outstanding students.
7. It is true that this system allows free play to the chance factor, but it is also true that hardly one or two out of thousands of students are able to pass without studying the books.

8. Examinations teach the student to organise and utilise his knowledge effectively.

Recommendations

Some of the suggestions preferred by the Secondary Education Commission are-

1. The number of external examinations should be reduced.
2. The form of questions should be changed; there should be fewer essay-type questions.
3. At the time of examination, the student's work throughout the year should be considered.
4. In order to. implement suggestions for improving the examination system, teachers should participate in the meetings of the secondary Education department and the External Department of the Central Education Ministry.
5. Before embarking upon the teaching of a subject, it is necessary to determine the increase in the child's knowledge which must be aimed at, as well as the changes in his behaviour to be brought about through the teaching.
6. Examinations should include New Type Tests, among which Objective Tests, are of considerable importance.
7. In testing a student, the focus should be on what and how much the student knows, not on what he does not know.
8. The examination should be treated, not as the end, but only as the means, since the purpose of examination is to aid education in achieving its primary goals.
9. Oral testing should be given a suitable place in the system of examination.
10. The teacher's advice is also important in this system.
11. There is great need for reform and improvement in the question papers employed under the prevailing system.

12. The questions should be so designed that the child is stimulated to think for himself in seeking for the answers.

13. There is a great need to bring about a decrease in the various kinds of public examinations, because they have a detrimental effect on the child at a time when he is passing through a sensitive age and growing quickly.

There can be no denying that teaching and examination are intimately related, and that examinations have always influenced teaching. By modifying the examination system, it is possible to spread education in such a way that it may be instrumental in the comprehensive development of the child.

Review of Examination System

According to the Kothari Commission, it is universally accepted that evaluation is a continuous process, which is an inseparable part of the educational system. It influences the student's habits as well as the teachers' mode of teaching. The techniques of evaluation are means to the preparation of a record of the child's development in the desired directions.

The following are the suggestions of the Kothari Commission with regard to reform in the system of examination-

1. Written examinations should be improved.

2. New testing techniques should be devised for testing those abilities which cannot be suitably assessed through written examinations.

3. In external examinations, questions should be of the objective type.

4. Various kinds of standardised tests should be employed for internal assessment by the teacher who can create new tests, oral tests, practical tests, and thereby evaluate the child's inclination and attitude. The results of these tests should not be compared.

5. The certificate issued by the Board after a public examination should contain the marks obtained by the student in each

subject, but it should carry no statement about whether the candidate has passed or failed.

6. The student should get his school record in addition to the Board's certificate.

7. The Commission has always been committed to the improvement of public examinations by removing their defects. It has even recommended that in the event of responsible evaluation, the education department should have the authority to suspend aid to such an institution.

The existing educational system aims exclusively passing the examination and thus it fails to bring about the mental and moral development of the individual. Hence it fails to aid and guide teachers as well as famous educational institutions. It is stated that the importance of modern education lies not merely in the intellectual attainment of students, but also in the emotional, social, mental and physical development. Social adjustment and other aspects of life are also important. As a whole, education should aim at the comprehensive development of personality.

Hence, the objective is to make the child a successful citizen, a fine soldier and a great leader. Hence, education in the country must make continuous progress towards improvement and reach the peak of success. In view of this, the existing system of education deserves criticism.

Vocational Aspects

In the changing concepts and beliefs of the modern age, our country lags behind other countries in terms of hundreds of years in the race for progress. We want to achieve equality with the developed countries but in this process, as we move forward, the developed countries move even faster and go ahead of us. The reason for this is that our knowledge has not been related to modern science and technology. In view of this, the education commission has proposed the vocationalization of education at every level, not only at the secondary stage. The Commission has sought to base this vocationalization upon production. Hence, after considering the mutual relationship between education and production, it has proposed the basis of the scheme for the restructuring of education in the following terms :

1. Science should be the basis of education and culture.
2. Work experience should be an integral part of general education.
3. Education at the secondary level should be vocationalized in order to meet the needs of industry, agriculture and trade.
4. Laying special stress upon agriculture and related sciences, scientific and technological education at the university level should be developed.

For vocationalizing secondary education, the Commission has considered in detail the vocationalization at both its levels—the lower secondary and the higher secondary. In the Commissions' view, 20 per cent students in classes 8 to 10 should obtain vocational training. In the same way, 50 per cent of the students in classes 11 and 12 should receive vocational education. The Commission clearly accepted the principle that among the most important reforms is that of vocationalization of higher secondary education. 50% of all students should take admissions to the vocational courses. The views of the Commission regarding vocationalization at both levels are as follows-

High School Level

1. Industrial training centres have courses suitable to post-primary educational levels. If the age of admission to such courses is set at 14 years, the number of students entering such institutions after completing primary education will be very large. (This age limit was 16 years, and was subsequently reduced to 15).
2. Students who stop studying after class 7 or 8 usually take up their family profession, while some of them hope to set up a small scale industry of trading organisation. For such people, arrangements should be made for short term or part-time syllabi so that they may be able to develop their abilities and skills. The Commission purposed that a separate department should be set up within the education department to keep in touch with youth and provide them with suitable opportunities for

receiving vocational training on a part-time basis, along with their general education.

3. Most students belonging to the rural areas will work on their ancestral fields. They should be given opportunities for general education, professional skills, etc.
4. A large number of girls get married soon after leaving schools. For them, arrangements should be made to provide them general education as well as education in domestic science.

Intermediate Level

At this level, the Commission has made provisions for, a very large number of vocational courses.

1. Along with an expansion in facilities for full-time study, there should be provisions for part-time syllabi at the higher secondary level, though it may be arranged through industries, evening classes, part-time or correspondence courses.
2. The syllabi in the industrial training centres should be such that the minimum qualification for admission to them should be class 10.
3. These syllabi should provide training in health, trade, administration, small scale industries, etc., through courses lasting for six months to three years. At the completion of the course, students should be given diplomas or certificates.

In view of the importance it has attached to the vocationalisation of secondary education, the Commission has proposed that the central government should aid the state governments in implementing such a programme. Citing the example of the USA, the Commission has thrust the entire responsibility for the vocationalisation of secondary education upon the Union government.

At present, the existing system of secondary education does not make provisions for vocationalization which will satisfy the needs for skilled workers in the next twenty years.

At the secondary level, these schools satisfy only 3% of the need. In 1965-66, there was increase of 2.2%. The Commission projected that by 1985-86, there should be an increase of 20% at the lower secondary level. For the next twenty years, the Commission made provisions for the admission of 24,13,000 students to vocational schools. In the same manner, the projected figures of admission to professional universities is 6,87,300 students, which is 43% of the total number of students. The Commission set for itself the target of 50 percent.

Professional Education

Regarding the vocational education at the school level, the Commission has expressed the following ideas :

1. The Central government should introduce a variety of courses for boys and girls in 14-18 age group. The responsibility for this should fall upon the Union government, thus creating a parallel with the Smith Hughes Act of the USA.
2. As far as the question of outstanding students is concerned, instead of putting them into special courses, they can be made to do intensive work within the same syllabus thus the deficiency can be made up.
3. At present, there are 356 polytechnic institutions in which 1,13,000 students can study.
4. The Commission recommended that the name of Junior Technical Schools should be changed to Technical High Schools.

Past Experience

The Commission has suggested that work experience is essential for arousing loyalty towards the vocation. In its view, work experience can be defined as any productive activity which contributes to productive work in the school, house, laboratory, fields, factory or at any other place.

The Commission has recommended that work experience should be introduced at every educational level. The concept of work experience is based on the principle that the process of generating knowledge and wealth should be co-extensive.

The reality is that work experience evolves an attitude of loyalty towards the profession. Because of this liberal attitude, it , is proposed that, at the higher secondary level, a variety of specialized courses should be available. The student should be allowed to make his choice from among them according to his interests and inclinations, and thus be prepared to choose a career of his liking. This will also facilitate his adjustment in life.

With reference to this attitude, as regards the higher classes, the Commission has argued that in these classes, it can take the form of teaching of art which will lead to the development of the student's creative ability and technological thought. Work experience can be imparted in the actual circumstances of real life, for instance, working in fields at the time of sowing or harvesting, or engaging in productive work in a family unit. Such situations can be exploited to the maximum possible extent.

The Commission has declared that, in the coming years, one workshop should be arranged for every school, or at-least for a group of schools. At the lower secondary level, work experience can take the form of laboratory training. At the higher secondary level, where students are more mature, and they are comparatively less in number, they can be given work experience in workshops, fields, industrial and trading enterprises.

Many kinds of materials are needed in school teaching. Work experience relating to the production of these materials should be available in schools and institutions. It has been suggested that (1) in some selected institutions (scientific and technological) students should engage in full-scale production. (2) In some institutions the apparatus used in school and college laboratories and workshops should be produced. (3) Some institutions should manufacture some things like furniture, etc.

The Commission has suggested that arrangements for scholarships on a large scale are desirable with a view to promoting vocationalization of secondary education. It has said that in vocational colleges, there are more provisions for scholarships, and that the proportion there is greater than in general education. For future progress, the following principles should be adopted (1) Liberal policy in granting admissions, (2) An increase in the amount of the scholarships.

In a country like India, the majority of parents cannot, afford a vocational education for their children because of poverty. It is because of this that the Commission has sought to make the programme of vocationalization of education successful through liberalisation of the number and amount of scholarships.

Goals Attained

Many problems will come to an end with the vocationalization of secondary education, though at present, these problems have a gigantic and daunting size. The Commission has not encouraged employment, as was the case in Basic Education. It has opined that every individual should work to fulfil the needs of the country, and every aspect of his work should contribute to national development. The fruits flowing from vocationalisation will be the following:-

1. There will be a direct relationship between employment and education.
2. The individual will depend, for his livelihood, upon his limbs rather than upon offices.
3. The country's economic condition will improve and its manpower will be put to constructive use.
4. The Commission hopes that, in this way, every educated individual will be given a job along with his certificate.
5. Students will be convinced that education is purposeful, and that they, too are needed for the building of their nation. The Commission views this change as the most profoundly significant.
6. The vocationalization of secondary education will make possible the best utilisation of the country's resources and circumstances. In 1882, the Hunter Commission had proposed a plan of education very similar to the present one.
7. Science and technology will be accepted as the foundation stones, and so, in modernisation, religion and work will be harmoniously blended together.

However, the important question is : when and how will these achievements take a concrete shape? Reflection upon this question turns our attention towards the following proposals of the Commission : (1) It is essential, for the vocationalization of secondary education, that vocational courses should immediately be made available to at least 20% of the students, and 50% students should be admitted to the higher secondary level. (2) At the secondary level, the opportunities for education should be available equally to everyone. A comprehensive programme of scholarships should be introduced.

Steering Group Report

The goal of vocationalization is to train and develop one stream of the educational flow in the country, in the context of the country's manpower and economic development. Through the development of vocational skills and suitable training, students are prepared for Middle Level employment in agriculture, industry, commerce, etc. The introduction of such courses in polytechnic institutions and provision of suitable training results in the student coming into direct contact with the employer. Hence, in secondary schools, educational and vocational guidance should be organised and provided so that students obtain awareness of training in various skills. Educational departments should develop vocational skills particularly in those areas in which institutional facilities are not available. These courses should be organised in cooperation with units which can provide employment. The experience obtained from multipurpose schools indicate that vocational training cannot be effectively organised until they are in close contact with those employers who will provide employment to the students trained in such schools.

Variations and modifications in vocational courses should only be made with the greatest care by highly skilled and qualified persons. However, geographical mobility among qualified people is quite limited, and so, vocational courses should be given a shape in accord with local circumstances and requirements. For this purpose, it is more convenient to carry out surveys at the district level before framing schemes for educational and vocational courses providing training in specific skills.

A powerful programme based on work experience and vocationalization can be effective in this direction. For this, contact between institutions and government agencies must be maintained. At various administrative levels, organisational facilities should always be available. At the national level, the NCERT can function as an effective clearing house and source of information for programmes of vocationalization and work experience. At the State level, independent man-power cells should be created under the management of the chief minister or the planning minister, and these cells should make, from time to time, declarations of policy on manpower. The state education institutions should take the help of employing authorities for creating research blocks, training blocks, extension blocks, etc. At the district level, project officers should be appointed for establishing harmony between work experience, teacher training and polytechnics. An employment committee should be set up under the chairmanship of the district magistrate.

Planned Changes

In the plans work experience and vocationalization have been conceived of as mutual complements. This view finds expression in the plan in the following manners:

Work Experience. It has been presented from the perspective for development. Provisions have been made in the plan for initiating work experience in 50,000 schools, strengthening state educational institutions, employment of district project officers, training of one lakh teachers, and the setting up of 125 Common Facility Centres. For this purpose, a sum of Rs. 10.60 crores has been allocated.

Vocationalization. At the secondary level, the programme of vocationalization has been implemented in many parts and regions. It has been extended to take within its purview health, agriculture, labour and employment and polytechnic education. An additional provision of Rs. 1 crore has been made for setting up institutions for survey, collection of information, training, etc., at the district level.

Counselling. In order to strengthen vocationalization and make it effective, provisions have been made for the training of 20,000 teachers as career masters. There are arrangements for the appointment of State

Bureau and District Guidance Officers. Rs. 2 - 5 crores will be spent upon this programme.

In reality, the vocationalization of secondary education is not a novel scheme but, in view of the country's present circumstances, it is essential that we provide employment to every individual according to his innate abilities. This will become feasible only when vocational education is available at every stage of the educational process. And, of all the stages of education, the secondary stage is the most important because 50% of the students have to struggle for employment and livelihood after completing their secondary education. If they are denied jobs at this stage, it will mean a wastage of valuable manpower, and this wastage represents a great loss for the country. From this point of view, the vocationalization of secondary education is of the utmost importance.

Schools with a Difference

In India, the process of setting up multipurpose schools was set in motion by the recommendations of the Mudaliar Commission. Supporting the idea, the Kothari Commission opined that it was their purpose to introduce varied courses which would be taught in multipurpose schools. It stressed the need for establishing such institutions.

It is obvious that provisions were made for the teaching of various subjects in these schools. Even before the appointment of the latter commission, there were numerous subjects and also considerable diversification in the syllabus, but there was no school in which every course or subject was taught. The Secondary Education Commission laid stress on the creation of multipurpose schools so that all the varied objectives of education could be achieved in a single school.

The term 'multipurpose school' applies to that school which makes arrangements for the teaching of all kinds of courses which can satisfy the interests, objectives and talents of the students. It inspires the students to choose courses of study according to their interests. The Mudaliar Commission, too, said that the purpose of the multipurpose school is to provide for the education of students according to their interests and abilities. These schools should try to provide students with opportunities to develop themselves in harmony with their nature, tendency, attitude and abilities.

The Mudaliar Commission stressed the need for establishing multipurpose schools on the basis of the following arguments :

1. In the USA multipurpose schools had proved more successful than schools which had only one purpose.
2. These schools destroy the feeling of inequality in the child's mind and help to develop human equalities and values in them.
3. In such schools, the child is free to choose subjects in accord with his interests.
4. Students who fail to progress in one class can easily be transferred to a more suitable class or course, without their being any need for the student to change the school.
5. In multipurpose schools, there are arrangements for teaching every course, and so the students undergo comprehensive development.
6. Multipurpose schools can fulfil the country's need for technicians and contribute to the development of technical education.
7. In such schools, it is possible to organise courses of study which are in harmony with social, economic and psychological needs.

Objectives of Schools

K.G. Saiyadain expressed the profound view that if a student; in the absence of proper counselling, takes up humanities instead of science, or vice versa, it is not only his school life which is ruined but also his entire future life, because he chose the wrong profession. It is in order to overcome this shortcoming that stress has been laid upon the setting up of multipurpose schools.

The main objectives of multipurpose schools are the following :

1. Making continuous efforts for the multi-faceted development of schools.

2. Guiding them to train the abilities and talents of students for the creation of national character and national wealth.
3. Creating skill in handicraft work.
4. Providing education in social and constructive or creative activities.

Their importance has been accepted in the Third Five-Year Plan, in which it was stated that although the concept of multipurpose schools had been accepted immediately, and the scheme had progressed rapidly, there were a few obstacles. It was argued that the attention of planner should be focussed on strengthening the institutions which had been established so that the whole scheme may rest on secure foundations.

Problems of such Schools

While multipurpose schools can be credited with achieving a comprehensive development of the child's personality, it is also obvious that they suffer from certain problems. These difficulties are :

Difficulty in Converting a High School. Generally speaking, there is great difficulty in converting a high school into a multipurpose institution. And, where some high schools were given this form, there was no real need. The difficulty arises because of local conditions, lack of adequate space, buildings and facilities for travelling or materials needed for teachings.

Opposition from Parents. Parents often express their opposition to multipurpose schools if these institutions do not provide course of study related to local needs. In the absence of a definite policy on the teaching of crafts and industry, many problems are generated.

Division of Time. In multipurpose schools the problem of division of time is a very complex one, because it is a very difficult task to arrange a suitable and convenient timetable in such a vast programme.

Lack of Text Books. Multipurpose schools have had to face great difficulties because, so far, they have lacked both in suitable text-books as well as trained teachers.

The Principal's Problem. Very often, parents do not agree with the course of study selected by the teacher for their children, and this leads to a conflict between the parents and the principal of the institution.

Economic Difficulty. These schools need buildings, laboratories, workshops, teaching material, etc. The government has faced great difficulty in making all this available, because in the absence of adequate finances, the government failed, on the one hand, to equip them with good laboratories, and on the other, to make them so attractive that students could be attracted towards the courses.

Ignorance of the Method of Working. Multipurpose schools can be successful only if a particular method of working is adopted but since the staff in many of them was not acquainted with it, they have had to face ignominious failure.

Difficulty in Changing Courses. If a student of a multipurpose school wishes to change the subjects of study, he has to face many difficulties.

Lack of Conformity with Local Needs. When the multipurpose schools were established, attention was not paid to local needs, and the result was only a wastage of money and manpower.

The government should consider the following facts in setting up new multipurpose schools

1. Multipurpose schools should be set up in prosperous regions because it is possible to get local help and cooperation in making school building and other activities.
2. Before setting up a multipurpose school in a particular place, it is essential to carry out a survey of that area. A school should be set up there only if the locale is suitable, and if such a school is really needed there.
3. Initially, multipurpose schools should be started as an experiment. They should be made permanent only if they are successful.
4. Guides should be appointed in multipurpose schools so that they can test the students and give them useful advice on the selection of courses.
5. It is not possible to meet the need for teachers for all multipurpose schools through four Regional Colleges. Hence,

either the existing colleges should be expanded or new colleges established.

6. Suitable text-books should be published.

Hence, it is obvious that although multipurpose schools are necessary for our country, there is need for necessary reforms and improvements in them. They will prove useful for the country only if these reforms are carried out.

Various Syllabi

It is ironical that, in our country, considerable thought has been devoted to the syllabi for boys and girls. The views of the Secondary Education Commission on the prevailing system were that political, social and economic circumstances had changed and new problems had emerged. It was, therefore, necessary to, make a careful study to determine the objective of education at every level. This idea was felt to be applicable not only to the existing situation but also to the direction of development, - nature and the determination of the future of our social structure, which itself had to be changed.

The Secondary Education Commission has determined the objectives of education in the following terms-

1. Students must be given training in character so that they can take a constructive part in our democratic social structure.
2. Students must be given practical and vocational training so that they can help to make the nation prosperous.
3. Students should be given training in literary artistic and cultural interests which may contribute to comprehensive human development and self expression, because without this, the culture of our country will be annihilated.

In addition, the Kothari Commission tied the objectives of education into a five point programme

1. Linking education with production.
2. Strengthening national unity and social unity through educational programmes.

3. Strengthening and vitalising democracy through education.
4. Evolving social, moral and spiritual values.
5. Modernising society through the development of skills by exploiting curiosity, inclination and values.

When we reflect upon these objectives, many questions arise to confront us. For instance: Is it necessary to differentiate between the syllabi for boys and the syllabi for girls ? Is co-education a solution to this problem ?

The Mrs. Hansa Metha Committee expressed its views on the question of differentiation between a syllabus for boys and that for girls in the following terms- (1) In the democratic and socialistic society of which we dream, education will be linked with those individual abilities, inclinations and interests which, in reality, have no relationship with difference in sex. For this reason, in such a society, there is no need to create different syllabi for the two sexes. (2) In a changing situation, it will be necessary to accept the fact of certain psychological differences between men and women. It will also be necessary to accept the fact of certain differences in their respective departments of work, and to make such differences the basis upon which the syllabi for them should be framed. However, in doing so, it should be kept in mind, that the desired and necessary values and attitudes should be evolved both in men and in women, with the passage of time, but that no step should be taken which may help to harden these differences between men and women or aggravate them.

In order to get an adequate answer to these questions, we must turn to the survey carried out by the Secondary Education Commission. During this survey, the following criticisms came to light (1) The present syllabus is narrow. (2) It is bookish and theoretical. (3) It has a long list of subjects which are not useful. (4) It leaves no scope for practical and other kinds of activities; it also lacks the necessary facilities for the proper development of personality. (5) It neither satisfies the needs of youth nor develops its abilities. (6) Excessive emphasis upon examinations is harmful. (7) It lacks technical and vocational subjects which are necessary, both for the student and for the country's economic development. The Commission's view is that the first thing, which should be clearly comprehended, is that, according to the most enlightened modern educational thought, the term syllabus does not apply to the subjects traditionally taught in schools, but rather the sum total of the various experiences gathered by students through varied activities, the experiences they gather from the school, art, liberary, laboratory, the playground, and even the mutual relations between themselves and their teachers. In this way, the entire life of the school is comprehended in the word 'syllabus', which helps the students in the development of their personality at every point.

The Secondary Education Commission has suggested a syllabus for the Middle level consisting of the following subjects- (1) Language, (2) Social Studies, (3) General Science, (4) Arithmetic, (5) Art, (6) Handicrafts, (7) Physical education.

The Commission's views on this issue are the following :

1. (a) Mother tongue, or regional language, or both, or a mixed programme.

(b) One of the following languages should be selected

(1) Hindi, for those whose mother tongue is not Hindi.
(2) Elementary English, for those who did not study English upto the Middle level.
(3) Advanced English, for those who studied English.
(4) One modern Indian language (in addition to Hindi).
(5) One modern foreign language (in addition to English).
(6) One classical language.

2. (a) Social Study (for the first two years).

(b) General science, arithmetic (for the first two years).

3. One handicraft from the following list should be chosen

Carding or weaving, wood working, metal work, gardening, stitching, practice of typography, workshop, modelling, etc.

4. Three subjects are included in these groups :

Group. 1. (Humanities). 1. One classical language, or one language from group (a), which has not been studied in the past. 2. History. 3,

Geography. 4. Economics and Civics. 5. Psychology and Logic, 6. Arithmetic. 7. Music. 8. Domestic Science.

Group. 2. (Science). 1. Physics. 2. Chemistry. 3. Biology. 4. Geography. 5. Mathematics. 6. Health science and Anatomy.

Group. 3. (Technical). 1. Practical mathematics and geometrical drawing. 2. Practical science. 3. Mechanical Engineering. 4. Electrical Engineering.

Group. 4. (Agriculture). 1. Harmonised Agriculture. 2. Veterinary. 3. Horticulture and gardening. 4. Agricultural chemistry and Botany.

Group. 5. (Commercial). 1. Commercial Practice. 2. Book-keeping; 3. Commercial geography or economics, or civics 4. Short-hand and typewriting.

Group. 6. (Arts). 1. Art and history. 2. Drawing and (aale-khan). 3. Painting. 4. Modelling. 5. Music. 6. Dance.

Group. 7. (Domestic Science). 1. Domestic economics. 2. Nutrition and cooking. 3. Maternal care and child welfare. 4. Domestic organisation and home nursing.

In addition to the above subjects, a student can also take one alternative subject from the above groups, irrespective of whether he has chosen any other subject from that group or not.

A syllabi is always the foundation of education. It is through a syllabus that we seek to fulfil the desired objectives. Educationists have, for long, been harping on the fact that the syllabus, which has been made the vehicle of education, has imparted inertia to education. The Commission has given careful thought to all the possibilities inherent in the syllabus.

Reforms Needed

The syllabus is one of the three pillars of education. It influences the entire educational process. Hence, in order to reform and improve, it is essential that the following steps be taken

1. Education departments must prepare the syllabi for schools on the basis of research.

2. Frequent revisions should be carried out in this research.
3. Text-books and reading materials should be created.
4. Teachers should be made to undergo refresher courses through in-service courses.
5. Schools should have the freedom to experiment with new syllabi. Thus work should be done particularly in schools attached to training colleges.
6. The state board of school education should prepare syllabi for every subject and implement them in schools which posses all facilities.
7. The syllabi should be prepared with the help of teacher councils, national councils and State institutions for various subjects

Preparation of the Syllabus

The syllabus should be compiled with the objectives of education in view. For this it is necessary that :

1. In non-vocational schools, a syllabus of general education should be the basis of education for 10 years.
2. At the end of this period, the level of achievement of the syllabus should be found out.
3. At the primary level, a heavy load of subjects should not be imposed upon the student. Subjects pertaining to language, arithmetic and environment should be taught.
4. The syllabus at the higher primary level should be more comprehensive and intensive. Methods of teaching should be systematically employed.
5. At the lower secondary level, the teaching should be in detail and indepth.
6. There should be diversification in subjects at the higher secondary level.
7. At the higher primary level, brilliant children should be given more facilities. They can be taught one subject in depth.

8. At the secondary level, there should be two kinds :

   (i) Ordinary. (ii) Advanced.

Teaching of Languages

1. In the context of education, there should be a new language policy.

2. The language formula should be structured as follows :

   (1) After the mother tongue, Hindi should be assumed to be the language of the Union.
   (2) Practical knowledge of English is useful for the students.
   (3) The development of language depends upon the teacher and his abilities.
   (4) By the 10th class, the child should have knowledge of three languages.
   (5) Two additional languages should be taught.
   (6) Hindi and English should be applied where they are needed.
   (7) At no stage should four languages ever be made compulsory.

3. *The three.language formula should be based on the following principles.* (1) mother tongue and regional language. (2) The official and the semi-official language of the Central government. (3) One modern Indian or European language which is not covered under either (1) or (2) above, and which is used as a medium of education.

4. (1) At the lower primary level, in general, one language should be taught: it should be either the mother tongue or the regional language. (2) At the higher primary stage, two languages should be taught - mother tongue or regional language and the official language. (3) At the lower secondary language, three languages should be taught- (A) mother tongue or, regional language, (b) official or semi-official language, (c) modern Indian language,, (d) At the higher secondary level, two languages will be compulsory.

5. The study and teaching of modern literary languages (with the exception of English) should be made available in selected schools. In non-Hindi areas, arrangements should be made for the teaching of Hindi and English.
6. Hindi or English should be taught respectively for three or six years as the official and semi-official languages.
7. The study of language should not be compulsory in higher education.
8. Efforts should be made to propagate Hindi at the national level, but it should not be forced upon those not willing to adopt it.
9. Good literature should be published in the Devnagri and Roman scripts.
10. The teaching of English should not begin before class 5.
11. The classical languages (Sanskrit, Arabic, Persian, etc.). should be introduced as alternative languages from the eighth class.

Teaching of Mathematics and Science

Every student should be made to study science and mathematics as part of his general education.

1. At the lower primary stage, science should be taught as environment education. In class 4, knowledge of roman numerals, charts, maps, etc., should be imparted.
2. At the higher primary level, logic should be developed. It is necessary for the child to develop his power of logical thought and deduction of conclusions.
3. In a lower primary school, it is necessary to have a science corner, while in the upper primary, there should be a laboratory and an auditorium.
4. At the lower secondary level, science should be developed as a form of mental discipline.
5. At the lower secondary level, there should be provisions for an advanced course for brilliant children.

6. The education of science should serve to relate and link agriculture and technology with each other.
7. Proper attention to the teaching of mathematics is essential for mental development.
8. At every educational level, the courses in mathematics should be modernised.
9. The methods of teaching science and mathematics should be as modern as possible.

Teaching of Social Sciences

1. Social study is essential for good citizenship. The course in social study must lay stress upon the strengthening of national unity and unity of man.
2. At all levels, the method of social study should be infused with a scientific spirit and temper.

Successful Experiment

Work experience implies taking full advantage of past experiences and linking education with production. Through work experience, the country can hope to achieve self-reliance in foodgrains, economic development, expansion of employment, social and national unity, political development, industrial progress, etc. For this reason, the Commission has made the following recommendations with regard to productivity :

1. At the primary level, a programme of work experience should be introduced. At the secondary level, it should function as a workshop. It should provide for work in agriculture, industry, etc.
2. Where a workshop does not exist, sets of tools and apparatus should be made available.
3. The necessary literature should be created, teachers should be trained and workshops established.

In the opinion of the Commission, work experience means being engaged in productive work at home, in school, in a shop, field or workshop, i.e., anywhere. Mahatma Gandhi introduced a revolutionary experiment in the form of Basic Education, and in fact, the concept of work experience is very similar to Gandhiji's concept. It can even be said that the kind of education which Gandhiji had envisaged for a society standing on the road to industrialization was similar to the notion of work-experience.

In Service of Society

1. A social service programme should be introduced to achieve community development. It should be introduced at every level of education.
2. Camps should be organised for labour and social service activities.

Physical Fitness

Physical education should be imparted to bring about formation of character and to maintain mental awareness, physical ability and physical skill. This education, which is based on the principles governing the development of the child can be modified.

Moral Education

1. In an organised manner, the provision of moral education should lead to the creation of spiritual values.. For this, both direct and indirect methods of teaching should be used.
2. There should be at least one or two periods per week in the time table for the development of moral and spiritual values. The subjects through which these are inculcated should be related to the syllabus.

Hobbies

1. The government should set up a committee to examine the potential for the teaching of art.
2. Children's Homes should be established in every part of the country with the help to local groups, or organisations.
3. In selected universities, departments of art should be established.

4. Co-curricular activities should be encouraged for self-expression.

On the lines laid down by the report of the Hansa Mehta Committee, the Kothari Commission has stressed the principle that there should be no differentiation in the syllabus on the basis of sex. Domestic science should be available for girls, but it should not be compulsory. Encouragement should be given for receiving education in music, the fine arts, science and mathematics.

New Curriculum

The basis of Basic Education is production, the idea that the syllabus should forge ahead through productive activities. The child should come into contact with the community. It should assume such a form that the method of education at every level should become definite. Every stage of education should be a basic one. There is no need for a separate class of education in the name of Basic Education.

The Kothari Commission devoted serious thought to the problem of preparing the most appropriate syllabus. Fresh suggestions have been invited. There is still a difference of opinion on the subject of language. Some people argue that Hindi is being throttled. In reality, however, the difficulty is that we are unable to grapple with concrete facts. The formula compounded above is similar to the Russian formula for doing away with linguistic disputes. We should take care to deal honestly and fairly with the languages of our own country.

Education for Girls

A committee was set up, under the chairmanship of Shrimati Hansa Mehta, to bring about development in the education of women and to formulate a suitable syllabus. The committee has held the view that in a democratic society, education is related to individual abilities, interests and bent of mind, and hence it emphasised the view that differentiation in the syllabus on the basis of sex should be avoided. Because of this, the Education Commission has formulated a common syllabus upto class 10. Despite this, it is desirable that the syllabus should conform to the tastes and interests of both boys and girls.

1. Home Science should be kept as an optional subject upto the Higher Secondary level. Though this subject is very popular among girls, it should not be made compulsory for them.
2. Special facilities should be provided for the study of music and fine arts.
3. Girls should be encouraged to study science and mathematics.
4. Lady teachers proficient in science and mathematics should be trained.

In addition, these suggestions should be given importance so that the education of women may gain strength and develop.

Accepting the recommendations of the National Council on Women's Education, the Commission has said that :

1. The gap between the education of men and women should be removed as soon as possible.
2. A special fund and special schemes should be generated for this purpose.
3. There should be a separate department at the Centre as well as in the States looking after the education of women.
4. Arrangements for vocational education of every kind should be made as part of women's education.
5. Vocational training courses should be initiated for adult women also.

The Commission has given great importance to the suggestions of the National Committee on Education for Women. The main suggestions are the following-

1. In the coming years, more emphasis should be laid upon the education of women so that the difference between men and women, from the educational viewpoint, can be eliminated.
2. Special programmes should be prepared for this purpose.
3. Both at the State and Central levels, there should be special machinery to supervise the education of girls and women.

From this, it is evident that attention should be paid, in preparing the syllabus, to differences in interest and ability.

Educational Counselling

There is now a crying need for educational as well as vocational guidance because of the individual differences among students. Stressing the need for a programme of guidance, the Secondary Education Commission has elaborated that because of the multipurpose syllabus, the teachers and managers of schools have an additional burden of responsibility, the responsibility of providing proper guidance to students in their educational and vocational choices.

The Kothari Commission, too, has voiced similar views on the questions of guidance. According to it, at the secondary level, the main function of guidance is to recognise the abilities of youth. It will help the students to understand their abilities and limitations, to make a proper choice of academic subject in view of their qualities. Besides, it will provide them with educational as well as vocational information, make education realistic and also provide a sound basis for individual and social adjustment in the school.

The following are the purposes of setting up a guidance programme:-

1. Collecting all relevant information about the student.
2. Providing opportunities for participating in all intellectual, social and cultural programmes.
3. Providing guidance through information about educational and vocational matters.
4. Establishing a service centre.
5. Solving problems through collective and individual guidance.
6. Creating an atmosphere suitable to guidance in the school.
7. Winning the cooperation of students and parents.
8. Winning the cooperation of the entire community.

The purpose of guidance is to discover the abilities of a student which may aid him in his individual development. Three kinds of activities are important for the individual-educational, personal and vocational. Hence, guidance also takes three forms :

Educational Guidance. In such a programme, the students are given guidance regarding the syllabus. It is needed for the following reasons-

Individual Differences. Suggesting a syllabus on the basis of the child's interests and ability.

Intellectual Differences. Providing guidance on the basis of intelligence quotient or level, of the individual.

Syllabus. Guiding the students in the choice of a suitable syllabus in view of the varied courses of study available.

Polluted Atmosphere. Guiding the students to overcome the polluting effect of the unsuitable atmosphere prevailing in the school or at home.

Vocational Guidance. The purpose of this is to guide the student in his vocation while he is still at school and also acquainting him with the opportunities open to him. Its need is for the following reasons:-

1. Vocational guidance is necessary for proper choice of career.
2. Special training is necessary for specialised vocations.
3. Creates an opportunity for choosing careers on the basis of individual differences.

Individual or Personal Guidance. The purpose of such guidance is to eradicate tension, frustration or conflict.

A guidance programme can be organised in the following manners:-

Director. It is necessary to have a Director for a guidance or counselling programme. His task is to bring about harmony between the teachers and workers.

Psychologist. His task is to identify the individual qualities and abilities of the student.

Psychiatrist. His function is to diagnose, identify and carry out treat of diseases among the children.

Counsellor. The function of the counsellors is to- (i) organise psychological tests, (ii) collect data, (iii) collect information about the defects of the syllabus, (iv) provide information about various professions, (v) provide vocational guidance, (vi) organising and implementing a follow up programme.

Social Worker. He is needed to study the social and family circumstances and situation of the children in school.

Teacher Counsellor. In schools, the task of counsellors should be performed by the teachers.

The guidance cell or department should make an effort to implement its programme in each school.

Suggestions

The view of the Mudaliar Commission is that the secret of good education lies in the fact that it must acquaint the students with their inclinations and tendencies and also generate in them the power of social adaptation and finding suitable employment. In this regard, its recommendations are as follows:-

1. Administration in education should pay more attention to educational guidance.

2. Films should be made to create awareness in the students regarding various industries, their sphere and nature and importance. In these films, the method of working in many industries should be brought to light. The films should be based on direct observation.

3. The services of trained counsellors or career masters should gradually be made available to all educational institutions.

4. The Centre should shoulder the responsibility for setting up training centres for training counsellors and career masters in various parts of the country. Able individuals can be sent to such institutions from each state.

A guidance and counselling programme makes a very important contribution to education since it recognises the students' abilities and tendencies. The main purpose of such a programme is to recognise the talent of every student in the secondary schools. Dr. Vimleshwar De has offered the following comments upon the recommendations of the Kothari Commission on the subject of counselling.

He has argued that the Commission has not done justice to the particular nature of education, along with counselling, by regarding it as a process, (*abhikrama*). This has been done at a moment when the objectives of counselling were said to be adaptive and developmental. The preface declares that guidance or counselling should be regarded as an inseparable part of education and not as a special psychological or social service which merely assist in the fulfilment of the objectives of education. Everyone agrees that counselling should be inseparable from education, but this does not mean that counselling is not a special kind of service, or that counselling maintains its position as a matter of right. Dr. De wonders whether the Commission has implicitly given recognition to the invalid views of John and Hand (1938), which declare that guidance or counselling is the pressure that is put upon the individual through the educational process. The writers quoted above also said that they could not implement their plan of counselling because of a lack of specialists, such as counsellors, school psychologists or other professional experts at the time in question. The Commission has clearly given considerable thought to the nature of guidance and counselling at the primary and secondary levels, but it has not laid sufficient emphasis upon their services. If guidance or counselling are not regarded as special services, one may ask what was the need for special courses for training in guidance programmes, which were organised at the post-graduate level? Hence it is difficult to conceive how the commission came to make such a fundamental mistake, though it is composed of eminent educationists.

Even more significant than this is the fact that more light has been thrown upon the search for talent and its development, the education of backward children, the guidance of retarded children. Unquestionably, a theoretical consideration of counselling and its importance is important for education. What is more important, in Dr. Vimleshwar's view, is the implementation of the schemes which give concrete shape to the counselling programme. Such programmes should work as powerful media to the extent to which they allow us to make progress towards efficient and effective counselling in the peculiar circumstances prevailing in our country.

The Kothari Commission has put forth the following suggestions for the growth and development of counselling programmes

1. Guidance and counselling services should be regarded as inseparable elements in education.

2. At the primary level, the following programme should, in general, be put into operation(1) during training itself, teachers should be made acquainted with remedial tests, (2) in-service courses should be organised for primary teachers. (3) occupational literature should be generated, (4) both students and parents should be given advice regarding the future education of children.

3. At the secondary level, such programmes should be conducted by trained individuals in the schools- (1) guidance programmes should function in every school, (2) in certain selected schools, intensive programmes should be made operative, (3) A bureau of guidance should be established and inspection staff should be appointed, (4) in training colleges, emphasis should be placed upon the importance of guidance.

Today, each one of us is aware of the fact that an organised movement is taking place for guidance and counselling. Hence in the present context, it has become necessary to provide the best possible guidance to students to ensure the suitable development of their innate capabilities. At least ten schools should take advantage of each counselling centre. There should be at least one central school in each district for organising a comprehensive programme. Inspection officers must be appointed to ensure that the programme gathers the necessary momentum. These centres should also provide vocational information and, in addition, make arrangements for part-time employment. Only then can the guidance and counselling programme achieve success.

Provision of Books

Text books are symbolic of national culture. It is necessary to study the text-books of any country in order to form an estimate of its culture.

The ideas, values and patterns. of a country can be known through its text-books. Though it cannot be denied that the teacher is of prime importance in the educational process, and that text books occupy the next place, the fact remains that during the early years of education, the child needs a teacher for such subjects as language, mathematics, writing, reading, etc., he still depends much more upon text-books after having learnt to read and write. Text-books perform the following functions: -

1. Even in the absence of a teacher, many more presons can take advantage of text-books.
2. The field of text-books is wide.
3. Text-books are helpful in the progress of individual as well as social life.
4. Text books hold a relationship with the parents, student, teacher, writer, the education department examiners and the publishers. Hence, they can be called the backbone of education.

Achievements

The need for text-books came to light during the period of the East India Company's rule. Prior to this, one or two books were used as fundamental books or text-books in the Sanskrit *pathshalas* and the Urdu *maktabs* and *madrasas*. In the absence of printing presses, manuscript books were more commonly used, but those were more expensive because of the labour and time consumed in their production. The Company administration and Christian missionaries set up schools at many places and to teach according to a pre-planned syllabus, they published text-books. In these text-books, the major portion comprised the writings of Europeon scholars. In 1825,, Mr. Elphinstone expressed the view that translations of particular books in specific languages should be prescribed for the literary development of the students. Adam had proposed that in accord with the Indian circumstances, European books should be made a part of the syllabus. He was of the view that the translation of European literature into Indian languages is compulsory so that Indians may be able to assimilate European literature through their own languages.

In 1854, in the Wood Despatch, too, emphasis was placed upon the translation of scientific terminology-into Indian languages, in addition to the establishment of oriental colleges. In 1882, the Hunter Commission commented upon the importance of text-books. It stated that scholars should be members of the text-book committees in various regions. These persons should be capable of representing the various classes of the community, as well as of reflecting upon the worth of the text-books in English and Vernacular languages put up for their consideration. In the same manner, the Secondary Education Commission, too made strong recommendation for the re-assessment and provision of text-books.

The Kothari Commission also expressed its dissatisfaction with the existing mode of preparation of text-books. Both the commissions on education have recommended that the text-books. Should be in consonance with the classroom situation and the child's mental ability should also be conducive to the achievement of the objectives of education. They also recommended that the production and publication of text-books should be nationalised so as to curb the willfulness of publishers. The secondary commission suggested that a committee should be set up for the production, selection and publication of text-books. It said that the committee should consists of the vice-chancellor of the state, one teacher, two educationists, one representative of the various classes of society, one judge. It should be presided over the director of education.. The Commission also recommended the setting up of a bureau for the production of text-books as well as the syllabus. This bureau is now known as the Department of Text-book Research and Curriculum. These recommendations of the commission were considered in depth by the government, and as a result, the state and central governments have published some text-books for certain classes. The Kothari Commission has almost repeated these recommendations.

However, we can see that the manner in which text books have developed in the, country has not helped in achieving the objectives of education. There is considerable scope for improvement and growth in this field.

Fundamental Issues

Text-books are important tools in the educational process. Today they are performing the role of a foundation for the development of education, but they have not succeeded in completely achieving the objectives of education. The main reason for this is that the text-books have not been prepared with the interest and inclination of the child in view. They have, therefore, failed to bring about the harmonious development of the child. In short, the following defects can be seen in most text-books:-

1. Uninteresting and unrelated lessons.
2. These are not useful for the student because they are lacking in the situation existing in the class-room.
3. In these books, the subject matter is put together unscientifically and unpsychologically, because of which the children do not understand the subject clearly.
4. These text-books are found lacking in the ideals of democracy, human rights, emotional and national unity, and international brotherhood.
5. Some text-books are written by foreign authors. These are not useful for Indian students. Besides, some of these books are written by the learned scholars of universities, who are completely ignorant of the real conditions obtaining in schools.
6. Till recently, the books were published by publishers who have been completely lacking in the necessary experience of publishing text-books.
7. They also suffer from certain technical defects such as inferior quality of paper, bad printing, weak binding, etc., which have an adverse impact upon the child.
8. Prejudice often mars the selection of text-books. Publishers get third-rate text-books selected by using unfair and unethical means.
9. Text-books of the desired standard in the regional languages have not been possible because of the absence of authors in these languages.

Guidelines

In view of these defects, the Secondary Education Commission had recommended the nationalisation of text-books. In its opinion, these text-books should seek to achieve the objectives of basic education, in view of the new educational policy. It suggested that they should be low priced so that cheap publications can be prevented, and also that the educational departments should not work with a view to earning profits on text-books.

The commission recommended that, in order to eradicate their shortcomings, a text-book committee should be set up. Its membership should consist of the judges of the state, one member of the public service commission, one vice-chancellor of a university of the state, one teacher (male or female), two renowned educationists and the State's Director of education. The committee should work exclusively upon the selection of text-books, and the prepared text-books should be sent to specialists without mentioning the name of the author or the publisher.

The commission also recommended that, if the education department does nationalise textbooks, it must fully implement its own policy regarding the quality of paper, the nature and quality of diagrams, printing and book-binding. The Central Government should set up a new department for the production of text-books based upon scientific research. Individuals should be given training for preparing art books to be used in Arts Colleges.

On the basis of these recommendations, a department for conducting research into text-books and curriculum was established. The department produced many text-books upto the secondary level, but it could not succeed in fulfilling the needs of the country.

The editorial comment in the *Times of India* (July 10,1964), lands support to this view. It says that children are compelled to read books which are inferior and in which hardly any sentence is grammatically correct. These books double the teachers' work, because they first have to correct them and then use them for teaching.

An almost similar comment was made in the Russian newspaper '*Pravda*' on November 30,1954. It said that in many countries the profession of text-books is not properly organised. At some places, there is a complete absence of such books while at others they lie unused in storing places.

The importance of text-books in education has been accepted by the Kothari Commission also. Text-books enlarge the mode of education, but unfortunately, the writing and publication of textbooks has not achieved the desired standard. In the opinion of the Kothari Commission, the text-book is that which is written by an able and talent specialist, properly published from the viewpoint of printing, etc., inspires the interests of the students and gives suitable help in the process of teaching. Many of the existing text-books are not only sub-standard, they are also very badly printed. In regional languages the condition of text-books is completely pitiable. Many reasons are responsible for this situation-

1. Scholars take almost no interest in text-books. Consequently the publishers get text-books prepared by inefficient authors at very cheap prices, but this economy proves very expensive for the country.
2. Many publishers adopt extremely immoral and unethical means in order to get their text-books selected, but these adversely affect both students and parents.
3. The use of unethical means in the selection of text-books is indicative of this tendency.
4. The absence of research in the preparation and production of text-books is painfully obvious.
5. Publishers get help-books, keys and other aids to study published. The evil consequences of these practices are self-evident.

Keeping in mind these glaring shortcomings, the Kothari Commission has suggested that the NCERT's work of preparing and publishing text-books must be encouraged. This council has made considerable progress even at the central level.

Having reflected on all these points, we are faced with the following questions-

1. Will the problem of text-books be solved through nationalisation?
2. Will the government not indulge in indoctrination of its own objectives and selfish interests through nationalisation?
3. Will such a step not hinder the development of the child's personality?

When we meditate upon these questions and seek answers, due attention naturally turns towards the Red Tapism existing in all government activity. The Madras government nationalized text-books, but because of this Red Tapism, it was compelled to have its text-books published by private publishers. Even in Punjab and Delhi, the official text-books are often not available even two months after the opening of schools. As far as indoctrination is concerned, it is possible to harbour the fear that the government may, if it is so inclined, inculcate only its own version of events and facts, as the Chinese Government does. However, in a democratic system, the opposition parties function as instruments of social control, proof of which lies in the storms of controversy that often arose, from time to time, on various lessons printed in official text-books. As regards the final question, we can answer it by saying the child's development of personality will not be imperiled if the text-books are objectively prepared, and if they are in keeping with the child's interests.

Production of Books

The National Book Development Board was established in 1967 for the preparation, printing and publication of text-books and other kinds of help-books. The Board also lay down certain guiding principles for the book industry. In 1969, the Central Government also set up the National Board of Text-Books. This Board is functioning as a clearing house for the book producing profession. In the 4th Plan, provisions were made for spending Rs.12 crores on this work. In the same way, the National Book Trust, the Children's Book Trust are performing similar functions. In the Fifth Plan, the following provisions were made for the production of books-

Expenditure on Book Production (Crores)

Sl.	*Standard*	*Amount*
1.	University Level	15
2.	National Training Centre	1
3.	Other Programme N.B.T., Low Cost Book, M.B.D.B., etc.	14
	Total	30

In this way, it becomes apparent that, if we want to impart dynamism to the important functions performed by text-books in the educational process, it is necessary to nationalise both their production and their preparation. For this purpose, the government can also seek the co-operation of reputed publishers.

Provision of other Teaching Materials

Both teaching and studying have become very scientific activities in the present age, and hence, teaching aids are no longer limited to a stick of chalk and a blackboard. Planning has become essential at every stage and at every level. It is only through planning that we can complete a given task according to our present time-table. In the field of teaching, the outline of the curriculum, which is to be completed in a given number of years, is reflected in the text-books.

At present, the teachers in India are almost completely lacking in proper guidance. In the view of the Kothari Commission, a good text-book, which has been written by a talented and brilliant specialist, and which is satisfactory from the view point of printing, diagramming and publication, inspires the student to read it, and also helps the teacher in performing his duty. Superior text-books and other suitable teaching aids play an incalculably important part in raising the standards of teaching.

The commission has also accepted the virtues and shortcomings of text-books in India. It has cast its eye upon the lack of interest among scholars towards the writing of text-books, corruption in the selection and prescription of text-books, corrupt methods used by publishers, absence of research, the exclusive concern with profit, etc.

The Commission has expressed some ideas on the setting up an institution in the public sector for this purpose. It has felt that text-books of the desired standard are not written because authors do not get an adequate return for their labours. To overcome this, many authors should be asked to prepare text-books in manuscript form for every subject.

Emphasis has also been laid upon supplementing text-books by guide books for teachers and other material aids. It has been suggested that the All India Radio and Doordarshan should improve the quality of their programmes intended for students.

In the publication of text-books, the needs of the teacher himself are completely ignored, a fact which has not been considered important even by the Commission. In fact, guides and useful material studies should be prepared for the teachers. The Kothari Commission's suggestions in this regard are-

1. It should be the prime task of the administration to ensure that text books and other teaching materials are available at low prices.
2. Teachers should fulfil the need for guides and teaching aids.
3. In every school, at every level, a list of the necessary teaching aids should be prepared, and these aids should be available in every school.
4. The teaching department should maintain contact with the All India Radio stations and provide information regarding the lessons to be broadcast, as well as the materials or books published for teachers and students. Special radio programmes should be broadcast in the mornings and evenings so that teachers may get help in preparing the lessons to be taught in the class.
5. For teachers, the teaching materials prepared by them should be available locally and at economic prices. If certain teaching aids are expensive, they can be purchased by two or three schools together.

6. Teachers should be trained in the art of preparing teaching aids.
7. The workshops of the school should be utilised for preparing teaching aids within the school itself.

The experience of the Commission in the course of its survey can be expressed thus,- it received many suggestions pointing out that new methods of teaching should be adopted. These methods use films, film strips; radio, tape recorders, audio-visual equipment, open and closed circuit television, language laboratories, programme instructional methods and many ordinary teaching tools. Most of these things can be made use of through a School Complex.

If we consider the suggestions put forward by the Commission, we will have to take up the following programmes-

Project and Experiment. In these, many subjects and programmes can be organised. Such programmes as Dalton, Projector, Open-air sessions, school seminar, domestic art, etc., can be taken up.

Extra-Curricular Activities. Extra -curricular activities are also an essential part of teaching, and so, such activities as cultural programmes, intellectual programmes, etc., can be taken up.

Audio-Visual Teaching. Audio-visual teaching should be encouraged, and it can be developed through the use of film strips, slides, camps, hikes, picnics, tours, discussions, debates, poetry and story competitions, school banks, etc.

Thus, it is evident that; in order to raise the standard of living, it is necessary to have proper guidance and teaching aids in every school.

10

Primary Stage

The Setup

In our country, there are two forms of primary education - (1) Primary education, (2) Basic Education. The first is called the general form. In it, there is provision for an education which achieves only the objective of intellectual skill. In John Ruskin's opinion, its objective can be described in the following terms. 'The meaning of education is not to educate people in the things of which they are ignorant. The real meaning of education is to teach people to conduct themselves in ways in which they do not behave.'

It has also been said in our Constitution- "The state shall endeavour to provide within a period of ten years from the commencement of this Constitution for the free and compulsory education for all the children until they complete the age of 14 years." (Article 5 of the Indian Constitution) Because of this, states and local bodies were entrusted with the responsibility of making all efforts to implement the seven-year plan of compulsory education.

In our country, general primary education is found to have different forms and names in different parts. The Kothari Commission suggested that this diversity should be ended and uniformity introduced but this uniform concept of education has yet to gain wide currency. For achieving this purpose, the Kothari Commission has put forward the following suggestions

The objective of primary education is to build up a responsible personality capable of functioning as a useful citizen. The Constitution provides for compulsory education of children upto the age of 14 years. The following programmes should be implemented for achieving this target :

1. By 1975-76, there should be adequate ar arrangements for providing effective education for every child for a period of 5 years. Providing effective education for every children for a Period of 5 years.

Existing Form	*Form Suggested by the Kothari Commission*
1. Pre-primary	1. Pre-primary
2. Pre-Basic	
3. Kindergarten	
4. Montessary, etc.	
1. Primary (in some states)	2. Primary
2. Lower Primary	Classes 1 to 7 or 8
3. Junior Basic	1. Lower Primary
4. Lower Elementary	Classes 1 to 4 or
	Classes 2 to 5
1. Middle (in some states	2. Upper Primar
eg., Punjab)	Class 5 to 7 or
2. Junior High School (U.P.)	Class 6 to 8
3. Upper Primary School	
(Gujarat)	
4. Senior Primary School	
5. High Elementary School (Madras)	

2. By 1986, every child should be given 12 years of education.
3. There must be very little wastage or failure in classes 1 to 7. The rate of success should be 80%

4. Children who reach the 7th class before the age of 14 and do not wish to study further should be kept in the same class. They should also be given a condensed vocational course.

5. Every state should prepare schemes for the growth of primary education.

6. A primary school should be available to every child within one mile of his residence.

7. Children between the ages of 5 and 7 should be admitted to class I.

8. The system of registering names in schools before actual admission should be introduced.

9. The rate of progress should be from 80% to 100%. A child should not be failed without sufficient cause.

10. The recommendations of the National Committee of Education be implemented.

Basic Education

In his book *To students*, Mahatma Gandhi has written that every individual who wants to do something for the students, and every educationist, has felt that our educational system is defective. It does not satisfy the needs of poor India. It fails to establish harmony between home life, village life and education. In his analysis of contemporary education at that time, Gandhiji has said that the prevailing system was defective in three major ways-(1) it was based on a foreign culture and had no relationship whatsoever with Indian culture; (2) it neglected the culture of the heart and the hand, and limited itself solely to the culture of the mind; (3) it was impossible to have real education through the medium of a foreign language.

Gandhiji expressed his views on education on-22nd and 23rd October 1937 at the Wardha Education Conference. For him, education meant the comprehensive and integral development of the individual and the child, in other words, the development of the brain, body and the spirit. Literacy in itself does not constitute education. For this reason, he wanted education to begin with handicrafts, and he wanted such an education to be productive from the very beginning. In this way, every school would become self reliant.'

Zakir Hussain Committee. A committee was setup under the chairmanship of Dr. Zakir Hussain for reflecting upon the concept of Basic Education. Its main suggestions were :

1. Provisions should be made at the national level for providing free and compulsory education for every child.
2. The medium of education should be the mother tongue.
3. The medium of education should be productive handicraft industry.
4. The educational system, should be self sufficient itself to pay the salary of the teacher.
5. Great stress should be put upon labour, and dignity of labour should be inculcated among students.
6. Education should conform to the child's natural environment.
7. The child should be transformed into a good citizen.
8. Curriculum. (1) One of the handicrafts- such as weaving and spinning, carpentry, gardening, agriculture, leather work, or other productive industry. (2) Mother tongue. (3) Mathematics. (4) Social studies (history, geography, civics). (5) General science, practical botany, biology, hygiene, etc,) (6) Drawing and painting. (7) Music. (8) Hindustani (in the Devanagari or Urdu script).

This scheme began to be implemented in 1937. In 1939, a committee was organised under the chairmanship of Shri S.G. Kher to evaluate the system of Basic Education.

The Kher Committee. The then Chief Minister of Bombay (1939) was made the chairman of committee to evaluate Basic Education. The Committee stressed the implementation of the scheme in rural areas. Its main suggestions are:

1. In the absence of adequate finances, it is not possible to arrange for basic education. Despite this, provincial governments should establish creches and also encourage voluntary organisations in doing the same.

2. The period of Basic Education should be increased from seven to eight years, of which the first five years should be for junior basic, and the last three for senior basic.

3. At the conclusion of this education, the child should be possessed of full potential for further development.

4. The advisory board for central education should establish a permanent committee for the supervision of basic education.

Sargent Plan. In the Sargent Plan of 1944, the importance of basic education was accepted. The recommendations of the Kher Committee also found a place in this plan. It was accepted by the Central and Provincial governments.

Kher Committee 1948. Accepting the recommendations of Sargent Plan the Kher Committee recommended that basic education should be introduced throughout the country in 16 years. It was also said that non-basic schools should be converted into basic schools, and the central government should bear 30% of this expenditure on education.

National Basic Education Board. This board came to be established in view of the suggestion for establishing a permanent commission for basic education. Although the government accepted Basic Education as national education the system failed to make encouraging progress. The responsibilities of this board include research concerning basic education, training of examiners and officials, advising governments and institutions, organising seminars, and organising laboratories.

Merits

The characteristics of basic education can be stated thus :

Psychological Basis. In basic education, attention is paid to the interests of the child. Stress is laid on the natural development of the children's personality.

Social Basis. It is on Indian culture and its needs, which it successfully satisfies.

Economic Basis. Basic education makes an effort to ensure that child should be able to meet the expenses of his own education. The real truth of the matter is that the system is a great scheme for putting an end to unemployment.

Importance of Labour. Basic education has always been alive to the importance of physical or bodily labour.

Social Synthesis. It also achieves a harmonious relationship between the home, the school and the society as a whole because it is based on the foundation of reality.

Centred in Industry. The entire process of education is based on industry. Thus, the child receives a practical education because he learns by doing and thus gains experience.

Comprehensive. Being a comprehensive collection of numerous subjects, basic education makes lessons interesting, and the child obtains a knowledge of numerous subjects simultaneously and without effort.

Centered on the Child. The basis of this system is the child itself. According to H.R. Bhatia, in the basic system, the child is regarded as the customer of education, and hence it becomes necessary to study his requirements and understand them, make provisions for them and satisfy them.

Independence. Both students and teachers have a very large degree of freedom in their activities.

Many tests and experiments have been conducted to evaluate the success of Basic Education. In every state, basic schools, training centres, teacher training programmes, etc., were initiated. Many such experiments have been conducted at Assam, the Kumar Mandir, Ahmedabad, Gujarat, Navyug School, Bombay, Graduates Training Centre, Dhaarwara, Basic Training Centre, Kalmore, Poona, Basic School, Sevagam, and at other places.

Demerits

Many charges have also been levelled against Basic Education. The allegations are as follows :

Craft Centered. Some people are of the view that the defects of basic education lies in the very fact of its being centered in craft and industry. The child begins to take more interest in the industry than in education.

Impracticable. Some people consider it to be impracticable. The reason for this is that it is not easy to impart this kind of education.

Lack of Self-reliance. One major charm of basic education is self reliance, but in reality children waste the materials given to them, and thus the objective of self-reliance is not achieved.

Lack of Religious Education. Gandhiji did not include religious education in basic education because the prevailing view of religion is an extremely narrow one, and it is more likely to cause harm than good.

Lack of Interest. Although basic education conceives of many industries in a single, school, it is not possible to make arrangements for every industry in every school, and hence students often lack interest in the industry available in a particular school.

Lack of text books. Since the basis of this system is activity, there is a lack of text-books.

Lack of Enthusiastic Teachers. The most serious shortcoming of basic education is the lack of enthusiastic teachers, and it is because of this that Basic education has proved a failure.

Review by Education Council

In 1965, the Central Education Advisory Council accepted the following recommendations of the National Basic Education Council—

1. Basic education should be given recognition at the primary level throughout the country.
2. Existing basic schools should be strengthened.
3. Primary schools should be converted into basic schools.

4. Crafts should be necessarily available in all new schools.
5. At the secondary level, post basic schools should be an inseparable part of education.
6. Post-basic schools, in particular, should be strengthened.
7. Training institutions should have facilities for providing training in basic education.
8. The knowledge and experience of administrators of education should be imbued with service and sacrifice.

Mahatma Gandhi's concept of basic education is a milestone in the history of education. It was, in fact, a revolt against the prevailing passive, book-centered education, an education dominated by examinations, and also against a tendency to blind limitation of the British government's traditional educational pattern. At the primary level, it gave birth to a national stream of thought, and it has become an important current in the stream of our national educational system. Mahatma Gandhi has clarified that our objective is not to create skilled workers or even skilled artisans and artists. What we want is the harmonious and comprehensive development of human beings.

The Education Commission (1964-66) has stated that it is our firm belief that its basic principles are sound, and that with due modification it should be closely associated with the national educational system, not only at the primary level, but at every level. Its important elements are-(1) productive activities in education, (2) correlation of the productive activity with the material and social environment, (3) close relations between the school and the community. In view of these ideas, the Commission has laid stress on work experience at every level of education. In it, education is closely related to handicraft. The Commission, too, has accepted its comprehensive form.

The Commission has caused harm to Basic Education by accepting the programme of work experience, since it is only on this basis that the National Basic Education Institute has been shut down. Having put an end to the very life of national education and its original and natural sources of inspiration, we have tried to fulfil our goal of national development through an imported and borrowed educational process.

Criticising the Kothari Commission's concept of work experience, Jugatram Dave has brought out the following points : According to him, the Commission claims to have accepted the basic principles of Basic Education in the total educational programme. These basic principles are identified as : (1) Productive tendency in education, (2) correlation, and (3) contact between school and society. These elements have been accepted at the top, and this is desirable. One additional element, a very important one, should also be included-and that is, love of country, love of indigenous things, self-reliance, courage, sacrifice, etc. The tendency towards social service has also been accepted. But these qualities will be absorbed by the children only when there is a concrete objective before them. Of course, there can be social service tendencies which can operate without giving too much importance to love of country. During Gandhiji's days, all tendencies were focussed upon the national movement for independence. Now, this movement is 20 years old. For the younger generation, it is a part of history, and it has not left its impress upon their minds. In our present day society, instead of love or worship of nation, the ideas that are present before almost every individual are those of wealth, honour, self seeking, etc. Consequently, there must be special efforts in our curriculum to introduce national ideas and patterns of conduct into our education. If this is not done, the most significant aspect of basic education- formation of character- will remain indistinct.

Shri G.N. Acharya holds the view that the Basic Education which was developed by Zakir Hussain and others was an attempt at the implementation of Gandhiji's ideas. In the preceding session of the Rajya Sabha, the President had sorrowfully declared that Gandhiji was the father of a new-born infant — basic education: The declaration of the Commission could be regarded as the death certificate of that infant basic education.

Every point in the criticism of Basic Education applies with equal validity to the concept of work experience also. The question is whether teachers want to make the child a human being or a skilled mechanic. If the child becomes a human being, he can become everything, but if the child is to be developed into a machine, then the social system will be dominated by a few who will never allow the majority to prosper. Hence, government should have no hesitation in accepting basic education as a system of mass education.

What is needed today is that the system of national education propagated by Gandhiji should be accepted as an instrument of social change. Its aim is to instill such experiences in the child as will persuade him to remain honest. Indian villages are a formidable instrument for a national social system, since they fulfil a social need. Through it, dignity of labour, social responsibility and a liberal attitude is developed.

Fundamental Issues

Like the numerous other problems facing our country after independence, our schools also faced the problem of education. The freedom from slavery made it necessary to evaluate education afresh. Hence, in this evaluation, the problems which had made this country illiterate once again ,came to the fore. Despite the introduction of a new educational policy, the progress was not satisfactory. Many factors lay at the root of this situation. In the process of evaluation, the following problems of primary education came to be identified distinctly, and these problems continue to exist even today, in one form or the other.

Problems of Administration. In India the responsibility for primary education falls fully upon the local administration and partially upon the State government. Both these administrative units manage primary education in their respective spheres in their own ways. There is lack of coordination between them, and the result is that the officials appointed by the State either fail to manage the schools established by the local administration or consider this unnecessary.

The responsibility for the conduct of education lies with the director of education in municipalities, the deputy inspector in the district councils, Communities in panchayats, and S.D.I. and Education Development Officers. All of them exhibit the tendency of passing on the responsibility to others. In America, the responsibility for primary education has been put upon the local administration, and it conducts education through the cooperation of the community. In the same way, in England; the Local Education Authority is responsible for primary education, and in both of these countries, state control is limited to providing funds for education. The local administration conducts education efficiently in its own way. Unfortunately, in India, there is a complete lack of efficiency. In this context, the Balwantrao Mehta Committee has recommended the complete decentralisaton of education at the primary level. Some of the suggestions given for bringing improvement at this level are the following-

1. The State's educational policy should be in conformity with the needs of the country.
2. The State should form a council consisting of governmental and non-governmental representatives for the development of primary education. Its prime function should be to ensure the uniform growth of primary education.
3. The State should lay down the minimum limits and standards which can easily be achieved by each school.
4. A strong administration should be formed in every State to provide compulsory education, and its aim should be to take advantage of every possible agency.
5. States should provide the necessary funds for the growth of primary education because proper management is inconceivable in the absence of funds.
6. The success of primary education depends upon administrators and inspectors. Hence, only capable and vigilant individuals should be chosen for this task.
7. On primary education, there should be uniformity in the policies of local administration, states and the Union government because, in its absence, the direction of primary education becomes lax.

Management of Schools. The 45th Article of our Constitution directs that education should be compulsory for all children, till they attain the age of 14. But this objective could not be achieved due to inadequacy of schools. Our schools are confronted with the following problems-

(*i*) *Problems of Primary schools in towns.* In towns, the number of schools is not in proportion to the population. for political reasons, many schools are set up at one place, with the result that areas requiring one school have two or three, and others which need two or three have only one.

Attendance is also a major problem in urban schools. In some schools, the number of students is so large that the teacher, after taking the attendance, has little time left for actual teaching. Such schools not only create an imbalance in the educational system, they also misuse and waste investment on education. In towns, there are very few schools near industrial establishments, though in fact more are required. In Mexico, there is at least one school with one industrial establishment. If such a policy were adopted in India too, at least one major problem would be overcome.

(*ii*) *Rural Schools.* In rural areas, the main problem of schools is the fact that they are scattered, they have dirty and kucha buildings, and inefficient teachers. The problems of housing for teachers and the indifference of parents complicates the situation.

Rural primary schools are in a much worse condition than urban schools. Since it is assumed that the reconstruction of the village is possible only through education. Education should be so organised that a child should find a school within one mile of his house. On the subject of rural schools, the editorial of American Education' opines that it cannot be said where the rural school ends and the villages began; neither can it be said where the life of the village begins and where it ends, because the school has created for itself a place as the basic or original office of the society and the community.

(*iii*) *Social Schools.* The third category of primary schools is of the schools found in tribal areas, backward mountainous regions and areas occupied by the erstwhile criminal tribes. These schools do not amount to even 5%, with reference to the population to which they cater, and consequently, instead of taking children out of the darkness of ignorance to the light of knowledge, they allow them to remain immersed in their darkness.

Provision of Finance. In India, money is spent extravagantly on every activity except education, and thus India's educational budget is much less than that of other countries. While Japan spends 6% of its national income on education, Russia 7%, England 4.5% and America 4.7%, India spends only 2.3% of its national income on education. This makes clear the financial condition of Indian education. Other countries spend 50% of the total educational budget on primary education; for India this figure is only 35%. It is obvious that unless this investment is raised, the growth of primary education will be below expectation. Without it neither the teachers will take an interest in their work, nor will the necessary means for it be provided.

Problem of Teachers. Some of the main problems being faced by primary teachers are(1) those concerning efficiency, (2) the problems of schools, (3) problem of equality, (4) problem of salary. As far as the question of efficiency and qualifications is concerned, for a primary teacher the certificate of the State Board is proof of the teacher being a matriculate and also of his being trained, but many teachers do not possess even this minimum qualification. This inevitably brings down the standard of education. Teachers in primary schools do not get an attractive salary. Consequently, they treat teaching as a kind of pension, and spend their time in other activities to supplement their income. Secondly, the salaries paid by the state differ considerably from those paid by institutions, with the result that there is widespread dissatisfaction. At places, a peon gets a better salary than a primary teacher.

The Kothari Commission has given numerous suggestions for the improvement of teachers at the primary level. Of these, the major ones, are :

1. Teachers in primary schools should be trained, as far as possible, and they should also have studied in a school for 10 years, i.e., they should be matriculates.
2. The Teacher should have gone through a training course for at least two years.
3. Untrained teachers should get an opportunity to improve their qualifications through in-service training programmes or correspondence courses.

Teachers should be aware of both urban and rural conditions, and their work should conform to it. In rural schools, it is best if the teacher belongs to the same region. Every school should have an adequate number of teachers because it has been found that single teacher schools are merely places where children collect together, but not places where they receive education. Teachers should be guided by the following motto-when you have more time, study more, but when time is short, do not study, but do. work industriously. China has organised its primary education on the basis of this principle. The immediate problem of shortage of teachers can be solved by following Denmark's plan. In this, a teacher takes one class on the first day, but a different class on the next day. Our schools at present need a minimum of 1,06,000 and a maximum of 2,64,000 teachers. Every effort should be made to fulfil this need.

Problem of Curriculum. Our schools lack a systematised curriculum. At some places, the load of work is so light that both teachers and students idle away time, but at others, children are burdened with books. In order to make the curriculum attractive, we should keep in view the needs of our country. The present curriculum does impart literacy to the child, but it cannot develop in him the qualities needed for achieving national goals. It fulfils the needs of neither the villages nor the towns.

The Kothari Commission has pointed out explicitly that students at the primary level should not be burdened with many subjects. They should be taught subjects imparting knowledge of language, arithmetic and the environment. At this level, the sole language taught should be either the mother tongue or the regional language. In arithmetic, knowledge of Roman numerals, the use of charts and maps, etc., should be imparted. Work experience should have a suitable place from the very beginning so that the child learns to work and develops the right sentiments.

The Commission says that all over the world, the curriculum is in a state of indecision. To improve the school curriculum, many steps, such as (1) research into the curriculum, (2) preparation of text books and teaching aids, (3) in-service training of teachers, etc., will have to be taken.

At the primary level, the Commission has divided the curriculum into two parts- (1) Lower primary stage (from class 1 to 4) - one language, arithmetic, study of the environment, creative activities, art, programmes, social service and health, (2) Higher primary stage (from class 5 to 8, - two languages, mother tongue or original language, arithmetic, science, social studies, art, work experience and social service, physical education, morality and spiritual values.

Problem of Space. Primary education invariably faces the problem of space. Most such schools operate in rented buildings, which usually lack adequate lighting. They are also not suitable from the environmental angle. They cast a deleterious influence upon the child's mental and physical health. At some places, such schools function even in huts and tents. During the rainy season, their difficulties increase manifold. According to Maulana Abul Kalam Azad, our attention should turn towards school buildings, the teacher and the method of education. He requests particularly the rural people to obtain construction materials from the government, and through local cooperation, construct school buildings for the community.

The Kothari Commission has recommended that state governments should provide some proportional aid for the construction of well-planned school buildings.

Problem of Resources. In primary. schools, there is generally a need for seats, blackboards, furniture and other useful materials. In addition, drinking water and urinals are also required. Experience shows that there are very few schools which have all these facilities and materials. In some places, students do not have even jute mats to sit on. At others, one finds the blackboards lying in the store. At yet others, there is a complete absence of maps and charts, and even if available they are not used by the teachers. This problem has two aspects, first, the lack of necessary materials, and second, the failure to use them when available. Regarding the first, the Kothari Commission has recommended that the government should arrange for the cheap production of good quality teaching materials. Whenever there is a lack of teaching material, it should treat the high school as an extension service centre and provide the necessary things. The second obviously depends upon the teachers.

Problem of Ancillary Services. The ancillary services concerned with education usually include- (1) arrangement for lunch, (2) free text-books, (3) free materials, (4) hostel accommodation, (5) medical facilities.

Regarding the first, it can be said with certainty that there are very few schools in India which provide lunch to children. Children who travel two or three miles to reach the schools generally have difficulty in carrying their lunch. They take lunch only when they return home after school hours. In winters, the period in school becomes even longer. Consequently, the health of children is adversely affected. Hence, the community should make such an arrangement that it should collect foodgrains and give it to schools, so that this problem may be overcome. In some schools, a substitute for lunch is provided in the form of snacks. The Central Social Welfare Board has prepared a budget of Rs. 3 crores for providing lunch to 119 lakh children.

It is the duty of the state to provide text-books and uniforms to poor children and to fulfil the requirements of Article 45 of the Constitution. If the government is able to provide housing for primary teachers, the cause of primary education will receive great strength.

Special Problem. The special problems of education include the problem of education of girls, training of teachers, attaining proper standards among teachers and preparation of suitable literature both for students and teachers. For the solution of these problems, the Kothari Commission has suggested that special schools for girls should be opened, but it feels that the majority of schools should be co-educational. Teachers should be trained through in-service training programmes or correspondence courses and literature suitable for them should be created. The materials necessary for the teaching of science should be available in every school, so that science rooms and science corners can be set up.

Problem of Research. Education is a dynamic process and therefore, at intervals research into it is essential. The sphere of primary education is riddled with problems, and they can be overcome only through adequate research. According to Shridharnath Mukerjee, this research should concern itself with the following spheres- (1) conversion of primary schools into basic schools; (2) implementation of compulsory education; (3) the attitude of uneducated guardians; (4) teaching of multiple classes; (5) proper adjustment of the school time table; (6) wastage and stagnation; (7) school buildings; (8) study of compulsory education as implemented in foreign countries; (9) construction of school buildings; (10) inexpensive tools of teaching or teaching aids.

Research can be conducted into many areas in addition to those outlined above. For this purpose, surveys into the educational conditions should be carried out periodically. The problem is that our legislators are concerned only with their own selfish interests. In the opinion of Shri K.G. Saiyadain, although the demand of the political conditions is the immediate implementation of plans, our politicians are in no position to achieve this. Hence, educationists, the government and administrators should seek solutions to these problems so that illiteracy may be wiped out from the country by 1985-86, the date set by the Education Commission.

Dominance of Politics. A survey of primary education in many states has revealed the fact the primary education has been profoundly influenced by panchayats. As a result, the teachers have become stuck in the quagmire of local politics. One Principal pointed out that his school was often visited by some local politicians who had managed to get many of the teaching staff involved in their own activities. He subsequently found it almost impossible to get any cooperation in teaching work from those members of his staff. Teachers took advantage of this situation to neglect the school and teaching work. this has not only led to wastage and stagnation, it has also become the cause of misuse of national funds and manpower.

Lack of Lady Teachers. Even today, many schools in India have closed their doors because of the lack of lady teachers. The main reason for this is an absence of mobility among lady teachers. The question of social security is intimately connected with the status of ladies, and the fact that ladies teaching in rural schools have no security worth the name hardly needs to be proved. Local politics creates further insecurity for a lady teacher.

Non-implementation of Plans. According to a survey in Rai Bareilly, there are 867 rural schools of which 15 are for girls. In urban areas, there are 10 schools for boys and 5 for girls. In these, the average number of teachers is five. Many of the state educational plans are not implemented in such schools at all.

Slackness of Law for Compulsory Education. For the success of primary education, it is essential that a compulsory education act be passed and implemented, but the entire administrative structure in the country has shown little inclination towards any concrete work in this direction. Hence, it is essential that the entire energy of the country should be directed towards this.

Pay Scales and Service Conditions. In primary schools, the service conditions for teachers and the arrangements for disbursement of salary are inadequate. At some places dearness allowance and village allowance is not paid at all, while the salary is disbursed at intervals of six months at a time. In such a situation, many District Boards constantly face hunger strikes by teachers.

Problem of Universal Compulsory Education. The 45th Article of the Constitution provides for compulsory and universal education for children upto the age of 14 years. Although this Article is mentioned frequently enough, it has not been possible to provide compulsory education till now. There are many reasons for this :

(*i*) *Economic Causes.* The first point is that the country as well as the population are steadily moving below the poverty line. Neither the government nor the people have the resources or the finances. Our economic structure has led to the steady enrichment of the rich and the deprivation of those already poor. In schools, students lack buildings and teaching materials. Only 30 per cent of our schools function in suitable buildings. According to governmental policy, there should be one primary school in every village with a population of 500. At present there are 3.5 lakh villages with a population of less than 500, and hence primary schools cannot be established there. Children thus have to trudge many miles to reach school. In hilly areas, the problem becomes an even more intractable one. Besides, guardians often keep the children away from school at harvest time, and consequently, their education is further curtailed.

(ii) Political Causes. Soon after independence, our country was forced to face foreign aggression on three occasions. In addition, it had to cope with the problem of refugees, and at the same time, frequent communal problems have further hindered the process of development.

A defective educational policy, defective administration and inadequate laws have created obstacles in the spread of compulsory education. The administration has failed to put pressure upon guardians to send their children to schools. And, as education is a state subject, state governments are not obliged to follow the dictates of the Central government.

(iii) Social Causes. Most guardians, being illiterate themselves, do not understand the importance of education. They regard the child as an economic unit, and hence they consider it better to engage the child in labour than to send him to school. The spread of compulsory education is further hindered by the caste system, untouchability, child marriage, dogmatism and many other social factors.

(iv) Educational Causes. The existing primary school does not conform to the child's natural environment. It does not conform either to life or to our land. It has neither utility nor creativity. There is also a lack of teachers. In remote areas, teachers do not even bother to go to school. Single teacher schools have proved almost a complete failure. The trained teachers do not teach on the basis of the teaching principles they have acquired, while the untrained teachers have no knowledge at all of such principles.

The absence of separate schools for girls is an obstacle in the path of their universal education. Lady teachers do not emerge from the rural areas.

(v) Geographical Factors. The geographical features of our country are such that a uniform system of education is not suitable for every region. Mountains, rivers, streams, forests, the weather and other geographical features influence the life of the school. At many places, it is impossible to send young children to schools.

The Difficulties

The 45th Article of the Constitution assures that the State will assume the responsibility of providing free education to all children between the ages of 6 and 14, within a period of ten years of the adoption of the Constitution. From this it is evident that India must aim at universal and compulsory education, but universality in this field is faced with three problems :

Absence of Universality in Facilities. There are very few children in India who can find a school within a mile of their houses. Many children have to walk many miles to reach their school.

Absence of Universality in Registration **.** There are many children in India who are admitted to a school at the age of 6. In many cases, children join the first class at the age of 10 or 11.

Universality in Drop-outs. This problem is related to the first two problems. The child joins a school, spends a few years in it, but then, for a variety of reasons, leaves. This practice leads to extravagance and a waste of resources. The draft plan for primary education states that education cannot be effective as long as every child does not obtain primary education. The removal of immature children from school leads to a waste of resources in education. Two problems can be seen in the process of leaving school- (I) Wastage, (II) Stagnation.

After 1921, the problem of wastage in education is becoming steadily more and more intense. Even the Hertog report made it clear that primary education would remain ineffective as long as each child did not remain in school for a minimum of four years and achieved literacy. The term 'wastage', in this context, means the dropping out of the child from the educational process, i.e., his leaving school at an unsuitable time. This wastage involves a waste of national labour and wealth and its long term consequences must necessarily be disastrous.

Single Teacher Schools. Schools with single teachers make a special contribution to wastage. According to the report of the Indian Education Survey, these schools have played a significant role in this matter. It is difficult for a single teacher to handle five classes simultaneously. If he goes on leave, the school closes down. This makes the students reluctant in going to school, and soon they drop out altogether.

Social and Economic Structure. India's economic and social structure is of a kind which encourages parents to send their children for general education. Even today, our rural population holds on to the belief that a child should only be educated to the extent of being able to read and write.

The Child as a Labourer. Children living in villages are the property of their parents who can compel their children to labour and earn on the fields. For such parents, the money earned by the child is more important than his education.

Schools without Resources. Many schools are almost completely lacking in the resource necessary for teaching, and in the absence of these means, the teacher cannot teach. Consequently, the children engage themselves in playing here and there, and in the absence of satisfactory results, soon leave the school.

Lack of space in Schools. Wastage also occurs in schools which have only make shift arrangements for housing the children.

Another factor contributing to wastage is the fact that children are admitted to schools throughout the year. Besides, lack of attention towards attendance is another factor. It has been observed that wastage reaches the figure of 36% by the time we reach class 3. About 50 per cent of the wastage occurs at the primary stage, but there is considerable difference between the wastages in the education of girls and boys. This is illustrated in Table.

Stage	*Rate*	
	Boys	*Girls*
Elementary	71.09	84.74
Primary	60.30	71.36
Secondary	20.43	25.95

It was stated in the Hertog Report that the term stagnation was taken to mean keeping a child in one class for more than one year. R.V Parulkar has explained that schools are established to provide education to children, and not to fail them. In other words, stagnation means the continuance of a child in a single class for two or three years due to failure. This too, involved a wastage of man's ability and the nation's energy, resources and manpower.

Besides, failure encourages a sense of inferiority in the child, and when children younger than him become his classmates, his abnormality tends to increase. Every year, the level of stagnation in primary classes is between 30 per cent and 50 per cent.

Defective policy of States. The policy of filtration which Lord Macaulay had planned in terms of providing education to a special class, and tacitly, even today, our education caters only to a particular class. In terms of proclamations on public education, our country has made spectacular progress, and in the present context, it wants to implement an idealistic policy, but it has made no attempt to keep reality in mind. There is much talk of financial restraints, but no one is ready to consider educational expenditure in the light of an investment, whereas it was the famous economist Adam Smith who pointed out that the money invested in education is returned with interest by the future generation. Besides, educational departments have not even taken the trouble of formulating a policy for combating stagnation.

Inefficient Administration. Having thrust the entire burden of primary education on local bodies, the state governments sleep the sleep of the just. But local bodies lack both finances and adequate means of raising resources, and hence they also lack any enthusiasm for the spread of education. If the local bodies serve notices on the local population for the compulsory registration of children in schools, they cannot hope to obtain popular approval in elections. Besides, the presence of inefficient and negligent officials in the local administration further encourage stagnation. Besides, schools are set up in an unplanned, haphazard manner, and this also adds to stagnation. In some areas, there are so many schools that the average attendance in them is only 100. Besides the inspecting staff is also over-burdened as it is expected to make a survey of 100 schools every year.

Lack of Money. The main stumbling block is the lack of finance. Local administration cannot spend adequate sums on education. In order to obtain grants from the state governments, it has to live at the mercy of the government. Because of this, there are difficulties in arranging not only the salaries of teachers, but even the materials needed for teaching.

Social and Religious Problems. Social and religious problems also contribute to stagnation. In schools which have a dominance of children belonging to a particular caste, tribe or group-such as tribals, scheduled castes, minority language groups, etc., other groups are neglected, and this itself becomes the cause of stagnation.

Physical Facilities. The high percentage of stagnation is also accounted for by the fact that, from the educational view point, rural areas, hilly regions and forest regions are neglected.

Educational and Economic Factors. Low standards of teaching, inadequate and unsuitable curriculum, the poverty of the people, etc., are also factors in stagnation. The two latter factors help, to a very great extent, in lowering the standard of education.

The problems of stagnation and wastage at the primary level can exist only as long as we are unable to develop the facilities for education, and fail to implement the educational policy in the right manner. Hence, this problem can be overcome if suitable efforts are made in every sphere of education.

The conclusions of a study conducted by C.M. Mehta are very revealing-

1. The annual wastage is 28%, 14.5% students do not participate in examinations, and hence, their comparative percentage is 39%. Of these 81% pass and 19% fail. Stagnation amounts to 19%.
2. Both wastage and stagnation are of the order of 57%. No distinction has been made between boys and girls.
3. Those failing twice had completely different causes.

Mehta has put forward the following suggestions for overcoming these difficulties, appointment of attendance officers, efficiency, regular attendance, appointment of excellent teachers, abolition of admission at a delayed time, in-service teacher training.

Kothari Commission's Report

The history of education establishes incontrovertibly that wastage and stagnation have always existed in one or the other form. The general education imparted for individual development does create or rear the common man, but it has failed to develop the individual in accord with his qualities, interests, bent of mind and innate tendencies. And, how could it do so, since how can possibilities for individual training exist in a system designed for mass education? As a consequence, under the conditions of a general education policy, the failure of certain children to develop due to some specific factors, gives rise to the phenomena of stagnation and waste. In general, the term 'wastage': is understood to mean the dropping out of the child from the educational stream without completing his education, while stagnation refers to his failing in any class.

The Hertog Commission was the first to consider this problem. Since then a number of studies have been conducted. J. Paul Leonards has expressed his view on the subject by saying that stagnation and wastage imply the absence of the child from the school at some times, his becoming an obstacle in the fulfilment of society's needs (6 to 14 years), and the individual's failure to develop his powers in his preparation for a profession.

After independence, we breathed the pure air of a free atmosphere, we got freedom of action and thought, but education could not mould itself to this environment. Education continued to face the same problems. The country's legislators adopted ideals which led to the decline of educational standards. Various curricula based on English and Hindi were alternately formulated, some small, others large, sometimes the accent shifted to social studies, at others it was general education which underwent cruel surgery. But we miserably failed to adapt the means to our ends.

Today, we are neck deep in problems. The increasing population has brought with it the problem of food, the administration's lax policies have brought corruption, and our ideal of a socialistic pattern of society has left us in a dream-world. When our sovereignty was endangered, we opened our eyes and realised that every pore of our body was stuffed with debt. Mahatma Gandhi had once said that if God were forced to come to India, he would have to be reincarnated in the form of a piece of bread. In a democratic country, every individual enjoys his own separate existence, and our educational system aims primarily at the development of his individuality. The Education Commission, too has observed that in democracy, the individual himself is the end or goal, and the purpose of education is to give the individual extensive opportunities to develop in accord with his abilities. India's future is being shaped and moulded in class rooms. This statement is undoubtedly true. Education alone can safeguard the individual's prosperity, welfare and success in this constantly developing world of science and technology. It is the prime tool or instrument of social change. It is always in the forefront in providing various means for the development of material as well as human resources.

The Education Commission has opined, in one context, that the child's leaving the school is wastage. So far, educationists have continued treating wastage and stagnation as problems but we prefer to call it a process, an activity that continues to happen during the life time of a society. Wastages and stagnation have remained processes. A problem can be solved, but a process cannot be brought to an end. It continues as a stream of water continues to flow. The Education Commission itself has not been able to recognise the two firmly as problems, and the available studies lead to the conclusion that there can be no solution to a process which never ends.

The Education Commission has identified the following causes of wastage and stagnation-

1. The existence of discrimination between children of different ages in a class.
2. The admission of children to classes throughout the year, while this should occur at a fixed time only.

3. The irregularity in attending school.
4. Absence of adequate teaching aids and materials both with the schools and the students themselves.
5. Excessive number of students in classes.
6. The curriculum not being in conformity with needs.
7. The absence of ability and capacity in the teacher to teach through play, thus depriving school life of joy.

Though simple and ordinary enough, these causes compel us to think. These facts have become a part of the life of all those concerned with education, and often enough, it is felt unnecessary to devote thought to them. One often feels that if the problem had one or two causes, one might have exercised one's mind to solve it, but where the entire structure is vitiated, the exercise is entirely futile.

The following is a brief summary of a survey conducted by Leonard-

1. During 1950-1960, at the primary level, stagnation and wastage were of the order of 65.5%.
2. The rate of wastage and stagnation was highest at the primary level, it steadily declined towards class 8.
3. Both were found to be greater in the case of girls than among boys.
4. At the middle level, wastage and stagnation is 22%.
5. According to teachers and parents, the causes of this wastage and stagnation are - the involvement of children in other activities, low socio-economic level, lack of ability among students, low levels of health, lack of communication between schools and the community, indifference towards education in the family, corrupt administration and organisation of the school, defective curriculum, absence of a suitable environment for the students, absence of emotional maturity among students, lack of motivation, etc.
6. In the rural areas, the percentage of wastage and stagnation at the primary level is 73% and at the middle level 50% among

low income families, while an additional wastage of 15% occurs because of residence in towns.

This study also establishes the point that wastage and stagnation have progressed constantly, and that they themselves are not problems, but indicators or symptoms of a problem.

There is a crying need for giving a new direction to the process of stagnation and wastage. This is possible only when we decide upon the proper planning for manpower. In society, every individual is not meant for every kind of work. Each individual should be so educated that he should be able to fulfil some specific need of society. In the statement of the Education Commission, R.A. Gopalaswami has laid great emphasis upon the correlation of education with manpower planning. In this view-

1. There should be projection of the available manpower possessing higher education so that it can be utilised effectively.
2. Highly educated manpower should not be allowed to remain unemployed or be wasted.
3. Curriculum of education should be moulded in accord with social change.
4. Extension services should be organised for progress.
5. One tremendous advantage of manpower planning will be that, irrespective of the education received by an individual, his abilities and powers will be utilised efficiently in the national interest.

Stress has been laid upon work-experience by the Education Commission for reducing the incidence of wastage and stagnation: According to it, work-experience can be defined as cooperation in some productive work, in school, at home, in a place of work, in a field, in a factory or in any other productive environment.

1. No other reform or suggestion is as important as the linking of education with the individual's life, needs and ambitions so as to make him a powerful instrument of social, economic and cultural transformation, and to fulfil national objectives through

him. This is possible only when education is linked with productivity, social and national unity and strength, the state cooperates in the development of a truly indigenous life- style, the process of modernization is speeded up and importance is given to the formation of character through stress on social, moral and spiritual values.

2. The various sources of human development should be developed.

3. Efforts should be made to discover how the best form of educational development can become possible.

4. There should be planning to ensure that the right kind and quantity of education is made available to every person.

5. Suitable Traits should be generated for the development of ability.

6. The power to provide facilities should be generated.

7. Manpower should be utilised suitably.

8. Vocational and professional education should be developed.

9. The Education Commission's concept of life-long education should be followed.

10. A clearly defined national educational policy should be framed.

11. There should be rigorous control over schools.

12. The curriculum should be reformed and made useful for life.

13. Arrangements should be made for the training of teachers.

14. Laws should provide punishment for those who do not send their children to school.

15. Adult education should be extended. Education for girls should be expanded.

16. 50% of the total educational budget should be spent on primary education.

17. Classes 1 to 4 should be regarded as a unit.

18. Local cess should be imposed for financing education.
19. There should be uniformity in education throughout the country.

The Education Commission has clarified that there should be overlooking the fact that wastage and stagnation are not illnesses like headache and fever, but the symptoms of other diseases concealed in the educational method. Of these the main are lack of proper harmony between education and life, and the defective management of schools which fails to attract the students towards the school. Wastage and stagnation are not, in themselves problems. In fact, it is a process, the sources of which are defective system of education, absence of objectives, and narrow mindedness of our law-makers whose selfish interests have blinded them to reality. There is no need to solve the problem of wastage and stagnation. What is actually needed is a change in the nature of its source so that these symptoms of a deep malaise may disappear and every child may be able to make his own contribution to the development of the nation.

Positive Attitude

Till today, the two noticeable levels of India's educational systems are - (1) the school level, and (2) the higher level. The former is divisible into the pre-primary, the primary and the secondary levels. All these three levels lack any relation, although the three levels provide education for the periods of infancy, childhood and early youth. So far the assumption was that the primary level was the education of the masses with the secondary level provided education to a class. Primary education was imparted through the mother tongue and the regional language while the secondary level was dominated by English.

These various dividing lines and boundaries ruined the social context and many problems emerged. Of these the main was the problem of alienation, which increased to such an extent that it made the problem irremediable. For this reason, the Kothari Commission has treated primary education as a single, composite unit, consisting of the entire educational process comprehending the pre-primary, the primary and the secondary levels.

The integrated approach can be defined as the process by which various elements are collected together, or brought near to each other.

The integrated approach can be seen as an attempt to link education to life. This concept has been evolved by the Kothari Commission, and according to it, education should be transformed in such a manner that it should come into close relationship with the needs and ambitions of individuals, and also become a powerful medium of social, economic and cultural transformations.

In the context of education, the concept can be elaborated in the following manner. The boundaries between pre-primary and primary or between primary and secondary are purely arbitrary, and so they can be changed or even eradicated. In the same manner, people no longer cling to the traditional view that a general undifferentiated education should be imparted under primary education, while variety should be introduced at the secondary level with the interests, inclinations and abilities of the children. In Russia, a curriculum was introduced to encompass pre-primary, primary and secondary education on the basis of this concept.

With the change in time, the assumptions regarding primary and secondary education have also undergone transformation. In accordance with the new light, the entire education before university education is now regarded as belonging to the same level. This, in effect, is the integrated approach.

The Basis of the Integrated Approach. In India, many false notions have arisen about the boundaries of primary education. Till the present, it was generally accepted that there should be pre-primary, primary and secondary education corresponding to the infant, childhood and early youth periods of life. for each separate level there were distinct concepts. Primary education has been regarded as that education which was to be imparted through Indian languages.

Another assumption current till the present is that primary education fulfils the needs of the masses while secondary education fulfils those of a specific class. But these false notions of classification acted as obstacles in the child's integral development. Hence, it has now become clear that it is wrong to consider each level of education as a separate and independent entity. It is, in reality, a continuous flow which flows uninterruptedly as does a stream. Consequently we regard integrated approach as that form of education in which the entire education from infancy to early youth is regarded as a composite of various streams of the same continuum. Under this, the curriculum is so designed that it is similar in every class for every age group. Thus, it does not give rise to alienation.

The foundations of the Integrated Approach are :

Achievement of National Objectives. If we want to achieve national objectives and ideals, we will have to transform the structure and approach of primary education. What it should be, depends to a large extent upon our national educational system. The Education Commission has started its entire argument by stating that, at present, the future of India is being shaped and moulded in its class rooms. The prosperity, wealth and level of security of individuals, in the modern world based on science and technology, depends upon education. Our success in the supreme work of national reconstruction depends upon the quantity and quality of our students emerging from our schools and colleges.

Educational Reform. The formation of the new generation depends upon our goals and ideals. Pointing to the basic objectives of education, the Kothari Commission has declared that the most important reform in education is concerned with its transformation into something which can be related to the life, needs and ambitions of our people, so that it can thus be used as a powerful instrument of social, economic and cultural transformation, which is essential for the achievement of national objectives.

View of Knowledge of a Unit. The main plank of the integrated approach is the view that knowledge is a unit. The famous educationist Jecktot also regards knowledge as an integral or composite unit. All the subjects that are taught are the various branches of knowledge, but each one aims at human development. Since we have been holding different views on the concept of primary and secondary education, we have been facing difficulties in adopting the integrating view.

Programme. Not only at the primary level, but at every level of education, what we need is a comprehensive viewpoint. The programme of the integrated approach should be the following:

1. Linking education with production.
2. Laying emphasis upon national and social unity through the educational programme.
3. Uniting and organising the population through education.
4. Developing social, moral and spiritual values.
5. Modernizing society through the development of skills on the basis of curiosity, inclination and values.

The Integrated Approach and the Curriculum. During the last ten years, considerable thought has been given to the curricula of the primary and secondary levels from the integrated viewpoint. In this context, the Kothari Commission has pointed out that a single, undivided curriculum for providing general education to everyone for the first seven years should be formulated. With regard to those students who continue their education beyond the seventh class, it is hoped that full-time or part-time professional education will be provided to 20% students. The other students should be given another three years of education under a single, general and undivided curriculum. In simpler words, what this means is that there will be a single indivisible curriculum from class 1 to 10, and this will come to an end at the time of the first external examination. In this general continuity, there will be no streaming of any kind.

Integrated Approach: Comprehensive, Varied Programme. The development of integrated approach depends upon the curriculum and a comprehensive programme. In the opinion of the Kothari Commission, the education of the first ten years includes four years of the lower primary level, three years of the upper primary level, and three years of the secondary level. But, there should be no break in the continuity of education at any stage. At the same time, however, at the conclusion of each partial stage, the level of knowledge obtained by the student should be clearly specified. Keeping in mind the comprehensive objective of school education, the levels of attainment should be made clear from the viewpoint of knowledge, skill, ability and attitude or tendency. The National Education Commission has suggested the following programme for giving concrete shape to this educational programme:

(*i*) *Science Education* . Education in science should be an inseparable part of school education.

(*ii*) *Work Experience* . Work experience should be brought into close contact with the curriculum, that is, there should be greater stress on activity than on theory. This should necessarily include the following four things - (1) Literacy or knowledge of language, humanities and social sciences. (2) Arithmetic and natural science. (3) Practice, (4) Social service. Every effort of industrial education should be such that it should influence the process of technology, science, and agriculture, because only then can principle of production be satisfied.

Development of Human Values. The integrated approach also makes possible the growth and development of human values, national unity and national awareness. Thus, the very values of development can themselves be evolved and developed through this approach.

Social and National Unity. Education should be so structured as to bring about growth in social and national unity. For this it is essential that the integrated approach be adopted. Nation building is possible only when the system and organisation of the country is satisfactory, and for creating such an organisation, the following programme should be adopted :

Common School. Social and national unity can be achieved within a short period of only twenty years through the effective means of the common schools intended for mass education. In such schools, every child will receive education without discrimination on the basis of religion, caste or class. This education will be completely free, and this will give relief to the parents.

Social and National Service. A programme of social and national service, should, in general, be adopted in every school. This activity should be part of the curriculum at every level ,of education. Such a programme can include the following activities: (a) At the primary level, work of social service should be introduced on the basis of basic education. (2) At the secondary or lower levels, students should be organised for social service for 30 days. At the higher level, this period should be 20 days. (3) At the degree level, students should be required to pursue social service for a minimum of 60 days. (4) Every educational institution should try to ensure that activities for the service of society and community should be organised for the students in their own regions.

Language Policy. The growth of a suitable language will contribute to national unity. It has generally been accepted that the mother tongue should be made the medium of education, and it has already been the medium in schools as well as higher education. Hence, the language policy should be conducive to the development of national unity.

Growth of National Awareness. Through the medium of education faith in and awareness of literature, language, philosophy, religion, India's history, India's past glory, sculpture, art, music, dancing, drama, etc., should be engendered.

Education and Modernization. Today, society is changing at a very rapid pace because new inventions and new possibilities are bringing changes in the structure and beliefs of society. Through an integrated approach, we can keep pace with time in the process of education and modernization. In this context, the views of the Commission are that- (1) In modern society, knowledge has grown at an amazing pace. This has brought farreaching changes in the educational sphere also. Proper development in interests, mental inclination, values and skills becomes possible when curiosity is aroused. All these things should be kept in focus both in teaching and in the training of teachers. (2) Society will have to obtain education for itself in order to bring about its own modernization. Education should also be productive of an intellectual class in society, a class which should come forward from every part of India to achieve the reconstruction of our nation.

Social, Moral and Spiritual Values. The educational system can contribute to the creation of social, moral and spiritual values in the following ways. (1) The central and state governments should implement the suggestions of the University Commission in education to bring about social, moral and spiritual development. (2) Private schools and colleges should also accept and implement these suggestions. (3)

Provisions should be made in the time-table of schools for various kinds of programmes introduced by various teachers for this purpose. (4) Universities should introduce comparative studies of various religions.

Religion and Education. In a multi-religious country such as India, there is pressing need for the sympathetic study of all religions so that the country's citizens should fully understand each other. Selected ideas from these religions should find a place in the teaching of civics and general education. Such an effort will be of great aid in the comprehension of the world's fundamental beliefs,. assumptions and ideals.

The achievement of the objectives of the integrated approach, as defined and clarified by the Commission, need unremitting effort, in the sphere of primary education. For this purpose it will be necessary to change the entire form of context of primary education for the comprehensive approach: And for this, it is essential that attention should be paid to the following elements

Democratic Education. Primary education should be such that it develops democratic values. In a democracy, the individual himself is the end, and therefore, the prime objective of education is to provide him with the greatest opportunities for developing his innate powers. This view contains a great deal of truth, and hence, at the primary level, democratic qualities should be evolved in the child from the very beginning.

Relationship between Education and Production. One of the charges against Indian education is that it has helped to create unemployment. In order to overcome this shortcoming, it is essential to relate it to production. This will also create a potential for an increase in national income and wealth.

Check upon Wastage and Stagnation. In order to place a check upon wastage and stagnation, it is essential that there should be a check upon the method of examination and evaluation. Evaluative methods should be developed, but classes or divisions should not be mentioned in the certificates.

Curriculum. Reflecting upon the condition of the curriculum, the Education Commission has opined that glancing at it in the light of significant reforms in curricula in other countries, it is found that the school curriculum in India is both extremely narrow and obsolete.

The curriculum of primary education is both narrow and one-sided. It fails to attract either the teachers or the students. It also fails to bridge the gulf between the home and the school. For this reason, it has been suggested that the rural community should be brought into the school through the project method. Hence, it is clear that the social system can never change as long as the curriculum and the modes of evaluation at the primary level are not drastically transformed. These suffer from the following defects at present :

(1) A narrow approach, (2) stress on learning by rote, (3) stress on achievement of high academic levels, (4) too theoretical, (5) lacking completely in any professional tendency, (6) inattention towards the interests and inclinations of the students, (7) lack of emphasis upon manual work and practical education, (8) completely lacking in any relationship with life.

The curriculum of modern primary education is restricted and biased. It is also negligent of the child's integral development. It only determines to make the child an intellectual creature but it avoids the responsibility of making the child capable of adapting to every circumstance of life. The whole curriculum is entirely bookish and theoretical. The attempts at reform in this direction include a change in the curriculum of primary education on the basis of the concept of Basic Education. This attempt was made in the third plan. As a result, handicrafts were introduced into the curriculum. The curriculum of basic education differs in some respects from the common one. Dr. S.N. Mukerjee's view is that, at the primary level, the project method will prove more fruitful. The project should be founded in local requirements. It should be concerned not only with general agriculture, but also with handicraft industry, development of the community and the home, health, hygiene and personal cleanliness. The Education Commission, too, has felt the same. It says that since the existing curriculum does not give adequate stress to the development of productive skills, proper kinds of interests, tendencies and beliefs, it is completely unrelated not only with modern knowledge but even the real lives of individuals.

Bases of the Curriculum of Primary Education. Representatives of governments in Asia determined the objectives of primary education in the following terms in their conference, held at Karachi in January 1980-

1. Providing opportunities for learning control over the fundamental tools of teaching.
2. Bringing about the comprehensive and integral development of the child's personality through opportunities for physical, mental, intellectual, emotional, aesthetic, moral and spiritual development.
3. Preparing the children for good citizenship, and arousing love, respect and sympathy for the nation's traditions and culture.
4. Evolving the ideas of world brotherhood and international understanding.
5. Creating a scientific attitude.
6. Arousing respect for and faith in labour.
7. Preparing the children for life, providing practical experience; creative work, and work experience.

When these principles are applied to our own curriculum, it does not appear suitable or adequate. It reveals the following defects- (i) It throws light on only one aspect of life. (ii) It fails to harmonize theory and practice. (iii) The curriculum does have variety and it is also not productive of either national unity or international understanding. (iv) It fails to bring about a proper development of mental and physical powers.

Education must be related to life, because only then can education undergo a qualitative development, and also fulfil the ambitions of life. The modern explosion in knowledge is causing rapid and farreaching social changes, but we have not brought about changes in our curricula which can keep pace with the changing times. Thus, the curriculum should be made to change in step with time.

In this context, we are bringing out the suggestions given at conferences organised by the NCERTs for improving the curriculum-

1. The curriculum of primary education should conform to local conditions and requirements.
2. Its level should be nation-wide. It must bring about a growth in knowledge, awareness, skills, values and attitudes.
3. Schools should be assisted in the formulation of their curricula by administrators of education, educationists, guardians and planners.
4. The educational process should take place in the context of the individual's development, universal brotherhood and the student's attitudes.
5. State educational institutions should formulate the curriculum for the desired levels in consultation with the NCERT.
6. There should be a proper place for the enrichment of Indian culture, democratic citizenship and economic development.

The Recommendations of the National Education Commission. The suggestions of the Kothari Commission for developing a suitable curriculum of primary education are as follows-

1. At the Lower Primary level, the child should acquire control over the basic tools of learning, such as reading, writing, counting, and in order to adapt himself to the environment, they should study, in elementary terms, the social and material environment.
2. At the Higher Primary level, education should be imparted in one language other than the mother tongue, arithmetic, natural and physical science, history, geography, civics, creative and constructive skills, and physical education. The Commission's outline for such a curriculum is as follows-

Lower Primary (class 1 to 4) Level. (1) One language- mother tongue or regional language (2) arithmetic (3) study of the environment (class 3 and 4) (4) creative activities (5) work experience and social service (6) health education.

Higher Primary (class 5 to 8) Level. (1) mother tongue or regional language (Hindi or English) (2) arithmetic (3) science (4) social studies (5) art (6) work experience (7) physical education (8) education in moral and spiritual values.

According to the Kothari Commission, the first two classes of the primary school should be dovetailed into a unit, and wherever possible, the same arrangement should apply to the third and fourth classes also. For these classes, the proposed curriculum is very simple, and it reduces the burden of prescribed courses. In order to develop learning, it is necessary to include in the curriculum such activities as a study of the environment, conversation, social studies, science, self-expression, music, art, drama, handicraft, etc. It is also necessary to discover the student's eagerness for studying, as well as his ability.

As far as the higher primary level is concerned, at this level the study of the languages, arithmetic, science, social studies, art, work experience, physical education, and teaching of moral and spiritual values should be included in the curriculum. According to the Commission, students should be given education in moral and spiritual value in order to form their character and also to generate respect in their minds for other religions. for this, one or two hours in the week should be fixed, and the activities for social service should include participation in the local social life.

In this way, we can observe that if the suggestions of the Kothari Commission for the reform of the curriculum at the primary level are accepted, there is no doubt that the standard of teaching at this level will improve.

Assessment

Evaluation is a necessary evil. In India, every one is aware of the shortcomings of our system of evaluation, that is, examinations. From time to time, numerous committees and commissions have expressed their views on these defects and methods for their eradication.

Secondary Education Commission: Evaluation. The Secondary Education Commission has thrown light on the defects of the system of evaluation in the following terms:

1. The student depends upon keys or help books, and he is required to demonstrate his skills only at learning by rote and writing essay-type answers.

2. Teachers, too consider it their objective to ensure the passing of the student in the examination, instead of seeking to develop his qualities.

3. A teacher's success is judged by the number of his students who pass the examination.

4. The attitude of the guardians is that their children should, by any means, pass the examination and secure a suitable job. Those giving employment also base their judgment on the candidates certificates.

These are some of the defects found in the existing system of examination and evaluation. But examinations inspire the teacher, provide a uniform standard, form a medium for the achievement of the objective, and provide social acceptance. For this reason, this Commission offered the following suggestions for eliminating the defects of examination and evaluation :

1. The number of external examinations should be reduced and objective testing should be introduced. The form of questions should be changed. Dependence on essay-type tests should be reduced.

2. The school record of each student should be kept systematically in order to find out his over-all progress and also to determine his future. The record should demonstrate the work done by the student and his achievements in various spheres.

Kothari Commission Evaluation. Evaluation is inseparably linked with the system of education, and it is a continuous process. It is influenced by (1) studies (2) teaching (3) method teaching. In order to arrive at a realistic evaluation of the student, we will have to modify the prevailing general method of written examinations. There are many aspects of the student's growth which cannot be tested by this technique. Hence, evaluation must be made objective. Reflecting upon the problem of evaluation, the Kothari Commission stated that in India every individual is aware of the defects of the examination system, and it is generally believed that the examination is the criterion for testing both the student and the teacher. In this, the students learn by rote the questions usually asked in the examination, so that it is difficult to assess their real intellectual development. At the primary level one major objective of the evaluation, in the light of the objectives of teaching at this level, is to discover the extent to which the student has improved his achievement in basic skills and developed the right habits and attitudes. The evaluative technique should assist in this measurement.

Concerning the criterion of evaluation at the primary level, it can be said confidently that there can be no change or improvement in the mode of evaluation as long as the teaching methods remain unchanged. For this reason, the Education Commission has put forward the following suggestions :

1. The size of the class should be around 45 to 50 students. In the lower primary, the maximum number should be 50.
2. Evaluation is an inseparable part of teaching, and hence there should be improvement in the written tests. New techniques of evaluation should be evolved.
3. At the primary level, the evaluation should concern itself with basic ability, attitude, inclination and habits.
4. Classes 1 to 4 should be regarded as a single unit.
5. At the higher primary level, written tests should be accompanied by oral tests, and there should be internal assessment. Cumulative records and diagnostic testing should be devised.
6. Evaluation should be done in a uniform manner at the end of the primary level. The techniques should be applied throughout the country.
7. Education officers of the district may organise a general examination at the conclusion of the primary level. This test should be more valid and reliable than the existing examinations.

After the test, the result should be accompanied by the student's school record.

8. For grant of scholarships, there should be separate tests.

If the Kothari Commission's suggestions are put into operation, there will undoubtedly be a rise in the standard of primary education and the coming generations will be able to make our nation strong.

Working Group, Planning Commission. The working group of the commission has also suggested, with reference to improvement of evaluation that the importance of the method of continuous testing is self-evident. Planning, practice or active implementation and evaluation are organically related to each other. Evaluation tells us how we can overcome our failures. Hence, three kinds of testing have been in practice

1. The simplest evaluation is carried out by the teacher, institution and administrator. The system of evaluation is of particular significance in any scheme of education.
2. The process working at the state and district level is responsible for creating the collective standard.
3. Evaluation of educational programmes at the highest level.

Thus, if we want to strengthen the concept of evaluation, it is essential that we maintain a balance between the various tools of evaluation.

Is the Primary External Examination Inevitable? For the last few years, it has been noticed that the district education officers, at the behest of some official directives, organise a general external examination at the primary level. Its outcome is that the ratio of wastage and stagnation rise. The arguments given in favour of it are that (1) it maintains a uniform standard, (2) it helps in the selection of the curriculum, (3) it improves teaching.

These arguments do not establish the inevitability of an external examination at the conclusion of the primary level. For maintaining uniform standards, other means can be adopted: Hence, such a test should not be regarded as unavoidable. The desired results at this level can be obtained through effective tests and proper surveys.

Autonomy

Dr. Devendradatt Tiwari express the view that decentralisation means handing over the focii of authority and responsibility to basic units or individuals, instead of allowing them to rest with one or a few individuals. In considering decentralisation, both authority and responsibility should be considered. A distinction between them is essential, because it is usual to trust responsibility upon the lower units, without providing them the necessary authority to carry out the responsibility effectively.

The decentralisation of education finds mention in the Constitution also, and as a result of this, education was made a State subject, and thus they got the responsibility for it. Each state is trying to fulfil its responsibility in its own region, in its own way.

Origin and Development

Efforts at the decentralisation of primary education have been continuing since the last century. In 1882, the Indian Education Committee had put forward the view that local institutions should be given the maximum possible autonomy. Latter on, the Hertog Committee evaluated the achievements of decentralisation, but it found the results dissatisfying.

According to the Statutory Commission, it was felt that changes were necessary for the progress of primary education. In its view, it was correct that, in local matters, the efforts should be made by the local institutions themselves, and it is not unnatural that mistakes may be made, initially, in the absence of experience. Despite this, the commission felt that education was national service.

After independence, great importance was attached to primary education. In 1951, a committee of the states and union was appointed. It recommended that local institutions should be given the power to exercise the maximum possible control and also to improve their resources in certain specific fields.

The Balwantrai Committee suggested to the Indian government in 1957 that a three-tier system should be adopted. In its report, it said that there should be local panchayat at the village level, a regional committee or panchayat committee at the block level, and a district board at the district level for controlling education. The main difference in this case was that, while the district had been the fundamental unit in decentralisation in the past, this report gave prominence to village panchayats and areas or regional committees, in view of the increasing population of the district and the large number of problems being thrown up because of the developmental process.

The Education Commission has also stressed the fact that the local community should prefer its active and direct cooperation in the question of education. Secondly, the district should be the basic unit in the work of planned development.

Kher Committee Report

The following were the suggestions given by the Kher Committee with regard to decentralisation

1. The prime objective of decentralisation should be to encourage the growth and expression of leadership, initiative and a sense of responsibility, but this objective has never been adequately stressed. On the contrary, decentralisation has so far been taken to mean nothing more than freedom in the raising of funds.

2. One general conclusion which emerges is that little attention has been paid to eliciting cooperation from the local population in matters of educational administration. Whatever little attention was given was casual, rather than determined. Almost the same situation obtains even at present.

3. History tells us that the suggestions put forward by Lord Rippon in 1882 to make this experiment a success were never put into practice by the administrators. He had made it explicit that the experiment could succeed only if- (1) local institutions were given adequate materials, (2) additional work involving additional expenditure was accompanied by additional grants of financial aid, (3) government officials engaged themselves devotedly and enthusiastically to the small efforts in the beginning of an independent political life, and they came to feel that, because of these efforts, a better sphere for utilising

administrative power management had been discovered. In such a situation, the effort could be pushed further. Unfortunately, these suggestions were consigned to oblivion very quickly.

4. People have generally been convinced that the root cause of all the trouble is the handing over of primary education to local institutions. They feel that its success is possible only if its control lies in the hands of the state government's education department. But history has completely confounded such a view.

Arguments in Support of Decentralisation. Dr. Devendra Dutt Tiwari holds the view that there are many questions which can be adequately answered only at the central level- security, national unity, national development, etc. Unity and development are spheres which comprehend every aspect of human life, and consequently, the intervention of the centre in all matters pertaining to the individuals and local units becomes unavoidable. Education has been recognised as the most significant means of social change and development, and hence the direction of education should be in the hands of the centre alone. It is for this reason that the states have implemented most of their developmental programmes under central direction. Not merely this, the centre has come to control even the awareness or consciousness of knowledge, but this can prove fatal for local enterprise. One example of this is the National Institute of Education, which has innumerable futile and meaningless departments.

Basis of Decentralisation. Decentralisation is extremely important for a country with India's diversity because the differences in culture and social traditions give rise to different local needs. Hence, decentralisation should be based on the following points :

1. Decentralisation is essential for maintaining national unity and achieving social and cultural development. Those who argue that decentralisation hurts national unity are mistaken. We must focus our attention upon the fact that decentralisation is to be accepted in the form of the objectives of a democratic nation.
2. Decentralisation brings about the development of the individual at the national level, but in consonance with local requirements.

In a decentralised system, power rests in the hands of the common man, whereas centralisation leads to the concentration of power in the hands of a few.

3. In the opinion of Dr. Devendra Dutt Tiwari, the first question to be decided is the nature or form of administration in primary education. Some people argue that primary education is very important for the success of democracy. And, since the Constitution stipulates the introduction of free and compulsory primary education, it is the duty of the centre to carry out this task. Such an argument implicity strengthens the case for the centralisation of primary education. On the other hand, at the state level, many people are convinced that the Centre should not interfere in educational matters, and that the entire direction, control and guidance of primary education should be in the hands of the state governments.

Some Aspects of Decentralisation. Decentralisation is one of the fundamental problems of our state. Its numerous aspects influence it. These are :

1. Our nation is a democratic one, and our Constitution has given importance to the dignity of the individual. Hence, democracy should be guided by the dignity of the individual and his dedication to duty.

2. At present, decentralisation is taken to mean the collection of money, and not the direction of education. The result of this is that political and economic rights are not divided on the basis of suitable administration.

3. Decentralisation brings about the expression and development of the individual's innate powers and abilities.

4. The curriculum should be formulated in accordance with local needs. Our nation is marked by wide diversities, and hence the curricula here should be constructed on the basis of local needs, not an imitation of the patterns of education in Britain or the United States of America. This will become possible only when decentralisation becomes a fact.

5. The preparation of text books should also be guided by local needs and contexts. Though the Kothari Commission has recommended flexibility and lack of compulsion in matters of preparing the curriculum, some of its suggestions implicitly support the centralisation of the curriculum, text-books and methods of examination.

6. Decentralisation should permeate not only the administration but also the school so that they can be freed from official domination.

7. The most distressing situation is opposed to decentralisation- that is, the centralisation of examinations. According to Whitehead, the ability to evaluate a student lies only in the teacher who educates him, and in no one else. As far as the question of uniformity of standards is concerned, that entire notion is an illusion. The standard indicated by external examinations is merely imaginary, not real and it only turns the entire teaching process into the wrong channels.

Significance of Education Commission

The Kothari Education Commission appointed in 1964-66 has proved to be something of epic proportions in the educational field. It will always be remembered by the future generations. It was at this time, that our leaders became conscious of the need for farreaching changes in the sphere of education. For the first time after independence, they came to lay emphasis upon the necessity of educational planning in consonance with the stream of social transformation.

According to Dr. Sampurnanand, the commission opines that education should develop so as to bring about an increase in production, to achieve social and national unity to give impetus to the process of modernisation and to generate social, moral and spiritual values.

The Kothari Commission has offered revolutionary suggestions for bringing about wide-ranging and fundamental change in the country's educational system. These suggestions will undoubtedly prove valuable and fruitful if they are accepted without modification by the Government of India. In its reflections, the Commission has laid the greatest stress at the following four points :

1. The various angles of the pyramid of education and their mutual relationship.
2. The total time-period of education keeping in mind its various stages.
3. The qualities of teachers, curriculum, method of teaching, evaluation, buildings and resources.
4. Utilisation of the available facilities.

These four elements create the entire structure of education for which it is necessary to consider the means and the total time period of the educational process. The Kothari Commission opines that the two efforts which need immediate attention at the school level are - the adoption of a utilitarian approach and improvement in the quality and quantity of all available things, apart from time. Through these, it will be possible to increase one year in the achievements of the school curriculum. In addition, the period of the higher secondary stage is to be increased to two years, which is to be achieved, through a continuous programme, beginning in the fifth plan and achieving completion by 1985.

New Educational Structure. The new structure of education should have the following pattern -

1. Pre-school education of 1 to 3 years.
2. 10 years of general education, which includes 7 to 8 years of primary education- 4 to 5 years for the lower primary stage, and 2 to 3 years for the higher primary stage. After this, at the lower primary level, there should be general education for 2 to 3 years, or vocational education for 1 to 3 years. The total number of students in the vocational courses should be increased by 20%.

Qualitative Aspects, Curriculum, etc. An improvement in the qualitative aspect of teachers, teaching methods, school buildings, evaluation, presentation and curriculum should be brought about. These should also be utilised to the maximum possible extent.

Utilisation of Resources. According to the Kothari Commission, the greatest shortcoming of the existing educational, system is not its structure, but its powerlessness. Hence, it is essential that greater stress should be placed upon the maximum utilisation of things usable in extra-curricular activities, and especially upon the programmes for the improvement of teachers. These form a part of our schemes for educational reconstruction. It is essential to adopt these facilities and suggestions.

1. Importance should be given to the intensive exploitation of the facilities implicit in various schemes.

2. Period of study should be divided in the following manner

School	39 weeks
Primary	36 weeks
College	36 weeks

3. The ministry of education should prepare a calendar of holidays in consultation with the State government and the U.G.C. The loss of teaching days due to examinations and other causes should not be more than 21 days at the school level and 26 days at the college level..

4. Students should fully utilise their vocations. This utilisation should be in the form of participating in social service camps, obtaining of production experience, participating in literacy campaigns, etc.

Some of the important suggestions of the Education Commission regarding primary education are-

1. There should be complete freedom from fees in schools run by local bodies and private institutions by the end of the fourth five year plan.

2. At the lower level, attention should be paid to the fact that no promising student abandons education due to lack of

resources. Arrangement for necessary scholarships should be made.

3. Provisions should be make for Ashram Schools at the primary level in regions where the backward classes, the Scheduled Castes and Tribes predominate. Such schools should be located in far-flung places. For the first two years, education should be conducted through the tribal language, and later on, knowledge of the regional language should be given.

4. Objectives should be determined in the following manner for the progress of primary education- (1) There should be good and effective education for five years for every child in the country. (2) The same kind of education should become available for seven years by 1985-86. (3) Stress should be laid upon the eradication of wastage and stagnation. (4) Those children, who at the end of 14 years, have, completed seven years of education, but do not want to study further, should be given a choice of various vocational courses.

5. The spread of primary education should be planned in such a manner that every child should have available a primary school within a mile of his house. A higher primary school should also be available within a maximum range of three miles.

6. By the end of the fifth plan, the transference from class I to class 4 should reach 100%.

7. In order to get rid of wastage and stagnation at the primary level (1) classes 1 and 2, and if possible, classes 1 to 4, should be regarded as a single unit. (2) there should be a one year programme of pre-school training. (3) In class I, the play-way should be adopted.

8. At the primary level, students should be taught either the mother tongue or the regional language. At the higher primary level, two languages should be taught. mother tongue or regional language, and the official or semi-official language.

It is evident from the foregoing elaboration that the Education Commission has attached the greatest significance to the growth of education at the primary level. The need is for a proper understanding of the demands of our times and of implementing programmes in agreement with it.

Role of Plans

As soon as our country became independent, the responsibility for the introduction- of free, compulsory and universal education, fell upon the shoulders of the popular government. During the five year plans, primary education progressed in the following manner :

1. In the first five year plan, provision was made for compulsory education, according to the Constitution for children of the 6 to 14 age group. Rs. 93 crores were allocated for this purpose.
2. In the same way, Rs. 89 crores were allocated in the second plan for the spread of primary and basic education.
3. In the third plan, Rs. 209 crores were invested on education. Arrangements were made for 76% of the children in the 6 to 11 age group, and 28% in the 11 to 14 age group.
4. In the fourth plan, Rs. 322 crores were provided for primary education.

Primary education is the basis of country's development. Its growth leads to the emergence of awareness in the social environment.

Enrolment. The major objective in primary education is to fulfil the directives of the Constitution, under which provisions must be made for the free and compulsory education of all children upto the age of 14 years. By the end of the fourth plan, it was expected that 88% children in the 6-11 age group and 44% in the 11-14 age group would receive education. In the former group, one fourth of the girls could not be enrolled by 1974. By the end of the third year of the plan, half the boys and three-fourth of the girls could be enrolled. The environment for enrolment which was created in the third five year plan (particularly for the 6-11 age group) was favourable, and as a result, during this plan, the annual enrolment for classes 1 to 5 was 17 lakhs, in excess of the expectations. From 1969 to 1972, this annual increase was found to be

27 lakhs. Under the employment scheme the appointments of 75,000 teachers was approved in 1973-74.

Enrolment has varied from state to state, district, block, city and village. There is need for a special effort at enrolment for classes 5 to 8. In many states, the percentage of girls enrolled is very low. For India, the percentage is 71.9, but in Assam it is 58.6%, in Bihar 52.3%, Haryana 58.4%, in Kashmir 79.9% in Madhya Pradesh 14.6%, Orissa 18.6%, in Rajasthan 14.0%, and in Uttar Pradesh 13.8%. In the classes 6 to 8, the percentage of girls is less than 20.

Institutions. The increase in primary schools has not been in proportion to the rise in population, but the disparity has been somewhat compensated by the setting up of Single Teacher Schools. By 1972, there were 25% of such schools, though in some states they formed 60 to 70% of all schools. These schools meet only a fifth of the demand. The reasons for this are : lack of proper training, for running such schools, lack of technical facilities, lack of insight in the surveying or inspecting authorities, and lack of necessary materials.

Teachers. Although the ability of teachers has undergone suitable improvement, on the whole, most teachers do not possess the requisite skills. Till 1968, 41% of the teachers had not obtained higher secondary education. It is estimated that, by the end of the fourth plan, about one fourth teachers were still left untrained. Training facilities have increased but the state governments could not provide the required number of jobs. Besides, private institutions too give priority to appointment of untrained teachers. According to the figures published by the Directorate of Employment and Training 1.5 lakh trained teachers were hunting for jobs, and in 1968, their number registered an increase of 25%. In 1971, 31,000 trained teachers were on the rolls of the employment exchanges. In Andhra Pradesh, Haryana, Kerala; Tamil Nadu, Punjab and Uttar Pradesh there is widespread unemployment among trained teachers. It was expected that under the educated unemployment scheme, 75,000 teachers would be appointed, and the situation brought under control.

Buildings and Equipment. The state of buildings and equipment in primary schools is depressing. According to the Kothari Commission, only 30% of school buildings can be said to be in a satisfactory condition. As far as the question of basic equipment for teaching is concerned— a proper blackboard, satisfactory library, necessary maps and charts, general scientific equipment, and materials for exhibition or demonstration— the situation is truly deplorable.

Finance. The direct expenditure upon primary education has been steadily declining from one year to the next. In 1951, the total expenditure on primary education was 38.2%, but in 1966, it had declined to 32.5%. The total additional expenditure was 22%, but on primary education, it was 8.4%. The figures for the third plan are even lower. The amount allocated for primary education was 56% in the first plan, 35% in the second, and 30% in the third plan, and now in the fourth, it has declined to 29%. What is even more surprising is that even this meager amount is not fully utilised. Comparatively speaking, during the first four years of the fourth plan, the amount not spent was of the order of 82%, whereas 67% of the educational budget had been allocated for basic education. Even those states which should have made the greatest efforts to fulfil the obligations of the Constitution have proved most lax. The reasons for this failure to utilise the allocated funds are numerous.

Quality. The teaching method at the primary level is completely lacking in quality. No significant change in wastage and stagnation is evident in this education. There is no decline in the number of students who fail or drop out without completing their education. Making the child remain at home before the proper time is clearly indicative of economic handicap. Stagnation can certainly be reduced at the school level by means of attractive teaching programmes. Success depends upon such elements as work experience, the solution of local problems, making necessary changes in the curriculum, etc.

The following efforts for the spread of primary education have been planned, in view of the shortcoming and facts outlined above :

Expansion of Facilities. The fifth plan will attempt to ensure that by its end, 100% of the children in the 6-11 age group should be able to get primary education. At the primary level, the enrolment is one-fourth, while at the junior level it is 41%. This ratio should be decreased.

States made certain rules concerning compulsory element and provided uniformity in the age structures. The result was that in 1974-79, the enrolment was of the level of 120 lakhs in classes 1 to 5,165 lakhs in classes 6 to 8, and 45 lakhs in part-time classes. Numerous tests were carried out to check the facility and success of part-time classes, and it was found that radio, television, etc., had played an important contributory role.

Social efforts were made to provide educational extension and facilities in states and districts which were backward from the viewpoint of education. Provisions were made for free text-books, free lunch, free uniforms, etc. It is also evident that the benefit of these facilities should go to the rural population. Even today, in villages with a population of less than 200 there are 80% of the children who are denied education. The same situation exists with regard to middle level education in villages with population of less than 5000. The needs of such regions and people will have to be met through radio and television, and the cooperation of the educated people in the community will also have to be sought.

The proportion of additional enrolment of children belonging to the Scheduled Castes, classes and regions is fairly large. Such children not only have to be enrolled, but actually kept in the schools. for this, the following schemes will have to be implemented :

1. Free distribution of text books, stationery, writing materials, etc., to the weaker sections.
2. Establishment of 500 Ashram Schools for the tribal and socially backward children.
3. Distribution of free uniforms to 25% girl students by the end of the fifth plan.
4. Provision of free lunch to 61.5% children.

In this plan, special attention has been given to providing extra facilities for girls, because, as a result of social prejudices, they are often deprived of education. For them, it is necessary to generate a suitable environment, and for this the cooperation of the panchayat and local community is unavoidable.

There are arrangements for providing free lunch to 12 million children, with the assistance of the famous institution, CARE. This institution will bear the entire burden of the programme. Provisions have been made for spending Rs. 40 per child or a total of Rs. 240 crores for 1.20 crores children. This will benefit half the children. The plan is that the burden of the free lunch should fall upon the local community, and for this schemes based on the school will have to be implemented. The basis for such schemes will be provided by agriculture, health, school agriculture, panchayat land to be used for farming for the school, collection of funds, etc. The state will provide animals, land, facilities, poultry, etc., for this purpose. Priority will be given to soyabean and other foods rich in protein.

Qualitative Improvement. For the growth and expansion of facilities, stress will be laid upon the source of equipment or means. For this, rural schools will have to play a special role for the uplift, social and economic, of the rural areas. These schools will build suitable citizens for the future, and therefore special importance will be given to their consolidation and development. Selected programmes will be introduced in these areas to ensure that the development is permanent, and that these programmes have a permanent impact.

Curriculum Reform. A major share of the problem can be solved through curriculum reform. It will have to be related closely to local needs and problems. They must be made comprehensive enough to include work experience, improvement in the teaching of science, personal and social health, information regarding control of population, the use of local resources and means, and development of civic consciousness.

Work Experience. Work experience must be recognised as the main element in the curriculum, and for this local resources and means will have to be organised and brought into use. In the rural areas, such programmes will consist of cleaning of the school and village, creation of soakpits, levelling of roads, working on the fields, etc. They will also include simple crafts not requiring expensive machines or tools.

This will help the programme of providing free lunch from the school.

In-Service Education. Apart from reforms in the curriculum, it will be necessary to provide in-service education to teachers to acquaint them with these changes. By 1974, 11.2 lakhs or 6% of the teachers will be given in-service education and training.

As a part of the same programme, there is a need for a clear policy on the selection of teachers. With the rise in the number of educated people, the basic qualifications for teachers have also been rising steadily. Some special efforts should be made to attractable; talented and well-educated people to come and teach at the primary level. They should be given the salaries they are likely to receive in any other sphere. In addition, the pay-scales, posts, etc., should be determined not by work alone but also upon qualification.

Improvement in Existing Schools. The buildings of most schools are in a truly depressing state, and they are also lacking in the necessary materials. Hence, it has been decided that 5% primary schools and 1% middle schools will be given financial aid for constructing buildings, and the aid will take the form of a matching grant. Half the expense will be borne by the state government and the other half by the local community. The success of this programme depends upon the organisation and collection of technological knowledge.

Development of Selected Schools. When a firm basis for the growth and expansion of primary education has been achieved, then efforts can be directed at their qualitative improvement, and for this, it is essential that technological guidance, inventive ideas and activities should be adopted for this purpose. For such a programme, the steering group of the Education Commission has come forth with the following suggestions

1. A relation between schools and technological institutions should be established at the district, state and national levels.
2. In the fifth plan, the management of this work should be concerned with the school, training school, state educational institutions, and National Teacher Education Council. The last mentioned should provide the technique to training schools and the benefit should then flow to neighbouring institutions.

On the whole, a School Complex programme should emerge, and in this, about 200 schools should be attached with the training schools.

3. These attached schools should perform, in addition to their routine work, the following activities also- adult education, pre-school education, distribution of literature to the newly literate, management of schools, etc.

4. 10 or 15 primary schools will be attached with the experimental schools. These will initially number 3000, and gradually they will expand themselves. They will receive developmental aid.

5. The experimental schools will get assistance from training schools and inspectors, with the result that a stream of emancipation and expansion will flow.

6. The state education institutions will require developmental aid, and for this expansion services will have to be provided in training schools. For technical and administrative assistance, a link between the training schools and the District Education Officers will be maintained.

Financial Implications. In the fifth plan, Rs. 1089 crores have been allocated for primary education. Table provides the details-

Expenditure on Primary Education

Sl. No.	*Programme*	*Amount (Crores)*
1.	Expansion Facilities	696 - 30
2.	Incentive to Enrolment	154 - 00
3.	Ashram Schools	26 - 25
4.	Teachers Training	45 - 81
5.	Qualitative Improvement of Schools	151 - 40
6.	Development of SIES	2 - 00
7.	Administration	13 - 32
	Total	1089 - 08

In the sixth plan, much thought had been devoted to universal education at the primary level. For this purpose, the following schemes were taken up :

1. Accepting the principle of average attendance to overcome wastage and stagnation.
2. Ensuring that a school is available to a child within 1.5 kilometres in a town and within 6 kilometres in a village.
3. Laying emphasis upon compulsory enrolment.
4. Bringing about the expansion of part-time, informal, education.
5. Eradication of the regional imbalances.